A Jubilee Journey

By

Kathryn Reese Hendershot

A Jubilee Journey

ISBN: 978-1-732529335

Empyrion Publishing
PO Box 784327
Winter Garden, FL 34778
EmpyrionPublishing.com

Unless otherwise noted, all Scripture quotations are taken from the New King James Version of the Bible.

KJV – King James Version

NIV – New International Version

AMP – Amplified Version

NASB – New American Standard Bible

NLT – New Living Translation

TPT – The Passion Translation

Printed in the United States of America

DEDICATION

To John, my consistent and compassionate cheerleader who carried me through the ups and downs of this crazy journey with grace and a quiet strength. I remember the Lord revealing years ago a picture of this leg of our life together: We were positioned securely within the boat (Jesus); you were the strong mast that held my sail steady while the wind of the Spirit guided us through uncharted waters. While your calling was behind the scenes, and mine more visible, Jesus was the Star of the show!! So grateful for the privilege of serving Him together!

I love you.

ACKNOWLEDGEMENTS

My deepest thanksgiving and appreciation for each one of you!

My son, Kevin, who prodded me to set writing goals at a time when I was ready to give up!

My editor, Donna Rees, for her servant's heart and persevering spirit in correcting my spelling and grammatical challenges. Gracing me with a glowing endorsement was the cherry on the top!

My friend, Janetta Hynous, and Pastor David Fultz for taking time out of pressing schedules to read my manuscript, and offer words of encouragement and endorsement!

My publisher, Judi Manis, for her sweet and gentle spirit, as well as her expertise in formatting my bizarre spacing issues. She turned fashioning the finishing touches into a joy!

Those who graciously hosted me along the way: Takako Yamashita, Yugi & Jerri Yasaka, Wendy Henderson, Tokorozawa Fellowship, Kent & Janet Norell, Jack & Celeste Ray, Operation Mobilization Team in Lucknow, Methodist Guesthouse in Nairobi, Operation Mobilization Guesthouse in Dubai, Bauta Motty, BORN Headquarters in Patna, Tammy Ma, and Rahab's Rope in Mumbai, Bangalore & Goa! I absolutely could never have survived without all of your tender loving care!

My husband, John, for patiently solving my seemingly non-stop computer challenges!

Jesus, You have been forever faithful in assuring me that nothing is ever wasted, and that I can overcome the enemy by the Blood of the Lamb and the word of my testimony. You are the One who has breathed life into my clay jar. Thank you for the gift of grace to complete this assignment!

ENDORSEMENTS

Follow Kathryn Hendershot as she travels on mission from God to countries around the world. She gives us insights to various cultures and what God is doing in them. Her insights on God's guidance are indeed valuable. You will be blessed by all she shares.

~ C. David Fultz
Associate Pastor, Church of the Savior
Author of *The Millennial Force*, and *Millennial Force II*

*****

Kathryn Hendershot has penned an inspiring account of God's continued fulfillment of Psalm 139:5 in her life as she has obediently responded to His call to "live a sold-out life for God." Taking Kathryn around the world as a teacher, encourager, pastor, seminary student, and servant of the Lord, her Jubilee Journey encompassed the twenty years that immediately followed a season of ministry via Christian Ministries, an organization founded by her husband, John. From dancing before the Lord with abandon in Canada to a sobering visit to the Wailing Wall in Jerusalem to ministering to eager listeners through instruction and counsel in Japan to distributing Bibles in China, God's hand upon Kathryn's exciting journey is evident.

Woven throughout her chronicles, Kathryn shares many personal visions and words of wisdom given to her by the Lord, indicative of her hearing heart and attentive spirit. Through these revelations and insights, her heavenly Father tenderly, powerfully, faithfully, and gloriously guided her steps as He "hemmed her in, behind and before, and laid His hand upon her" (Psalm 139:5).

True to the meanings of her names (*Kathryn* means "pure" and *Gayle* means "delight"), the author invites us to share her pure delight in loving and knowing Jesus and making Him known. Along the way, you will be introduced to individuals such as Dr. Mabel Lossing Jones, the wife of E. Stanley Jones and the subject of Kathryn's dissertation; Takako, who hosted the author in a "mystical, quaint neighborhood" in Japan; a "bag lady" named Joy who was the author's house guest for a season; Buford, an oversized suitcase who demanded lots of attention; Manal, a resident of Dubai who recently had been trampled on her pilgrimage to the Hajj; Antonia, a young, Christian woman in India who is on a mission to enlighten others regarding the abuse of the Brahman ideology, even among believers there; Manjula, who works for a mission organization as a matchmaker; and a little Bedouin girl who made an "eternal etching" on Kathryn's heart as they sat on a hillside together near Bethlehem at sunset. This is the account of a journey that was filled with surprises and delights.

Every unique, God-appointed encounter documented in *A Jubilee Journey* drew me to magnify the Name of our Lord Jesus, who orders our steps for His glory and our joy. *A Jubilee Journey* is a true celebration of our Eternal King, who calls His children to join Him in the work He is doing among His people and around the world.

~ Donna Rees
Senior Publishing Editor, EAB

*****

I love memoirs/autobiographies—but personally knowing the author made this a memorable, awaking, and inspirational journey with a dear friend.

I love the easy flow of Kathryn's thoughts, insights, and experiences. She makes the journey of her readers catch the supernatural revelation and awakening to the work of the Lord that needs to be accomplished.

The whole essence of Kathryn's travels reveals how faithful the Father is in "birthing" a vision and tapping an unlikely middle-age lady's shoulder to step out of her comfort zone and be led by the Spirit—empowering and encouraging to all of us in saying, "Yes, we can—with God!"

It is with certainty her mission has brought freedom and hope to those who are hurting and marginalized—she is a good and faithful worker. She truly has a heart of a lioness and my prayer is that she continues the hunt with ever more intensity of courage and purpose in the years to come.

~ Janetta Hynous
Friend of the Author

TABLE OF CONTENTS

INTRODUCTION

"Good grief! Where does the time go? It seems like only yesterday..." These trite truisms clamor to convey that life is but a vapor—vanishing in an instant! My days are winding down, so I ask myself: "What about my life would be helpful for you to know? Have I any life-changing wisdom or insight to impart? Any heads-ups on pitfalls to avoid or joys that would lighten your load? Any adventures that would spur you on to step out into the unknown? What victories would encourage you?"

It all depends on who you are and where you are in your journey. I trust that in God's masterful weaving of our ways, He has for us a truth or two, a key of sorts, to reveal His character and how He weaves our days into intricate patterns that often look like a mess from our earthly point of view but are, in reality, an exquisite tapestry redeemed by His loving touch.

"O Lord, You have searched me and known me.
You know my sitting down and my rising up;
You understand my thought afar off.
You comprehend my path and my lying down,
And are acquainted with all my ways.
For there is not a word on my tongue,
But behold, O Lord, You know it altogether.
You have hedged me behind and before,
And laid Your hand upon me....
For You formed my inward parts;
You covered me in my mother's womb.
I will praise You, for I am fearfully and wonderfully made;
Marvelous are Your works,
And that my soul knows very well.

My frame was not hidden from You, when I was made in secret,
and skillfully wrought in the lowest parts of the earth.
Your eyes saw my substance, being yet unformed.
And in Your book they all were written, the days fashioned for me,
When as yet there were none of them."
Psalm 139:1–5,13–16

Chapter One

ORDEALS TO OUTPOURING

This effort to chronicle God's goodness, faithfulness, and engagement in the lives of an ordinary couple is a continuation of our original account of early marriage and ministry.[1] Surely, if we were hearing and obeying God's voice, life's circumstances would line up with our perceptions of what "walking with the Lord" would look like. However, we quickly learned that the way in which to live a sold-out life for God created more of a challenge than we previously had counted on.

Let's begin with a brief summary of those earlier years of bedlam. Our souls survived a number of ordeals in shadowy valleys and on shimmering mountaintops—like a spiraling circle around the mountains—sometimes drawing us upward (via the Holy Spirit), sometimes spiraling downward (by the world, the flesh, and the devil).[2]

During those sixteen years, we relied solely on the Lord to provide the finances and grace to raise our three children while remaining obedient to a distinctive anti-the-norm drumbeat. John's vision was to minister to ministers, ministries, and missionaries—to serve and support them according to any feasible means. He planned to provide office space for young, struggling ministries, as well as secretarial assistance, professional legal advisors, computers, counseling, newsletters, printing, and shipping of enumerable ministry tracts to more than 250 nations.

He also planned to man the Christian Broadcasting Network's Operation regional prayer phones and duplicate and distribute teaching cassette tapes—all at no or minimal charge, via volunteers! He named his new labor of love Christian Ministries.

When the pastor of a local Baptist church caught wind of John's projected vision, he offered the use of an old, 6,000-square-foot house standing on its last leg. It once had embraced the life of overflowing Sunday school classes, and now, the broken-down beauty would be available for John to spread the love of God within its walls again—for as long as he wanted, and in whatever manner he saw fit. The once splendid showcase was recalled into service of the kingdom!

John's servant's heart and listening ear consistently drew the trust of pastors, missionaries, and ministry leaders who longed for a "safe place" to release the pressures of their personal and professional lives. An invisible shingle seemed to hang across the threshold of Christian Ministries, beckoning burdened souls to come in for comfort and counsel.

John often operated as a supply sergeant. He instinctively knew whom to contact or where to find the required resources to meet a myriad of needs. He especially delighted in networking across denominational lines, and his vision of "Serving Together" morphed into projects such as amassing medical supplies and shipping them to nations in crisis, establishing a thrift store to serve the poor, and managing massive parking-lot yard sales that served as fundraisers.

When the Lord confirmed that our ten-year season serving with CMI had come full circle, He sent another heart-servant to take the helm and transferred the ministry to Washington, D.C., while simultaneously leading us to align with another highly credible mission organization. However, this new organization's requirement that we raise support instead of trusting the Lord daily for supply set us up for a fret-filled year of fundraising, only to be received a year later by a left hand of fellowship.

On our initial visit to the organization's headquarters, the CEO indicated that John would be serving as the second-in-command at their Stateside office in Georgia. Unfortunately, as a result of burnout, this executive bid *adieu* to the organization before our arrival. The new CEO's perspective on our position fell far short of our expectations. Within the first few weeks, it became apparent to all, including John and me, that we failed to fit into the current agenda—we have yet to discern the source of discord in those circumstances.

Our hunt for employment in the area proved fruitless. Thankfully, John was able to resume his pre-ministry occupation in sales with his family's heat-treating company in North Carolina. At this point, both of us were at a loss mentally, physically, emotionally, and spiritually and bore the symptoms of post-traumatic stress disorder, although we did experience the assurance that God was still on the throne.

With John "on the road" most of the week and no friends or family nearby, I slid into depression. My mother had died the previous year, our eldest daughter had married, our son was serving in the military in Saudi Arabia (during the Gulf War), our youngest daughter was struggling with health issues in college, we had experienced a stressful year of fundraising, we had made significant changes in location and living accommodations in a matter of two months, and my grieving father was coming to live with us!

Out of brokenness and boredom, I took a job working for a temporary employment agency for a few months before accepting a teaching position at a private middle school—not my dream job! The transition took on further complications with a painful and prolonged bout of shingles across my midsection.

On January 1, 1995, the suffocating clouds began to clear when the Lord spoke to me—not in an audible voice, but just a breath away: "When you stand before Me you will not be able to say, 'But John didn't...,' nor will you be able to hide behind your skirts, saying, 'But I'm a woman.'" These words seared my spirit.

God continued to declare, "As you enter into your fiftieth year of life (in July), it will not be just a Year of Jubilee but a Decade of Jubilee." God was promising to *"restore to you the years that the swarming locust has eaten."* (Joel 2:25) Indeed, within those next ten years I would serve on a pastoral staff for three years, travel to ten countries, and earn a Doctor of Missiology degree[3]—none of which had shown up on my radar screen prior to this revelation.

My original call to public speaking, preaching, and teaching had been hushed under hierarchical pronouncements such as "a woman's place is in the home" and various Bible verses taken out of context, such as 1 Timothy 2:12[4] topics I will address later. Now, God was emphasizing accountability to use my gifts for His glory in spite of the chauvinistic consensus of the day[5].

Chapter Two

CANADA (OUTPOURING) 1995

My spirit was lifted, my mind raced, and my emotions soared as I counted the days until the calendar finally flipped to my forty-ninth birthday on the 16th of July. Rumors of revival in Toronto, Canada, had spread to North Carolina. John and I had already spent his vacation time at the beach that summer, so he wasn't available to travel to Canada, but the Lord fanned the flame in my spirit with a fiery expectancy. I knew He was wooing me to jump into the "River of Life" being poured out in Toronto. My hunger and thirst for more of God compelled me to accept the challenge of driving to Canada by myself. Even though I could afford only a three-day stay, I would celebrate my forty-ninth birthday immersed in the presence of God!

Upon arrival I heard the sacred sound of more than three hundred Christian voices from around the world surging in heartfelt prayer—praying in their native tongues and in their prayer languages, truly a reflection of heaven come to earth—extravagant praise. The Holy Spirit whispered, "Come with your heart."

Already deeply moved, I lifted my eyes to see a purpose-driven man weaving his way across the room—taking a distinct path straight toward me. He introduced himself as a pastor from Texas and said, "The Lord sent me to tell you that you are and always have been a good mother."

What?! How did he know that my heavy heart accused me of just the opposite? I slumped to the floor in tears—so blessed by the Lord's powerful, personal love that would whisper this message of hope into a stranger's ear to boldly speak His words of life and healing to me!

I experienced a considerable amount of "carpet time"[6] during those three days, as the Lord showed me visions and saturated my heart with His healing presence. On the lighter side, I saw Jesus "cutting a rug" in dance! It startled me because I had always pictured Him as being quite stoic. When I questioned the reality of what I was seeing in the Spirit, He assured me through the Shepherd's Heart translation of Zephaniah 3:16:

"He is cheered and beams with exceeding joy, and takes pleasure in your presence. He cannot contain Himself at the thought of you, and with the greatest joy spins around wildly in anticipation over you. In fact He shouts and sings in triumph, joyfully proclaiming the gladness of His heart in a song of rejoicing. All because of you."

The next day, on my forty-ninth birthday, a fresh fragrance of the Lord's Presence permeated my every move—a flow of worshiping, resting in Him, and sharing in the Spirit with my new family from around the world. The morning session unfolded much like a missions update of God moving mightily in Thailand, China, and England. Karen, a new friend from New Zealand, noted that during the two weeks before I had arrived, she had heard nothing about missions! Yet, everywhere I turned I heard of the latest life-changing experiences and encounters on the mission fields.

I so yearned to be one of God's mailmen—delivering His letters of love and promises to the multitudes! He was calling me to "come out of hiding, and don't let go—be a bulldog!" He pointed me to Philippians 3:14 (NIV):

"I press on toward the goal to win the prize for which God has called me heavenward in Christ Jesus."

And Isaiah 54:2 (NIV):

"Enlarge the place of your tent, stretch your tent curtains wide, do not hold back; lengthen your cords, strengthen your stakes."

It was no longer about me; it was about Him.

The theme of the Lord's outpouring—then and now—is a call to deeper intimacy with Him, individually and personally. He continues to search for an awakened Bride who loves Him. After all, what groom wants a bride who talks with him only when she wants something or only wants to spend time with him for an hour on Sunday mornings? God yearns to commune with believers who long to know Him more deeply, and above all, to spend time alone with Him in the secret place of His Presence.

Karen blessed me with a woven white bookmark honoring the holiness of this sacred celebration of my jubilee birthday. I wore a purple linen dress to the evening service that night—purple, the color of royalty, and linen, worn by the priests of old (a fabric that does not "sweat"), thus offering us a symbol of trust in God rather than self-works. The decision to wear the purple linen dress also conveyed my commitment to not buy any new clothes for a year, simply as a gesture of appreciation for what Christ had already clothed me with—Himself!

During the evening worship, I danced before God with all my might, in total freedom—joining other joyous souls doing the Jewish hora (a Hebrew dance), circling the front of the auditorium with abandon. Later, as I rested in the Spirit, I envisioned my baggage, marked "rejection," being parachuted from a plane flying over the ocean, diving down into the depths of its watery grave. The aircraft then slipped into a nosedive spiraling toward the sea with all my other baggage of lesser bondage sinking with it—another prophetic scene depicting my newfound freedom. God reminded me of Psalm 103:12:

"As far as the east is from the west, so far has He removed our transgressions from us."

I basked in the presence of the Holy Spirit for hours after each meeting, as the Lord brought up memories and brought healing to my soul as He filled me with His words of love and encouragement.

That week I started studying the Book of Philippians, which is the fiftieth book of the Bible and one that rings with JOY! Paul wrote this joy letter as a result of his journey of intimacy with Christ and obedience to Him. The words *focus* and *yield* leapt off the pages as words of instruction from God for the coming year, jogging my mind back to the issues of intimacy and missions that He had highlighted:

Chapter 1: JOY IN SUFFERING
Chapter 2: JOY IN SERVING
Chapter 3: JOY IN BELIEVING
Chapter 4: JOY IN GIVING

Chapter Three

FURTHER INSTRUCTIONS

En route to Toronto I pulled off the parkway for a quick view of Niagara Falls from a distance and within seconds popped back into the car, eager to press on—as is my usual mode of operation! On the way home, however, caught up in the atmosphere of my "honeymoon with God," Niagara Falls arrested my attention as it has for other lovers throughout the centuries. Hopping out of the car, I pressed in for a closer view. As sprinkles started threatening my sunny day, I thought, "I need to jog back to the car and grab my umbrella," but the Holy Spirit whispered, "Stop trying to protect yourself—the days of self-protection are over."

Almost at once the light rain stopped. Had I not heeded the Holy Spirit's voice, I would have been lugging my "protection" around all morning. This event was the first of numerous nudges through the years that would encourage me to give up trying to protect myself, and instead, to TRUST HIM to take care of me.

A cable train descended just feet from where I had stood on my first visit, but in my haste, I had been blinded to its existence—I had overlooked the opportunity right in front of me. However, this time I was much more alert to the provision. This scenario would play out over and over in the days to come as the Lord showed me His provision to care for me in ways I had never discerned.

The cable train landed me right in front of a variety of ferry-type vessels that would carry passengers up to and behind the waterfalls. Feeling a surge of bravery, I boarded the *Maid of the Mist*, a little tourist tugboat. Well aware that

I no longer stood alone on the edge of a cliff surveying the action from a safe place, I was engaging with the Lord's invitation to step out of my comfort zone.

As the tugboat moved close to the waterfalls, it was cupped within their cave-like covering. I felt the water spraying fiercely upon me and springing from a strong force flowing under me, around me, and over me—framing an amazing sense of awe and baptism and causing me to consider the resurrection power of the Holy Spirit and the new life He was creating within me!

After casting a few furtive glances around the vibrating vessel, I discovered that a delegation of Japanese people—about one hundred of them—was also on the tugboat. As I began observing them, the Lord breathed these words into my spirit: "You are going to draw a delegation of Japanese to the TRUE POWER SOURCE." Not understanding how this could happen, I reasoned that He was referencing my daily prayers. I had begun praying out of *Operation World* the year before, and since the first day when the country highlighted in the prayer guide had been Japan (on my birthday in 1994)—I had diligently prayed for them daily.

As I continued in my almost-stunned state, I became aware of my pocket burning with the last of my Canadian currency! I expectantly entered the souvenir shop, where my eyes immediately dialed in on a delicate, pastel-flowered pin. It spoke to me of my precious time with the Lord—but the sturdy navy tote bag with "Niagara Falls" stenciled in white seemed to be a more practical purchase—sold! Later, the Lord gently revealed that I often substitute the "practical" for the "beautiful" and miss the greater gift. Noted.

Approaching the cable train, which would return me to the top of the cliff and my parked car, it dawned on me that they charged a fee for this service—and my pockets had holes! The astute attendant recognized my predicament and took pity on me. He invited me to ride free of charge—just like Jesus! (Heaven is a FREE GIFT! There is NOTHING we can do to earn it or deserve it—Jesus paid it all!)

I continued my trek homeward, maneuvering my way through a maze of exits . . . "Oh, no! I am on a toll road!" Frantic to figure out what to do, I pulled over near a guard station—and wrote a check for $2.19 to the New York State Thruway. Next, I noticed the needle on the gas gauge hovered over "Empty." Thankfully, the famous orange-yellow glow of a Shell station saved the day. As I searched for my Shell credit card, I rejoiced in God's provision that had met my every challenge.

The Holy Spirit continued my "traveling tips" over the remaining eight-hour drive home. These lessons were not only relevant to my current road trip; He also compared them to my entire spiritual journey:

Make sure you have sufficient gas/oil.
Keep your focus on the road ahead.
Don't glue your eyes on the rear-view mirror!
No U-turns.
Watch for speed-limit changes.
You can't push the slow ones.
Others are following you.
If you follow the fast ones, be sure you have enough distance between you if they stop, swerve, or leave the highway.
Read the signs.
Obey the signs.
When you get distracted, you scribble!
One task at a time.
When you have made a wrong turn, you may have to go on a while until you find the appropriate place to turn around.
Know where you are going.
It doesn't matter how many mistakes you make on the way; if you will turn around (repent), you will reach your destination.
Don't give up!

"Let us not become weary in doing good,
for at the proper time we will reap a harvest
if we do not give up."
Galatians 6:9 (NIV)

John met me with a warm "Welcome home!" and a birthday gift from him and our children—a bicycle (Japan's number-one means of transportation)! The next morning while praising God I uttered, "My fiftieth birthday could not be any better than this." The Lord immediately dropped into my heart these words: "You will be in Japan on your fiftieth birthday."

LET THE FIRE FALL

During the weekend following my return from Toronto, our church hosted a "Let the Fire Fall" Conference. The soaking presence of the Lord saturated the sanctuary. While resting in the Spirit on the second day, I watched a large fishhook sink gently down into my heart and pull up an old, gunky bicycle chain. The Holy Spirit worked at cleaning it until it was transformed into a sparkling silver chain that then turned into pure gold. He was making all things new.

After attending the ministry team meeting and receiving healing for TMJ, I returned to resting in the Spirit. I tried to make myself repentant, but nothing specific came to mind. The Lord laughed at me and said: "Let Me lead. After soaking for a few days, it will come up easily, roots and all." I thought about how, in the natural realm, that is how we de-weed too—it's much easier to pull up weeds after a soaking rain.

During our afternoon intercession time, Kathleen Dillard shared about some housewives who had been using *Operation World* as a prayer guide. They had discerned a strong pull of the Spirit to linger on Albania and had ended up visiting there—was the Lord hinting that I may have a similar experience with Japan?

Later I had a vision of myself as a little girl dressed up in a wedding gown. I was approaching Jesus as a child. I had regained my sense of expectancy. I was recommitting to my First Love. As Randy Clark prayed for an anointing and commissioning for healing, the palms of my hands felt like they were on fire.

I had prayed about anger issues earlier and heard the Lord say: "Deal with anger immediately. Don't sell the enemy any real estate." After I had repented, I had a vision of a flower garden. The dandelions had been plucked up, and the garden flourished with gorgeous blooms of majestic colors. I recognized the Lord's provision. I could exchange my irritation for a flower from my inner garden and offer it to someone—or even enjoy a bouquet instead of clinging to my dismay.

"Do not be stiff-necked, as your fathers were; submit to the LORD."
2 Chronicles 30:8 (NIV)

"Finally, brethren, whatever things are true, whatever things are noble, whatever things are just, whatever things are pure, whatever things are lovely, whatever things are of good report; if there be any virtue, and if there is anything praiseworthy; meditate on these things."
Philippians 4:8

I saw my gold chain reappear. Its form had been changed, and it now looped like a conveyor belt running between my heart and my head. God aligned me for proper balance—a steady flow of the Spirit directing my soul (thoughts, emotions, and will).

A little later the Lord offered His hand and drew me into a dance—a flowing fantasy waltz through the universe. He wore a white tux, and I swayed alongside Him in a luxurious, long, light-blue gown. He asked, "Can you do this?" He clicked His heels in midair, and I followed with precision!

"Can you do this?" He inquired as He tumbled forward, doing a complete flip in midair. He laughed as I tried to imitate Him. I experienced Jesus in realms previously unknown to me: the joy of His intimacy, the surprise of His sense of humor, the thrill of hearing Him laugh, resting in His arms of love! He is life abundant!

"You turned my wailing into dancing; you removed my sackcloth and clothed me with joy, that my heart may sing your praises and not be silent. LORD my God, I will praise you forever."
Psalm 30:11–12 (NIV)

The Westminster Short Confession, which is basically the catechism teachings of the Church, clearly states, "The chief end of man is to glorify God and ENJOY Him forever!" How are you doing?

God continued to restore to me my First Love. As the days of "Let the Fire Fall" progressed, people who had known me for years did not recognize me! Apparently, the glow on my face reflected the intensity I was experiencing in seeking the presence of the Lord.

"But we all, with unveiled, beholding as in a mirror the glory of the Lord, are being transformed into the same image from glory to glory, just as by the Spirit of the Lord."
2 Corinthians 3:18

Another area the Lord drew my attention to involved my childhood memories of my family's makeshift bathroom. I had held onto shadowy memories of our dank, dark basement with its dirt floor and musty, damp walls. A small, bare, dim light bulb dangled at the bottom of the rickety, narrow stairway. My dad had mounted a dingy-looking tub and toilet onto a rough wooden platform in the back cobwebby corner. A cold chill gave me the creeps every time I descended into this dungeon-like setting in my memory.

While soaking in the Lord's presence, He suggested that we remodel the whole basement—HGTV at work! We installed a smooth and shiny hardwood floor and opted for a soft color pallet, bright artificial lighting, and glistening bathroom fixtures—including a lounge area with a comfy, contemporary chair and matching love seat opposite a mirrored vanity. A sense of peace and healing soothed my soul.

"I gave orders to purify the rooms."
Nehemiah 13:9 (NIV)

On the last day of the conference, Randy mentioned that his old roommate was from Japan, and I almost jumped out of my seat! There it was again! Japan. Japan. Japan. I detected a "Tinkerbell-like" light flying around within my whole body—bringing a flicker of light here and there. This was followed by an explosion in my heart that illuminated me completely. No more dark corners—I was clearly hearing God: Japan was officially on my to-do list!

After receiving prayer for those called into full-time ministry, I spied a ship in the background. I watched an image of me grip myself by the hair and violently dunk my being into the water—I thrashed around, fighting myself. All of a sudden, I relaxed and simply slid back onto a bright pink float and waved good-bye as the ship headed out to sea. What a relief! (I get seasick!)

The Spirit started gently steering my raft down the Yangtze River, into the Sea of Japan, and all around Asia, Europe, and Africa. I was assured that the Holy Spirit would not force me to go anywhere; He would gently lead me in the way I should go.

Then I heard Randy praying against the spirits of fear of poverty and inadequacy. I had a vision of being in a round room with towering walls, as though I were in the bottom of a well. Gold coins were falling on John and me, completely covering us. I had to find a place to breathe. I heard the words of Deuteronomy 28:2 (NIV):

"All these blessings will come upon you and accompany you if you obey the LORD, your God."

I saw John and me walking arm-in-arm along the shore with Jesus. Jesus drew our heads to His chest. John sobbed, then laughed. We became as little children playing with Jesus—dancing around in circles. He scooped us up into His arms and hugged us. Then we rolled down a hill, laughing.

"God has brought me laughter, and everyone who hears about this will laugh with me."
Genesis 21:6 (NIV)

Chapter Four

"HEY, YOU!"

Once the school year had started up again, there was little time for soaking in the Lord's presence 24/7. My passion was now focused on my middle school students, and my journal writings dwindled to scanty scratches: "Lord, please help me to continue receiving Your voice—like the steady rain running down my bedroom window. I don't want to hide under a shelter. (I saw myself huddled under a picnic shelter. There was no food under the shelter, but there was a tablecloth blanketed with a feast out on the open grass.) I heard Him reply: "Keep pressing into Me and moving out into the world. I have provided abundantly for you."

"Trust in the LORD with all your heart, and lean not on your own understanding; in all your ways acknowledge Him, and He shall direct your paths."
Proverbs 3:5–6

Several weeks later I had a vision of lambs frolicking in a field. As they settled next to me, one by one, I stroked their soft little heads and pulled out burrs buried in their fleeces. Just as Mary's little lamb had "followed her to school one day," these lambs followed me to school, and I taught them with joy. The Lord encouraged me, "You do not know how important your job is."

"Feed My lambs."
John 21:15

Our grandson's ETA into this world hovered around mid-September, which made me hesitant about registering for a women's conference scheduled for the second weekend of the month. But the Spirit kept nudging me, and I could not quiet my desire to experience more of what the Lord was doing among women. I drove the three hours to Montreat, North Carolina, by myself to make possible a prompt exit should Nicholas decide his time in the womb had come to an end!

During the first night of the conference, God confirmed my calling to Japan once again. As a young Japanese woman shared her story of salvation, the Lord spoke to my spirit: "I am delivering you from bondages that others have placed on you. I am burning them away." I saw myself being burned at the stake, but the fire did not consume me. I rejoiced, broke free, ran, and released others. The Lord continued: "I am putting My words in your mouth. They are words of fire. I am going to set your feet on foreign soil."

More than two thousand women listened to Fuchsia Pickett speak the next morning as she challenged us to be willing to change—from the women we are to the women God created us to be. She stressed that our level of repentance would determine how much joy we would receive in the process. I had no doubt about my willingness to change. More than anything, I wanted to be the woman God had created me to be.

June Evans taught the afternoon session, which was on the ministry and gifts of the Holy Spirit. At the end of her teaching, she stepped to the left side of the stage and said: "There is a woman here who has been absolutely paralyzed. God has a call on your life and your ministry, but the devil has shut you down. God wants you to know that He is starting your motor again!" She walked across the stage, pointed me out, and said: "I looked over at you while I was ministering—it was like I could see the Lord pouring a fresh oil of anointing upon your life. And the Lord wants you to know that the place where you are and the places you have been walking and ministering—that you are going to have to enlarge, and you are going to have to stretch out because God's vision for your life is broader than where you are and what you are doing. He wants you to lay hold and walk because there is a broadness, there is a width and a depth and a height that you have not yet reached, but you are about to go there, says the Lord!"

The crowd roared with cheers. June quietly closed her notebook and stepped off the stage. She did not speak prophetically to anyone else. The inspiring word carried a confirmation of what God had already conceived in my spirit.

A season of breakthrough had arrived. God exhorted me: "Use everything you have to build the kingdom, build lives. Find empty vessels and fill them, train them. Praise Me. As you praise Me, your face will shine like gold. When I see My reflection in you, I will know you are ready for more."

Once again the Holy Spirit shone His flashlight into my secret chambers. He nodded as He said, "It's looking good." Then He pumped my spirit full of fresh water. The bubbles of blessing blew through me, but the fire in my heart remained unquenched and stoked my soul with His Presence.

The following Sunday our pastor invited me to tell our congregation about my encounter with the Lord at the retreat. He summoned me, and three other women who had also been on retreats that weekend, to come to the altar, and called the men to stand behind us, lay hands on us, and join him in prayer, acknowledging God's moving among His daughters.

While praying for me, one of the men saw the word "LANGUAGES" written above my head. I, in turn, observed the letters of the word written on a blackboard. The letters began to drip down the board like tears, forming a river in France (to date I have not set foot beyond the Paris airport, but I am still expecting to). No doubt, the Lord's call was embracing several nations in the Eastern Hemisphere.

The next morning, while leisurely looking over pamphlets that I had picked up at the conference, I noticed mention of a trip to Israel that was scheduled for March. A trip to Israel was one trip my thoughts had tossed about from the time I had accepted Jesus as my Savior twenty-eight years ago. I instantly dismissed the idea—finding substitute teachers in our private Christian school had proved to be next to impossible even for a few days, let alone for two weeks. However, the Holy Spirit prodded me to pursue the possibility. God went before me, and the door flew open when a parent who had a teaching degree **offered** to fill in for me! March was six months away, but it would be worth the wait!

NICHOLAS

At the first notification that my eldest daughter, Kimberly, was in labor, I left school and scooted expectantly over to the hospital, only to end up spending the night in the delivery waiting room. Our youngest daughter, Christi, is a nurse and was given the honor of attending Kimberly and her husband during the lengthy labor. Christi would periodically update me on the progress, but the long-anticipated word didn't arrive until the next morning: "Mother and baby are well!" The wonder of it all swept over me afresh as I held Nicholas for the very first time—the blessing of a new little person to love!

A few weeks later, his mother brought him to visit me at school so that I could show him off. It was there that one of the most touching and lasting memories of God's love came as Nicholas stared directly into my eyes—connecting and smiling right back at me! He warmed my heart to the nth degree! I immediately heard the Lord say, "This is how I feel when you lock eyes with Me and SMILE!"

*****

The following months were filled with surprises and special words from the Lord. I experienced a recurring dream in which I stood dressed in white and speaking on stage in a huge auditorium. I looked like a tiny speck in the midst of a mass of humanity. God said, "It's going to happen someday."

A friend invited me to share about my Toronto "honeymoon with Jesus" at a small women's conference in Peachtree City, Georgia. Reverend Mary, a large, African-American lady who ran an inner-city ministry in Atlanta, came to hear me speak. She graciously encouraged me and also prophesied over me, assuring me that God would raise up young women to help me in my ministry.

The visions continued. I saw God stuff something into John's fist, and then a large stalk appeared. It bloomed into a bouquet of flowers that cascaded down a mountain into a valley. God explained, "John will bring comfort and joy to those in the valleys of life." Two weeks later, Bob Mumford used the same illustration to explain how God was moving the external into the internal.

God revealed that I was not relaxing in Him. He showed me a telescope. I was the wide end; He was the narrow end. The Lord said, "Turn it around." Peace came as I was reminded of the words of John 3:30: *"He must increase; but I must decrease."* That truly takes the pressure off.

I then saw a chain of Marines marching in step in my bloodstream. The Lord dismantled their ranks and devoured them like Pac Man, which was a picture of pharisaism, that is, legalistically going through the motions, trying to be perfect in my own strength.

I saw a fire gutting the school where I worked—it turned to ashes. The Lord reminded me of His promise to give us *"beauty for ashes"* (Isaiah 61:3). I knew my sojourn there was soon coming to an end—God was preparing me to sow in another field.

Chapter Five

ISRAEL (CBU) 1996

Off to Israel! Our entourage spent what seemed like an eternity at JFK International Airport before boarding the Israeli airline, ELAL, at 1:30 a.m., but not before a voice via the public address system summoned me to the baggage area to unlock my suitcase—my electric toothbrush was vibrating! My traveling woes continued in Tel Aviv when an old un-gentleman rudely cast me aside as I reached to claim my bags off the conveyor belt. Jet-lagged, exhausted, and disoriented—my dreams of world travel dissolved into the proverbial puddle of tears.

The evening had yet to ebb when our tour group, led by Jim Jackson of Christian Believers United, landed in Tel Aviv. Not wanting to waste waking hours, we bounded out to the buses and set our sights to go straight to Joppa. In Biblical times, the port of Joppa marked the northernmost border of the Philistines' territory. Solomon floated his cedars of Lebanon to this port, and Jonah bedded down on the ship here (the enemy always provides a ship—passage paid—to divert us from God's plan). Peter raised Dorcas back to life in Joppa, and he later received a visit from Simon the tanner, along with a lesson on unclean food. My photo album skips these historic scenes because my trusty camera had clicked to the wrong setting during the flight, which resulted in a dead battery!

On the first night, our hotel in Tiberias rested on the western shore of the Sea of Galilee. My assigned roommate, who was touring with a married couple, turned out to be a little eccentric around the edges. One unfortunate glance as she stripped to slide her nightgown over her head alerted my eyes to shield themselves! The next morning our incompatibilities put an insufferable strain on my senses as we took our assigned seats next to each other on the bus—until she fell asleep with her head cradled on my shoulder!

To my relief, the tour leader granted my request for a transfer to another bus. I realized the Lord has His hands full when it comes to my total transformation!

On the second day we toured Caesarea, which Herod[7] built reminiscent of a Roman city and named after you-know-who! Pontius Pilate lived in this commercial city when it served as the cultural capital, boasting of its amazing amphitheater dug out by hand.

Israel's international significance lies in its location as well as its religious roots in Judaism, Christianity, and Islam. This 400 x 80-mile strip of land links Africa to Europe and Asia. At one time, Israel's landscape teemed with tall trees, but when the Turks instigated an industrial revolution, they systematically stripped her land of this natural resource. In 1948, when Israel birthed their nation, they hand-planted 6 million trees, and continued to plant 3 to 6 million trees annually, yet only 5 percent of the country had been reforested by 1996.

I was privileged to participate in a tree-planting effort at Kiryat Menachem, "City of Comfort." In Isaiah 40:2–3, the Lord reminds us, *"Speak comfort to Jerusalem .... Prepare the way of the LORD."* These hills of Jerusalem, themselves, are our Christian heritage and our Jewish roots. I tucked ten seedlings in my arms while attempting to steady my footsteps as I stumbled down the rocky hillside with a goal of establishing personal roots in Israel. Each seedling signified a specific family member.

A holy hush enveloped me as tears trickled down my cheeks and my trembling fingers dug into the soil, preparing it to receive my gift—my heart, for in my heart I carried each family member before the Lord in thanksgiving and dedication. I prayed for God's blessing upon them and asked that they would become *"trees of righteousness, the planting of the Lord, that He may be glorified"* (Isaiah 61:3) and that each would *"be like a tree planted by the rivers of water, that brings forth its fruit in its season, whose leaf also shall not wither; and whatever he does shall prosper"* (Psalm 1:3).

Another sobering atmosphere settled over me at the Wailing Wall, which is close to the place where the Holy of Holies was situated in Jesus' day. The Jewish people say it is just a "local call" to God from there! It definitely held a sacred sense of His presence as I donned a black veil and added my laundry list of petitions into the slits between stones. It felt like God Himself was peering over my shoulder and smiling in response to my visit as I tiptoed the traditional seven steps backward on my exit from this holy ground.

A visit to Yad Vashem, their Holocaust Museum, also quieted my soul in remembrance of the horrors the Jewish people had endured. We must never forget the results of the menacing moral lapse that cost 6 million Jews their lives. In the silent shadows of the Hall of Remembrance, the names of twenty internment camps are etched in the flooring—an eerie evidence of the evil perpetrated against the Jews. Outside are twenty white, limestone, broken-off pillars of various heights, ranging in size from 8 feet and descending to 6 feet, 4 feet, and 2 feet. They portray a sense of the reality of the suffering—by all ages. The Nazis moved the Jews to ghettos, then concentration camps, then to extermination camps. I shall forever pray for the peace of Jerusalem as God exhorts us to do in Psalm 122:6:

"Pray for the peace of Jerusalem: 'May they prosper who love you.'"

I found the Old City intriguing. I could not take in enough of the sights and sounds of the Jewish community, garbed in authentic tradition that had remained through the centuries and calling out to one another in their native tongue. It felt like I had always imagined it to be when Jesus literally had walked these narrow pathways, which were the arms' width of two people. We literally were forced to press our backs to the walls so that cars could pass! Yet this was the hub and hum of their daily life—buying and selling their wares in the bazaar-type alleys. There were scarfed women in their street-length coverings and men in long, black robes with their heads wrapped in checkered scarves called kaffiyehs sitting on low stools and smoking their hookahs.[8]

We took Holy Communion by the Garden Tomb, drinking from miniature olive wood cups—so very thankful that the tomb is EMPTY! We crossed the Sea of Galilee and toured the ancient ruins and towns of Biblical times: Jericho, Capernaum, the Dead Sea, the fortress at Masada, and other well-known Biblical sites.

To my surprise, there were a few places that radically rattled my worldview. One was the Temple Mount. We had to pray with our eyes open to avoid being arrested by the guards. Christians are not welcome there! We could not read the Bible or touch one another. It felt evil and eerie as guards eyed us with suspicion outside the Dome of the Rock. Several pick-pockets were caught around us, causing a stir, so we politely left as the police approached.

Another discomfiting episode took place as we exited St. George's Restaurant on Bethlehem Square to cross over to The Church of the Nativity on the opposite side. The church was supposedly built over a grotto[9] where some traditions say Jesus was born. We were warned not to leave the restaurant alone but rather to walk closely within groups. The moment I stepped outside with two other women, men and boys of various ages were literally in our faces with their hands hovering around our bodies—threatening harm if we resisted their advances.

We ignored their menacing faces as best we could and continued moving forward with our arms firmly locked together until at last we reached the church. It is ironic that over the years of my travels in many different countries and in various dangerous situations, I never felt fear as intensely as I did in Bethlehem Square. Whatever happened to "O Little Town of Bethlehem"?

On the lighter side, I rode a donkey and a camel, and I also enjoyed listening to our tour guide, Rowan. As our crazy bus driver wound us around precarious places, she shared a joke about a priest and a bus driver when they arrived in heaven: The priest got a nominal reward. The bus driver got great riches. She explained that the people slept when the priest did his job, but they prayed when the bus driver drove!

A precious memory manifested on Shepherd's Hill outside Bethlehem at sunset. Flocks of sheep roamed freely around us as we rested on good-sized rocks scattered across the landscape. Several took turns reading the Christmas story while we listened to the sheep gently baaing as their bells tinkled in the soft breeze.

I was startled at first when a little Bedouin girl who appeared to be about seven years old climbed up on my lap. We watched the city lights slowly switch on. She snuggled close as we lit candles and sang hymns in what was to her a foreign language. My candle kept going out—I wasn't protecting it enough—but others were quick to come alongside and rekindle it, just as this little girl rekindled in me a love for Israel. I have since found that no matter where in the world I roam, it is the children (and the childlike) who make an eternal etching on my heart.

KATHRYN

Upon my return home from Israel, I continued to press in for a closer connection with the Lord and accordingly searched out several conferences to attend that spring. The women's conference at Morning Star was particularly life-impacting. In my usual manner, I sent a check with my registration form, signed with my full name, Kathryn G. Hendershot. When I arrived, they handed me a conference packet, which included an already-printed name tag: KATHRYN. Several women naturally began addressing me as Kathryn. I would reply, "Oh, you may call me Kathy."

Well, on the third day of the conference, one of the women countered me with "The Lord will not allow me to call you Kathy because that is not the fullness of who you are!" I was stunned, to say the least—blown away! My spirit aligned immediately with what she said. I literally felt the Holy Spirit shoot through my being. The Lord said, "I have healed the little girl, Kathy, and I am calling you forth as the woman of God I created you to be: Kathryn." From that time on, I have introduced myself as Kathryn, and I find that it does call me out of my childish ways into more mature ways of responding to life's challenges.

At another conference in Montreat, a stranger turned to me in the midst of a meeting and asked if the name Gayle meant anything to me. I replied, "Yes, that is my middle name." She said, "God wants you to know that no circumstance will be able to overtake you; you are a windstorm created to blow them away!" I later looked up the meaning of my names: *Kathryn* means "pure," and *Gayle* means "delight." *Reese*, my maiden name, means "enthusiastic." I am an enthusiastic, pure delight! Ha! Ha! That is my goal in life!

Chapter Six

JAPAN (50TH) 1996

By the end of the school year, my thoughts had ebbed back to Japan. I checked out the Vineyard's worldwide directory and found four Vineyard Fellowships currently meeting in this island country lying off the east coast of Asia. I contacted the pastors, explained my leading to celebrate my fiftieth birthday in their country, and offered to be of service in any way they perceived might be profitable for their congregations. My suggested possibilities included teaching, preaching, caring for their children, or prayer walking. After making my request a matter of prayer, Toshi Araki of Tokorozawa (near Tokyo) and Yugi Yasaka of Shimizu encouraged me to come; both expressed excitement about my travel plans.

Toshi arranged to meet me at the airport in Tokyo with Takako Yamashite, a married woman about my age who spoke English! After a warm welcome and a two-hour drive of delightful getting-to-know-you conversation, we arrived at her tiny traditional Japanese home. Just inside the front door, Takako presented me with a new pair of house slippers. She continued to dote on me with anticipated attention to my every desire. Nothing was too much trouble! Pastries and fresh fruit and vegetables were served seemingly without a struggle throughout my time with the Yamashites—I later was humbled to discover that the melon she served me every morning had cost $25!

Takako had prepared my room with an authentic tatami mat which, after being awake for twenty-seven hours, felt like a feather bed. It seemed that I was fitting into their true Japanese tradition without a hiccup, until on my last day

Takako confessed that her family slept on American-style beds upstairs!

On my first morning in this mystical, quaint neighborhood, we strolled through narrow lanes, then through a small farm area that transitioned into a busy commercial area, all within a relatively small number of steps—so much for the eye to take in! People of all ages and all walks of life maneuvered their bicycles among their fellow pedestrians—all were clad in a kaleidoscope of traditional and trendy fashions. Takako wore a simple, blue housedress with her white parasol splayed open in the sunshine. Other women cycled with their aprons draped over dresses on their daily routes to the fresh food markets. Men in suits, students in uniforms—it was an endless portrayal of the Japanese on the move.

Our mission that morning was to take a short train ride to Kokubu Station to reserve a ticket for my Bullet Train excursion to Shimizu, which would take place the next day. The logistical preparation necessary to transport me to the appropriate venues on a prearranged schedule was daunting. Takako was doing a helmsman's job, for which I was deeply grateful.

Once we had secured my ticket, we squeezed back onto the train to Kokubunji and began our reverse route back to her house. A light rain signaled both the cyclists and those on foot to unfold their umbrellas—another fascinating scene as a sea of umbrellas bobbed above cyclists and pedestrians hurrying off to their respective destinations.

On the slower side, as we approached the more rural area I spied a well-dressed little man facing the hedge along a path with his back to us. I found myself staring at him until I realized he was taking a leak! I swallowed my embarrassment and looked away. I was not sure if Takako had noticed him or me, but if she did, she took it in stride. Let's just chalk it up as "local color."

Mr. Yamashite joined us for dinner and an energetic evening of conversation. In response to his inquisitiveness, I pulled out a map of North Carolina and showed them the location of Greensboro, shared photos of my family, and presented them with gifts from home. It proved to be a perfect opportunity to share about my relationship with the Lord. He listened intently, asked questions, and seemed content with my answers. He allowed his wife to attend church, although he was not a believer yet. The Lord gave me favor with him, and hopefully He planted some seed in Mr. Yamashite's heart.

The next morning, Takako called a cab, and the three of us took an hour's ride to Tokyo Station, where they both escorted me to my seat on the Bullet Train to Shimizu. I felt like a child being tucked in by her parents—such a sweet couple tenderly taking care of me!

Breathtaking scenery zoomed past my window on the Bullet Train! Mount Fuji was the only thing that I was able to capture on film; everything else was out of sight by the time I had recognized it! I do remember being impressed with all the laundry hanging on lines outside windows—a sight that would curiously repeat itself in most countries I would be traveling in during my Decade of Jubilee.

Yugi and Jerry (a beautiful redhead from Alabama), along with their children Maria (7 months old) and Tyler (3 years old), met me at the Shimizu Station. I was pleasantly surprised to meet an American on this leg of my journey, although as our time together progressed, I found my American sister and her husband were not happy campers in Shimizu. They had been there for two years and only one couple had come to their house church—and Yugi was out of work. Their discouragement was palpable. We talked and prayed and prayed and talked. The Holy Spirit seemed to have the words they needed to hear and the hope they needed to focus on as I shared with them about my own journey—especially of our walking by faith for sixteen years while raising three children. God is faithful.

The next morning, six people came (with lots of little kids). This constituted a crowd for their little house church.

One by one, they gradually began to look me in the eye, as I shared the love of God with them. I was blessed to pray with several of them individually and watched the Holy Spirit bring them peace and smiles—their countenances lightened.

Jerry and I had some alone time that afternoon, and she was able to freely "unload" and receive some counsel. "Thank You, Holy Spirit, for the privilege of being there for her."

The next day, five young mothers showed up with their babies for a mothers' meeting. I encouraged them with the Word of God and prayed with each of them before departing on the Bullet Train back to Kokobunji.

Back in Tokorozawa, my spirit was refreshed when the opportunity arose to share with ten women at Takako's church. I taught on Deborah and God's call for women to step up into leadership positions. They attentively received the Word and engaged—asking questions with hungry hearts. Then I spent some private time ministering to Naomi, a young wife in need of the Father's love to lighten her load. That afternoon Takako and I enjoyed a sweet time of prayer together, and after I taught her "The Bridge"[10] method of sharing her faith, she practiced on me!

Reiko and Yuko were newcomers to Takako's English class. These pre-Christians eagerly engaged us in the classroom discussion and then whisked us away to a restaurant for crab croquettes and an opportunity to learn more about this "Westerner"—and to practice their English! Later in the week, Reiko arranged for us to meet with her and another friend, Akia, at a craft sale in a local home setting. Afterwards, she drove her Figaro (a fancy French auto) to Jonathan's (an upscale restaurant) for lunch. Although we never spoke directly about the Lord, I was able to reference His reality in my life. Reiko was intrigued and invited me to stay in her home when I return to Japan. I trust that the Lord was and is preparing the soil of her heart to receive Him as her Savior.

Mr. Yamashite kindly drove me to Hijama Chapel, about an hour's drive, on his day off. Takako made sure I made contact with Mari, a young woman sponsoring this gathering of young girls, before leaving me there. The pastor and his wife also joined the gathering and watched as we played some fun games, such as Chee Chicka Boom, and ate barbecue before I spoke on being confident in God's love. Their twenty-five beautiful faces focused intently on my every word.

Some were visibly shaken when they realized God's great love for them. One of the girls confessed she had cried the entire previous day because of a low score on an exam—there is remarkable pressure upon students to excel in their studies. Her relief of receiving God's love and acceptance for who she was—not for her performance—set her free and filled her with joy! Many shared how the message had impacted them and encouraged them. Sharon, their American English teacher, was touched, and the pastor's wife asked to copy my notes so she could pass on the message to their women's group.

It was thrilling to learn that initially they had gathered only because I was coming, but then they had decided to keep meeting together and encouraging one another in God's love. They presented me with a huge bouquet of flowers, which I took "home" to share with Takako!

It was humbling to see my likeness on posters that announced, "Kathryn is coming!" The Tokorozawa Vineyard Fellowship buzzed with anticipation that Sunday morning—talk about overcoming a lack of confidence with such a big buildup! Fortunately, the Holy Spirit showed up and saved the day. The congregation of about forty adults entered praise and worship with abandon. Half the songs were sung in Japanese and half in English.

Unfortunately, my interpreter did not know he had been assigned the job until the last minute. I don't know who was more nervous! We received a lot of laughs! Hearts were ministered to and encouraged. They brought in a cake and sang "Happy Birthday" to me. And guess who came to visit? Reiko!

After all the festivities, a group of eight singles entreated me to join them over lunch. For more than two hours they grilled me with questions about dating and marriage. They begged me to return in the near future to present my Premarital Seminar. I guess they thought an old woman (now 50) would have some answers!

My next stop was with a small group of seminary wives (and their babies). They were so excited to meet together—their conversation seemed nonstop. Takako fended well, but of course I failed to understand a word and found it difficult to join in the merriment until it was time for me to speak. Even then our interaction proved to be a bit perplexing because they hardly glanced at me, and the girl translating seemed rather rude. I do believe they were being respectful, but the lack of eye contact made it even more difficult to dialogue with them. However, Joy could speak English and felt that the Lord had sent me there just for her! It was, indeed, a joy to minister to Joy! The wives sang "Happy Birthday" and graced me with lovely gifts before I left.

From there, Takako and I sadly boarded our last train ride together. She then turned me over to Wendy, a single missionary from Canada who was craving American company. We talked into the wee hours, sharing about our respective journeys with the Lord. Her small but adequate apartment provided another opportunity for tatami comfort and countless lychee nuts!

My official fiftieth birthday finally arrived. My very first celebratory movement was a collision with Wendy's hamster's cage—thus inadvertently setting the captive free! I thought I could just corner him until Wendy woke up. However, he got away. My hostess was not happy. Thank the Lord for His quick response to "Help me!" Wendy found and contained the hamster before we left for the 7:30 a.m. train.

This two-hour trip consisted of four separate trains (one-way) to attend an Aglow leaders' meeting in a spacious, private home somewhere. After I shared a brief testimony, Wendy took over the ministry time. The ladies then circled the dining room table and commenced their planning meeting, while I sat and read the Book of Matthew for several hours—completely clueless about what was being said in their conversation. We finally left around 4:00 p.m., but Wendy failed to get us on the right train, so it took rides on five trains—for three hours—to find our way back to her apartment.

The extreme heat added to the tension of the day. We did manage to find some ice cream and a Coke between hopping trains. I bought some pretzels (my comfort food for the day) but was advised that it would not be polite to eat them en route. Wendy's friend Doris came to my aid and treated me to dinner at a nearby restaurant, which became the highlight of my celebration day—dining on octopus (which tasted just like fried chicken to me).

My last day in Japan started at 7 a.m. with a premarital counseling session with Chris and Iayco. I spent two and a half hours with them, convinced that this was a divine appointment. They truly may have loved each other, but they definitely were not meant to marry. The Holy Spirit led our time together and exposed obvious roadblocks. I was relieved to hear, several months later, that they had called off their wedding.

ALASKA

Yeah! A bulkhead seat! I stretched out with thanksgiving as we jetted off to Alaska on the final transpacific leg of my journey. By the time we had landed in Seattle, I'd been without sleep for more than thirty hours!

The airport buzzed with the normal "hustle and bustle" expected. A quiet corner in a TCBY/Taco Bell called out to me, "Come and rest." I read for a couple of hours and ate ice cream, Wheat Thins, chocolate chip cookies, tacos, Kit Kats,

Rolos, and some kind of toffee—just trying to remain conscious! The Lord was faithful to provide and protect.

I lurched into frantic movement when the attendants finally announced that the flight to Fairbanks was now loading. The fear of falling asleep and missing my plane was relieved; however, my expectation of counting sheep until dozing off didn't work—I was too cranked up on caffeine and sugar! My son, Kevin, and his family met me at Fairbanks International Airport and treated me to good ol' American pizza before our hour-long ride to their home, just a mile down the road from Eielson Air Force Base. It was such a blessing to be with family and not have to strain to understand the language!

At midnight my thirty-six-hour ordeal ceased—I conked out cold while the clock counted off the next twelve hours! When I awoke and looked at my watch, I thought the battery had bit the dust, but sure enough, it was noon.

This perfectly timed visit was an added birthday bonus—I had not seen these three for a few years—they "just happened" to live close enough on my flight path to make this a stopover. Melissa, my daughter-in-love, and Anna, my eleven-year-old granddaughter, took turns modeling my new kimono—complete with an ornate obi that wrapped around and around and around little Anna!

They drove me around the base and ushered me into the BX—my favorite major military installation! After loading up on familiar items of interest, we stopped by a lake to watch Kevin steer his little speedboat by remote control. It stalled in the middle of the lake a couple of times, but some kind canoers came to his rescue. My heart was filled with the peace of God in this quiet, still, secluded part of the world—content just to watch my son play and to be with them.

Later, Melissa and I napped while Kevin and Anna worked on their tree house expansion—talk about creative design! They even added Shaker siding. My exercise for the day turned out to be a challenge—jumping on the trampoline. It looked so easy when Anna did it, but I evidently had lost my sea legs in Japan, as well as my energy level! However, I provided lots of laughs for my attentive audience before passing up the "opportunity" to ride the go-kart! I thoroughly enjoyed watching them speed around in circles, while I sat on their back deck hoping to spy the moose that occasionally wandered into their yard. Soaking up the slow pace was the ideal scenario for regaining my strength.

That evening we began our Rummykub[11] marathon. Every night at eight o' clock we flipped the tiles and tried to win the battle of the mindful moves. Needless to say, my wit was not too quick at this point! Melissa cooked wonderful meals, but my favorite food memory is that of snacking on chocolate-covered M&M peanuts and animal crackers while playing Rummykub.

One afternoon we hopped on a train that took us through a permafrost tunnel to a place where some mining demonstrations were being presented. I actually panned nine dollars' worth of gold! Kevin gently guided me in transitioning it into a circular charm to be worn on a gold chain—a forever memory of our precious time together.

On another afternoon we enjoyed an educational riverboat ride and learned about the Eskimo heritage of the area. God's world is truly a work of art—with each ethnic subculture adding to the revelation of how BIG GOD IS—All-Powerful, All-Knowing, Everywhere Present! What an AWESOME GOD we serve!

My relaxing week eased me back into a relatively normal sleep pattern and an effortless adjustment back to Americana. I got home on July 24—the end of a WONDER-FULL three-week celebration of my fiftieth birthday!

Chapter Seven

RUSSIA (BOOK OF LIFE) 1996

Shortly after my return from Japan, an opportunity arose to join David Crabtree, the pastor of a local church that was organizing an outreach to Russia. The proposed agenda included distributing copies of *The Book of Life* (the life of Christ) in schools and inviting the children and staff to attend evening activities at the cultural center. The group also planned to host a brunch honoring female teachers and administrators, and that event needed to be orchestrated: gifts, decorations, food, music, and the sharing of the Gospel. "Ditty bags"[12] were waiting to be filled, and testimonies of God's grace were waiting to be written. A third part of the plan was to present both the gifts and testimonies to Russian prisoners.

Where did Tuesday go? We departed Greensboro at 2 p.m. on Monday. Chattie Parker, my 50-year-old roommate-to-be, and I were "joined at the hip" on all our flights: Greensboro to Atlanta, Atlanta to Amsterdam, Amsterdam to St. Petersburg, St. Petersburg to Arkhangelsk—a total of twenty-five hours of travel. Our experience aboard Aeroflot (*circa* 1946 airline) was not as terrifying as we had been told to expect—hallelujah! Seasoned travelers had "briefed" us about boarding the aircraft via a rope ladder, and we had been told to expect to see chickens running loose in the aisle! We were spared those scenarios but were still a bit startled when the seats in front of us flopped forward without warning. Chattie and I literally laughed our way into our well-worn seats while reciting Psalm 91:11:

"He will order his angels to protect you wherever you go."

Our rickety ride landed in Arkhangelsk (Archangel) on Tuesday evening—thankfully with all hands on deck (stomachs were churning somewhat, but there were no rope burns!). This timber and fishing center sits just below the Arctic Circle in Northern European Russia, on the mouth of the Northern Dvina River, which flows into the White Sea—except for the five months of the year when it is iced in.

The environment of this entire countryside exuded a 1920s–30s barren, colorless atmosphere. Our "luxury" hotel, the best Arkhangelsk had to offer, moped in the middle of an isolated, overgrown field. The hotel owned neither working lawnmowers nor gasoline to empower them. The originally ornate chandeliers were now mere wannabes that were missing half their light bulbs, thus creating a dark and dingy atmosphere in the lobby. The low wattage prevailed in our private rooms as well.

The elevator doors presented another unanticipated thrill: they opened or closed at will, usually not in accordance with one's first attempt to enter or exit the elevator's confines. We often took several trips up and down before the doors creaked open on the floor of choice, and even then the elevator floor and the hotel floor resisted alignment. Guests were required to either step up the 8–12-inch difference looming directly in front of them or at other times step down about the same distance.

Our guides/interpreters delivered dinner to all sixteen of us who were huddled (trying to get warm) in the second-floor lounge area. It was not your run-of-the-mill menu: liverwurst, cheese, bread, grapes, melon, and crunchy cookies. The temperature inside was 30° and dropping; they would not turn on the heat until October 15 (another two weeks), if then, since the coal miners were on strike. We slept with coats, gloves, and even hats on! A couple of the girls came up with a brainstorm—they borrowed my hair dryer to warm their sheets!

No hot water for bathing! Thankfully, later in the week a few of us found favor with some staff members who showed us how to sneak down to the boiler room one at a time for a shower—kind of scary, but well worth it. I kept wondering if the KGB knew what we were doing and would kidnap us en route.

As our relationships with the various staff members grew, so did our special privileges. On Thursday night, Chattie bravely asked for an extra blanket, and the chambermaid personally delivered "real" blankets to our room. Chattie blessed her back with some soap, coffee, and creamer from home. Later we found out that one gal on the team had brought an aluminum blanket purchased from a camp store in the States. She said it warmed right up. Note to self: IF I ever venture near the Arctic Circle again, I'll check out the camp store before embarking into the great unknown!

Our transportation consisted of either filthy, beat-up, old buses with rusty holes in the side and flooring; cracked, dirty glass windows; and ripped-up seats or private cars in similar condition. The guys on the team stood out in the middle of what they referred to as a "street"[13] and flagged down ordinary citizens to request rides. The drivers of those vehicles obviously were on their way to somewhere but eagerly accepted the negotiated financial reward to deliver us to our destination. We paid the equivalent of four American dollars for a ride a few miles across town.

David led our devotional time each morning before the individual teams departed on various assigned missions: schools, orphanages, prisons, hospitals. The praise and worship always united our hearts afresh—with one another and with the Lord, from whom comes our strength, provision, and protection. He always filled us with excitement and expectation about what God was doing in us and through us.

My team headed out to an elementary school on our first excursion: Dima, my interpreter, age 26; David, my teammate, age 27; and Sergei our "taxi" driver, age 26. I called them "my three sons"! Sergei (pronounced Sir Gay) forced my door open from the inside (the back, left door would not budge). The "roads" were full of potholes, bumpy, and lineless. We laughed and compared driving experiences as we zigzagged across what looked like a war zone. When they realized I had thirty-four years of driving experience under my belt, they decided I should drive! NOT!

Because of the poor economy, the teachers had not been paid since April (six months before our arrival). One teacher reported: "President Yeltsin is just a puppet. The Mafia runs the government. They make your American Mafia look like children. They stole 56% of the money taken in by Russia."

Of course the unheated school challenged our physical senses. The students wore their coats, hats, mittens, scarves, etc. in the classrooms. The principal escorted our team of four to a total of seven different classrooms and graciously introduced us to the children. I loved presenting myself as a *babushka*, a grandmother! They laughed and were so receptive!

I held up a copy of *The Book of Life* and explained: "This tells the story of Someone very special to us. His name is Jesus. He is our best Friend. If you read and answer the questions in the back of the book, you will understand more about Who Jesus is and why He came. We would like to give each of you a copy of this book and invite you to come to a Christian celebration tonight at the cultural center. We will have music, clowns, and puppets, and we will tell you more about Jesus. Bring your family and friends too!"

Tommy Powers videotaped each class. The children giggled in delight as they crowded around him to view the recordings of themselves on his camera. One group questioned us extensively about our personal lives—even asking our ages. They guessed David to be fifty-one and me to be twenty-two! Made my day!

One class extended our stay as they sang some songs for us. The assistant director pulled a shawl around herself and began to sing and dance—a hoot! The children gave each of us handmade gifts. Mine was a knitted elephant pencil holder—unique!

Snow White and the Seven Dwarfs showed up unexpectedly on the walls of a third-grade classroom! It seemed surreal to be sharing the Gospel with these Disney fans in such oppressive surroundings. The building itself may have been cold, but their beautiful hearts warmed our souls.

The principal and the assistant director served us tea, rolls, and chocolate after we had made the rounds. We sat around a table in their office, struggling to communicate through our interpreter, but the effort proved to be rewarding. Their hospitality humbled us.

David wanted to give one of the girls a calculator as a gift for posing for pictures like a professional model. The assistant escorted us to her classroom, knocked on the door, and beckoned the girl into the hallway. She kissed the child on the cheek and motioned to David to do the same—sweet. The little girl's face glowed with gratitude.

We hustled back to the hotel, leaving enough time to freshen up and eat dinner before boarding a bus to go to the evening meeting. We ate salads, fish/potato soup, fries, and peas at our hotel restaurant. Once again, I noticed their frugality—the napkins were torn into fourths.

About sixty people attended the crusade on the first night. The crowd of various ages was easily engaged, although we Americans found it a bit frustrating to follow our Russian partners without personal translators within earshot. Over the next two nights the attendance doubled, and by the last night the cultural center was packed to the point that we had to surrender our seats! Hundreds of men, women, and children received Jesus as their Lord and Savior.

By Thursday evening, children and teens had lined the street in anticipation of our arrival. They would crowd around the bus, making it almost impossible for us to move into the center. Inside, they backed us up against the walls in pursuit of our autographs! We signed autographs forever—both before and after the meetings. They thrust scraps of paper, books, and balloons at us to sign; some even begged us to sign their hands. Our "movie star" status wore us out and made moving to the bus a supernatural feat.

One night when David was trying to squeeze onto the bus, I jokingly stuck out my hand and pleaded, "Please give me your autograph!" I laughed and started to pull my hand back, but he grabbed it, saying, "Oh, no!" and scribbled his signature on my hand with a magic marker! The driver diligently maneuvered the bus, inch by inch, as the crowd continued to press in. He finally broke through, but they chased after us for several blocks!

These precious people were so thankful that we had come and were so blessed by the loving attention and the message of HOPE! How can we not go into a lost and dying world with the Good News? Lives are being changed for eternity.

AFTER THE CRUSADES

In preparation for the women's brunch on Saturday, we decorated the barren hall with balloons, crepe paper, tablecloths, and brightly colored paper bags filled with confetti. About forty-five women attended this special celebration in their honor. We served them tea and sweet cakes, while several Russian young women sang worshipful songs. Another lovely Russian woman shared her testimony of Christ's impact on her life.

Irene interpreted for me as I hosted a table of eight Russian ladies. This lovely young woman did not know Jesus—yet. The assistant director from the first school I visited sat with us. She abruptly voiced her disdain over the Russian woman leading the music: "It is rude of her to play her guitar while singing." During a ministry time I offered to pray for her. She quickly and stoically listed her requests: "I need healing. I need to be happy. I need my husband to love me." I prayed. Her countenance and demeanor distinctly softened.

After praying for Natasha, a middle school teacher, she whispered, "I felt like I'd been in a storm, but now I feel peaceful." She invited Irene and me to come to her home after the meeting on Sunday. WOW! What an amazing opportunity!

Another lady at our table was a high school English teacher. Aha! The Holy Spirit quickened me, "She is the one you toted that NIV Bible halfway across the world for." I just "happened" to have brought it with me to the brunch!

I ran to the coat room, retrieved it, and set it on the table in front of her, saying, "This is for you." At first, she appeared to be in shock, then disbelief, and then the tears began to flow. She tenderly took hold of it and hugged it to her chest. She reverently laid it back on the table and began caressing the pages one at a time, while sobbing, *"Spasiba! Spasiba!"* ("Thank you! Thank you!") A wave of conviction flooded my soul as I considered how casually I handle the Word of God—taking it for granted. My home library holds more than forty Bibles of various translations. I often lay them on the floor, leave them on the back seat of my car, forget them at church . . . "Lord, thank You for the reminder of how precious Your written Word is."

That evening I pulled out my suitcase that was stuffed with clothing I planned to share with several of the women whom I had met that week. Irene would look good in my black sweater and beige sweater vest. I decided to take two gray skirts, a gray sweater, a white turtleneck, a blue-green vest, and a white sweater to the teachers and take the green sweater to Dima's wife, Olga. What a joy to share my hand-me-downs with those who truly will be blessed by them.

The guys on our team had shown the film *The Cross and the Switchblade* to Dima and a full house of men on Saturday afternoon. Dima said he was "very impressed." We were excited to have Dima and Olga join us again on Sunday morning at Pastor Sergei's church. They agreed to accompany me to Natasha's home after the evening service too.

Natasha lived in what appeared to be a neighborhood of tall, cold-looking, concrete buildings. We cautiously climbed the steep, crumbling, concrete blocks to the third floor. The unlit hallways lent an eerie feeling to our expedition. Relief flooded our hearts when Natasha opened her apartment door and warmly greeted us. She proudly showed off all three rooms, plus the kitchen and bath. Not many Russians enjoyed such luxury. Her friend Irene lived in a rented room but had to go to a public bathhouse to shower.

Natasha's old upright piano provided her eldest daughter the opportunity to develop her love of music. The accomplished ten-year-old played "The Star-Spangled Banner" in my honor; they were so eager to please me. In "normal" times, Natasha would earn $160 a month, but this single mother had not been paid for six months. However, that did not stop her from rolling out a table FULL of delicious baked goods—so gracious!

She shared her family history and insisted on giving me samples of old Russian money that was now obsolete. Dima did an excellent job of keeping up with translating her stories for two and a half hours! I prayed with them individually before we left. Irene was awed that I prayed so many things over her that were true, exclaiming, "You must be a wizard!" Oh, no! I tried to explain the work of the Holy Spirit, but Dima was having a hard time translating what He did not understand himself. I have to trust that the Holy Spirit will encounter them as only He can!

On our last full day in Arkhangelsk, we visited a youth prison further out in the middle of nowhere. The loquacious administrator and his assistant gave us a tour of the dorms and boys' living quarters, which were much warmer than we expected. We were caught totally off guard when we heard a young prisoner play what sounded like a professional piano concert.

About one hundred boys crowded into the cafeteria for an assembly. We introduced ourselves, and there were more laughs over my being a *babushka*! I shared a message about not allowing our past to prevent us from making proper decisions in the future. David gave his testimony, and we prayed with them before distributing New Testaments and copies of the book *The Cross and the Switchblade*. The warden hosted us in his office over tea and thanked us for coming.

On our last night of meetings, we had to turn people away. We were beyond "standing room only"! When we returned to the hotel, we pooled our snacks and had a party in honor of our interpreters. Dima proudly showed me their wedding pictures, while Sergei's daughter sat on my lap, totally content, as Dima told me about his decision to follow Christ! Our maid had come to the evening meeting that night also, and back at the hotel she came running down the hall with gifts for me: a nesting doll, a linen towel, and a jar of cranberries.

Tuesday was one looooong day! I started by spending time with our maid, giving her my last sweater and a few small gifts. She was embarrassed at first, but I explained I just wanted to share God's love with her. She humbly accepted the gifts and opened up with more of her personal story. She had earned two postgraduate degrees, but because of the poor economy, she was forced to scrub floors for a living. Our hearts bonded in smiles and hugs.

The team squeezed in a sightseeing trip to an all-wooden village—made without a single nail! Amazing! Unfortunately, the below-freezing temperature prevented me from viewing the whole thing. Halfway through the tour I returned to the bus (before my toes fell off) and used Chattie's hand warmers on my feet. Then, on our way to the airport, we made one last stop at the Minister of Education's office to deliver some supplies.

At 6 p.m., we arrived in St. Petersburg, which seemed like a totally transformed world: first-class! cosmopolitan! manicured landscape! luxurious heated hotel with hot water! exquisite subway system—the ambience of a fine art gallery! grand architecture throughout the bustling city boulevards—

statues, cathedrals, museums! colorful, well-dressed citizenry! culture shock!

Wednesday's schedule centered on a trip to the Hermitage Museum. We arrived at 3 p.m. I was out of Russian rupees, out of energy, and out of interest. The others offered to pay my way, but my socialization skills were spent. I silently strolled the outside perimeter of the famous museum, stunned by the quaint, quiet scenes of canals, magnificent plazas, and bridges. My heart was filled with a sense of wonder at my "secret find," as if no one else had ever discovered the exterior treasure surrounding the Hermitage.

We flew out of St. Petersburg at 4 p.m. and arrived in Amsterdam four hours later for our last night abroad. Under other circumstances I would have been duly impressed with the super-modern airport hotel. Unfortunately, my focus was only on leaving for home first thing in the morning!

At check-in, the flight assistant inquired if I had checked my toolbox and Marlboro bag. I responded, "No. I own neither."

"Are you coming from Bahrain?"

"No."

Somebody had goofed! She had checked in a traveler named "Henderson" yesterday under my name. She informed me that the person who flew to Bahrain would be without his or her luggage for a few days, as it was flying on my flight to Greensboro!

Within the week I began receiving letters and pictures from my new Russian friends. Dima wrote:

I'm missing you very much and because of it I'm writing this first letter. Olga and I remember you every day, every minute and it's a shame of us but I must say that we were crying all of the night after your leaving, you know. And now I am sitting here writing this letter and your face is standing before my eyes. The time that I spent with you was like, you know, like a holiday of my soul. I don't know how to explain it, but something really changed in my life. We are reading

the books that you gave us. We also pray sometimes. I learned the song, 'Lord, I Lift Your Name on High.' I can now play it on my guitar... Oh, I nearly forgot to say that I don't smoke three days already! All the Best!!! Bye! I'll be waiting for a letter from you! And we'll meet someday, definitely! (At least in Heaven . . .)
Your Russian Buddy,
Forgive me my mistakes, please.
Dima & Olga

HOME FRONT

Irons in the fire were heating up as I returned home. I began having that recurring dream where I appeared as just a white speck on a stage of a large arena presenting a powerful message. As my mind picked it up and put it down, I questioned the Holy Spirit about its validity. When an opportunity to have personal prophetic ministry at a Morning Star Conference came my way, I participated—hoping to receive some insight from the Lord. I cautiously entered a small counseling room, where three people whom I had never met and who knew nothing about me graciously greeted me.

The first prophetic words felt like a peg driven into a sure place: "You are not having delusions of grandeur. God has a mighty calling on your life and He is going to complete it." I was stunned, to say the least! Here we are twenty-plus years later, still waiting for it to manifest. Have I missed it? Maybe. Maybe not. The vision still recurs.

After so many confirmations building my confidence to step out, I made an appointment with my pastor to run these revelations by him—to test the Spirit. Lee's spirit witnessed wholeheartedly, and he immediately invited me to join the pastoral staff of Gate City Vineyard. The next Sunday, the elders ordained me as the women's pastor. I was off and running—joyfully juggling brunches, retreats, prayer meetings, counseling, and leading Bible studies.

Chapter Eight

DOMINICAN REPUBLIC (YWAM) 1997

We organized our first official mission trip as a church outreach in 1997. Jack and Lisa Kody, members and former missionaries to the Dominican Republic, played a key role in identifying areas where our multifaceted group of sixteen could serve. We would be working with Dominican, Brazilian, and American missionaries—cooking, cleaning, singing, and constructing a new chapel, and Lee and I would be teaching and preaching in various venues. Arrangements for a couple of women's brunches topped my to-do list.

Our preparation meetings were paramount in forming team unity as we prayed together (for each other and for the people we would be serving), carried out exercises in working together, and became familiar with the culture of the Dominican Republic (including learning a little Spanish). We stuffed our suitcases full of gifts for our hosts as well as supplies for ministry and construction.

The YWAM (Youth With A Mission) base in Santa Domingo was our first destination. The base directors, Kent and Janet Norell, a young couple from the States, began orienting us the moment our boots hit the ground. After a "circle of sharing" and prayer, we received our assignments:

- Lee and Nathaniel—build something (?)
- Dave and Linda Jo—work on computers
- Josh and Sam—accompany Steve to wire a lady's house
- Lisa and Brooke—sort suitcases
- Adam, Luke, and Abbey—knock a hole in the wall for a fan to be installed

- Brie, Sarah, Paige, Afton, and Cara—work on the roof with Herman
- Jack—meet and plan with Kent
- Me—sit in a plush hotel lobby nearby to pray and plan for the women's brunch

That afternoon, Janet took me to scout out the brunch venue at the elegantly appointed "bakery." The Lord was obviously planning something special for these missionary ladies who were coming from stressful stations across the Dominican Republic.

Since our sleeping quarters were so hot, I set up shop in the base's air-conditioned office with Linda Jo and Dave. Linda Jo helped me blow up balloons, and then I created centerpieces and tried my hand at calligraphy on name tags.

The long tables that formed a square turned out beautifully! The twenty-two ladies were taken aback as they walked into the room set apart just for them—Methodist, Baptist, Four Square—such a variety of backgrounds coming together as sisters in the Lord. Each guest introduced herself and then told what geographical area she served in, the type of mission she was engaged in, and what she was doing when she was sixteen years old! The food was fabulous. The praise and worship were heartwarming.

After I shared my testimony of God's grace, they lined up around the perimeter of the room and shared laughter and tears as I anointed them with oil and laid hands on them in prayer. The Lord poured out His precious healing, blessing, and refreshing upon His daughters!

Lee and I shared the pulpit at a large Spanish-speaking church on Sunday morning, and then our team packed up and scrunched into a semi-retired minibus for a precarious pilgrimage up serpentine slivers called roads into the mountains of Jarabacoa. Mauro and Leonice Laranjeiras, the directors of the YWAM Mission Center there, greeted us with hearts of gratitude, and we greeted them with sighs of relief that we had made it alive.

The surrounding scenery was breathtaking—quiet, serene, and much cooler than Santa Domingo. We retired at dusk, and roosters woke us up around 5 a.m. every morning. Our prayer and praise time after breakfast was always anointed with God's presence brushing over our hearts anew. On our first morning, Lee and I had the privilege of releasing deliverance for Afton, who had been suffering from deep pain as a result of a previous relationship.

After our Spanish lesson and lunch, we prayer-walked the new property where a young couple, Tim and Esther, planned to build a church. After dinner we walked "downtown" for an outreach. Linda Jo and I teamed up, inviting everyone we passed on the dirt street to come join us as we gathered at a makeshift stage on the corner. The youths on our team performed mimes, Sam gave his testimony, Lee shared a short presentation of the Gospel—and two young men gave their hearts to Christ. Hallelujah!

The next morning, I met with Carol, a middle-aged lady missionary who was struggling with some relationship issues. The Lord met her need with His wisdom as we talked with each other and with Him. That afternoon we hiked up to Los Corales, one of the areas where she had faithfully sowed seed. It was about a twenty-minute trek up some rough terrain. We sat in wicker rockers on the dirt porch of a small shack. The nine ladies and several young girls with babies who gathered for the Bible study were deeply moved as I taught. One young bride was only fourteen years old. Afterward, they extended their hospitality via grapefruit juice. Carol said she had never suffered from drinking it previously, so I sipped cautiously, even though the swarming flies wanted to share my cup.

Bright and early the next morning, I jumped up, hoping to shower and wash my hair before breakfast—no water! I pressed on to wrap up my final preparations for teaching at YWAM's Discipleship Training School. I taught on the mind and the emotions for three and a half hours, but the students were so attentive that the time seemed to slip away. Before we had even blinked, the lunch bell was ringing.

After lunch, some of the gals helped me set up for the "Tea" on the staff porch upstairs. It was a lovely setting, even though we had to struggle against the wind to keep balloons and centerpieces from blowing away. The program was the equivalent of the brunch we had provided earlier in Santa Domingo. These missionary ladies were blessed and refreshed as well. I was so thankful for the opportunity to minister to them.

Carol and I visited another remote village, where I was blessed to teach the Word and pray with about fifteen ladies, one man, and several children. The sweet Holy Spirit ministered to their hearts and lives. In hindsight, I vaguely remember sipping some water offered to me. I began to feel puny, but God's grace was sufficient to see me through our time together.

As we reached the main road on our walk back, I realized I needed to use a restroom REAL SOON! I alerted Carol, "It would be nice if the team came along in Big Blue (YWAM's old minibus)!" Just then a young man from the mission came whizzing up on a motorcycle, I hopped on, and he delivered me without ado to my destination in the nick of time!

The next twenty-four hours were challenging. Linda Jo rounded up some extra TP and lugged several buckets of water to keep the drainage system from plugging up! I slept most of the next day but was appreciative of neck rubs and prayers.

It was kind of sad when we packed up Big Blue for our descent back to Santa Domingo, but once we hit the buzzing city life, our attention bee-lined to the local markets and an afternoon of shopping. I found some unique gifts for my family: a cow's horn ship, a colorful sponge doll, fresh vanilla, specialty blended coffee, bracelets, purses, hats, chimes, and maracas!

Our last stop was Boca Chica—a picturesque resort on the ocean. The white sands and see-through water were fascinating. Relaxing in the sun with refreshment cabanas providing cool drinks and snacks seemed surreal after our previously rigorous routines. Dinner reservations were for 7:30 at a fancy French restaurant. (We had to send the guys back to their rooms to change into long pants!) After dinner, Lee led an awards ceremony. I received one for "The Most Words Spoken in One Day!" (five hours on Wednesday).

PASTORAL TRANSITION

Sadly, within a relatively short period of time, our pastor made devastating moral choices. Jack Kody and I were ordained as interim associate pastors, which turned out to be a two-year assignment. My passion for preaching was released once a month. Keeping regular office hours, visiting newcomers, and making hospital calls required a sizable chunk of my calendar. Although I held a master's degree in counseling, that wasn't my favorite hat. Organizing outreaches, heading the missions committee, and overseeing the Sunday school program while working on a master's degree in theology was more up my alley.

One of the more challenging concerns I faced was a "bag lady" named Joy who regularly attended our church services and our women's meetings. She had a sweet, childlike quality about her and seemed to love the Lord. She approached me one day to ask if the church would buy a house for homeless women. She described how dangerous it was for them to live on the streets.

I knew that the church board was not interested in taking on a major project at this time. We were in a financial bind and dealing with a pastor who had been unfaithful to his wife. But I was concerned for Joy. She had a broken-down car full of junk parked in the church parking lot. It was the middle of July and we were experiencing a hovering heat wave.

I wanted to at least provide a break for her. John and I agreed to invite her to stay in our guest room for a couple of weeks. Unfortunately, our contrasting worlds began to collide on the very first night, when she did not show up before our bedtime. We waited up until about 2 a.m. because we did not want to lock her out (we had not given her a key). We discussed the possibility of an earlier curfew, which did ease the tension for a couple of nights.

I thought giving her a safe place with clean sheets and privacy was a gift, but she brought all her unclean belongings (literally a huge pile of trash) and deposited them in our home. She could hardly pass through the door of her room without pushing aside the clutter. She overwhelmed our guest bathroom with strange-smelling concoctions, and our refrigerator reeked with foul odors as well! She cooked up strange stews and absentmindedly left the burners aglow.

Our "act of kindness" quickly turned into a terrible nightmare. Her value system and worldview were definitely different from ours. I had been quite naive in my notion of creating a possible lifestyle change for her. My father, who was also living with us, was greatly disturbed by the discord.

Joy obviously enjoyed her routine on the streets and was not really looking for a change of environment. I think she was just hungry for some special attention. After the first week, we received a phone call saying a dear friend had died in Ohio, and we felt we were to go to his wife's side. There was no question—we could not leave her in our home with my father. I explained our emergency and that she needed to have her things out of the house within two days. The news did not seem to faze her; actually, I believe she was relieved to return to her old stomping grounds.

Looking back, I am glad that we reached out to her. It was a learning experience for us all. I believe she felt our open heart toward her, as we continued to have a special connection upon our return.

Chapter Nine

CHINA (BIBLES) 1997

China had been on my "bucket list" from as far back as reading *The Good Earth* by Pearl Buck in high school! When our children were school age, we'd gather them around the cassette player and listen to Brother Andrew's "Open Doors Ministry Reports" of smuggling Bibles into China. So when I received a flyer announcing that Wesley Smith was planning a two-week "Bibles to China" journey, my spirit stirred to attention. They were seeking couriers to carry Bibles from Hong Kong into Shenzhen and later to Beijing. I presented this opportunity to the church elders, who agreed that this was my time to travel to China. They sent me forth as an ambassador from Gate City Vineyard and released the finances for my trip!

I met eight of my nine teammates-to-be for the first time at the O'Hare Airport. Murray and his three parishioners: Theresa, Darrell, and Larry, flew in from Southwest Indiana. Mike Rhodes was traveling with his two teenage daughters, Emily and Dana, from Michigan. Pam, a young wife and mother from Elkhart, Indiana, was to be my roommate. Wesley would join us days later in Beijing.

After a few short, disjointed dreams on the fifteen-hour flight to Seoul, I sleep-walked the Kimpo International Airport a couple of hours before boarding for another four-hour flight to Kai Tak International Airport in Hong Kong. Our trek continued in travail as our contact, Mr. Cobb, did not greet us at the gate as planned. We hired taxis to take us to our hotel, only to find out after taking an extended, circuitous route that the taxi driver could not locate our new hotel! Eventually we *and* Mr. Cobb ended up at the Pearl

Garden Hotel for our pointless "briefing" (he had been at the airport but had neglected to have a sign identifying himself).

Unfortunately, the team did not bond as quickly as I had hoped for, which proved to be a teachable moment on how *not* to lead a mission trip! Part of the problem stemmed from the fact that for security reasons, plans were not released until just before we were to execute them. Murray served as our leader on this leg of the mission since he had been to Hong Kong previously.

The first item of business entailed walking several blocks to a tailor known all over the world for fashion. Custom-made suits could be created in as little as twenty-four hours from a large selection of materials (not exactly on my to-do list)! We ate dinner at a lovely restaurant with tablecloths—overpriced fried rice. Our stroll provided an overload of local color—bright neon-lighted signs galore, dirty bamboo scaffolding towering seemingly over every building, squeezed into narrow, crowded streets teeming with hurrying humanity.

We met the next morning at seven in Murray's room for a short prayer, then hopped a train, followed by a hike to the supposedly prearranged point of contact to meet our host-guide. We stood, anxiously waiting for an hour and a half. Murray had forgotten to bring his map, so he and Theresa took a couple of train rides back to the hotel to fetch it. We then transitioned (on two more trains) to the designated meeting place—two hours late and with no one to meet us.

Yep! Murray and Theresa hustled back to the hotel *again* to get Mr. Cobb's telephone number. The rest of us stayed at the last station, where we ate lunch, shopped, and people-watched. At 1 p.m., Sue, a sixty-five-year-old English lady, arrived on the scene. She graciously led us on an unusual walk through a Sha Tin slum and up a steep hill to the courier house. There she offered some simple instructions, the most important of which was "never refer to Bibles or tracts—they are referred to as "'Bread and crumbs.'" We were not to appear as a group but as independent individuals, and we were to watch over our words, especially in taxis and on trains.

We each loaded up two suitcases with Bibles and tracts; each suitcase weighed about 25 pounds! We had to carry them back down the hill and catch the next train to the Lo Wu border checkpoint, where we would cross over into Shenzhen (about a twenty-five-minute ride). On average, 157,120 people crossed this checkpoint each day in the previous month (September 1996).

We cautiously passed through Hong Kong customs, crossed a bridge, and then passed through Chinese customs—all the while shoulder-to-shoulder with thousands of Chinese in a mob-style movement that was occasionally halted by guardrails lowered in front of and behind us for about twenty minutes in several areas as a traffic-control measure. The armed Chinese military stood guard at incremental monitoring platforms. Our team had separated on purpose to avoid drawing attention to ourselves; hence, for several periods of time we were out of each other's sight—alone. It was hot. Humidity hovered at 98.6%. It took hours to get through. Once you cleared one side, you had to repeat those steps on the other side.

Once we arrived at the checkpoint, our bags had to go through X-ray machines. Detected Bibles were confiscated. In our suitcases, we had packed "distractions," i.e., suitcases that would help camouflage the contents, but only three of us got our Bibles through. The others were forced to unpack their Bibles and stow them in large plastic bags and leave them at the checkpoint to be retrieved on their return. Four hundred Bibles did not make it into China on that first attempt, but my fifty did! One of the guards spotted Darrell's video camera and stripped his film—but they did not catch his stash of Bread and crumbs!

Mine was the only luggage that made it through customs on all three trips that week. I attribute the success to strong prayer coverage from home. As disjointed as much of this excursion was, I always had a sense of peace that the Lord was there with me—guiding me, strengthening me, protecting me.

Once successfully in Shenzhen, we congregated at a corner bus station. Deep breath—so far, so good. We split into the appropriate restrooms and divided the remaining Bibles and tracts into duffle bags. Theresa and I accomplished our assignment in the ladies' room—hovering over a nasty, in-ground hole (their toilet). We then linked up with Murray and Sue, lugged the bags down the street to a second-floor massage parlor, and deposited our offering for future pickup.

We retraced our route back to the checkpoint crossing and waited as the six members of the group whose Bibles had been confiscated contended for a half-hour to retrieve them for a fee! After a short train ride back to Sha Tin, we wearily climbed the now dark path up the hill, unpacked the books, and then went back down for a couple more train rides and a walk to our hotel.

I became acutely aware of the importance of pre-experience team building. Now, without that, we were struggling to survive what was, for some of us, cultural shock. Murray had been to Hong Kong previously and obviously was enjoying himself. He and Theresa were inseparable. Larry and Darrell were both dairy farmers and had known each other for years. Mike enjoyed the companionship of his daughters, although he was disappointed that his bread did not get delivered. Pam was a free spirit, content to run on her own agenda. And then there was me.

On Friday morning, Murray announced that he and Theresa would be gone all morning on business—the rest of us were on our own. I spent the morning praying and resting in my room, desperately needing to be alone with the Lord. I did not sign up for a pleasure tour. I signed up to distribute Bibles and engage the underground church! An attitude adjustment was needed—I found this to be the case on many mission trips. I understand that a balance is needed between intense pouring out and R&R, but it is a challenge to not be in charge of your own agenda!

We met up at 1 p.m. for a tour of Hong Kong. It began with a jaunt to Hong Kong Harbor. Victoria Peak provided a unique panoramic view of the city and the harbor. The Aberdeen Fishing Village fleshed out the old way of fisher-folks' life in the harbor. We strolled around the stall shops of Stanley Market, which offered a variety of famous international name brands at bargain prices. Seven members of the group voted to return to Victoria Peak to view the lights after dark. Thankfully, Larry was running out of steam too and preferred the peaceful Pearl Garden!

The energized group gathered back at the hotel around 9 p.m. We all walked a few blocks to a spaghetti shop for dinner. Darrell and I were on our way back when sheets of rain started to pour down—of course this was the first time I forgot to tote my umbrella! Darrell and I ran to the hotel. Pam came running in a few minutes later—totally drenched. Somehow, we had missed each other in our mad dashes. She had raced to the hotel, grabbed my umbrella, and run back to the restaurant to rescue me! We spent the rest of our evening attempting to blow-dry her shorts, sweatshirt, socks, and shoes. We were bonding!

On Saturday things were looking up. We boarded the first train at 9 a.m. When we arrived at the courier house, we met several young people from the Philippines and Australia who were staying at the "guesthouse." These precious people gave up their two-week vacations every year to carry Bread and crumbs across the border. What a privilege to serve on the same team that day! We all made it through two round-trips, successfully depositing 650 loaves of Bread and crumbs to the massage parlor.

That night Sue offered a surprise trip to the "bakery" (where the Bread and crumbs were uniformly packaged for inland distribution). Sue paid for the services of an old battered minibus. We rode for about an hour before our driver suddenly stopped under an overhead freeway and stomped off into a field. What was happening? Were we being abandoned? Were we out of gas? No, he needed to relieve himself!

Sue strongly stipulated the protocol for our evening excursion. We arrived in a slum-tenement-type area, where we silently walked single-file through a narrow alley-type maze. We could hear the ebb and flow of Chinese conversations emanating from families who were bantering back and forth. Sue stopped at a darkened first-floor apartment, inserted her key, and we solemnly entered the bakery. The heavily draped windows prevented our presence from being detected by passersby. She pointed us to stacks of flattened boxes and demonstrated how to assemble them, insert the bread and crumbs, and secure them with wide tape.

Our crew of fourteen represented Christian men and women of various ages between twenty and sixty-five, from five different countries—working side by side in silence for about an hour. With the task completed, we joined hands in a circle and bowed our heads. The holiness of God encompassed us. The reality hit—we were about our Father's business. For every piece of Bread sent inland, there would be *at least* ten people who would come to the Lord. We silently prayed for them. Silently we wept. The glory of God filled our souls. We soberly walked single-file back through the narrow lane to the battered bus—RICH—one in Spirit. Our U.S. team transported over 230 loaves of Bread that week—that translates to at least 2,300 souls who would come to the Lord! [13]

BEIJING

The next morning, we packed up for our flight to Beijing. My elephant in the room at this point was Buford—my black, oversized, hard-sided suitcase. He did have wheels, but they didn't spin and hardly rolled. Plus, he weighed a ton with all my must-haves inside. I had yet to learn the tricks of a seasoned traveler. Crammed with my necessities, Buford became my mobility menace. I could hardly handle him, my carry-on, and oversized purse under “normal” conditions. Not only did I have to walk Buford through crowded airports, lift him up on check-in scales, and on and off of conveyor belts, but now we were forced to navigate city blocks, climbing up and down endless staircases at train stations and through throngs of fast-paced flesh!

More often than not, a Good Samaritan would take pity on me and usher Buford up or down to his destination. My teammates all had their own luggage to deal with and laughed at Buford. Thankfully, on several occasions Darrell stepped up with some gentlemanly compassion to help me out.

Wes met us at the Beijing airport around midnight and escorted us to the elegant Taiwan Hotel for a reasonable night’s rest before heading out to the Great China Wall the next morning. I was taken aback by the encroaching commercialism as our minibus maneuvered through the narrow, shop-lined street at the base of the Badaling section of the Wall. We spent only about an hour on the steep and windy Wall—most of the time posing for snapshots at the requests of Chinese tourists! We ended our excursion by eating at the Wall’s KFC. I became quite popular with the clientele when they learned I was from Kentucky!

By nine the next morning we were cruising the countryside on our way to a magnet factory that served as a cover for a missionary couple and their two teenage daughters. They had settled in a small village about an hour and a half outside Beijing about two years ago. It was a rather abrupt transition as we rode from the densely populated, cosmopolitan city into sprawling open fields and slow, wobbly wagons piled with hay or other commodities being pulled by frail-looking, hardworking peasants.

The humble little factory provided a living for about sixty people. Although the accommodations were rough, the workers had come from villages without electricity, and this factory accorded them a once-in-a-lifetime opportunity to earn money. Several evenings a week were set aside to teach English, and every other week (in order to not raise suspicion) the couple opened their home as a house church. Their home and offices have been bugged, so they must be careful. Karen puts on a teakettle as a noise buffer when they meet. The workers are accepting Jesus one by one.

On our factory tour, we watched them making molds and meticulously creating the designs they hand-painted on the magnets. We excitedly placed our orders, with the assurance they would be ready for us upon our arrival the next evening.

Before returning to the city, we ate lunch in a real rural restaurant: dirt floor and a rickety, makeshift, bare, unfinished wood table, with food that was questionably hygienic and somewhat unrecognizable! But we all made it out alive!

We spent the remainder of our afternoon touring Tiananmen Square and scooting through the Forbidden City as it was closing, the highlight of the excursion being our four rickshaws racing back to the hotel. What fun to watch Larry hilariously and hopelessly pedal for a few blocks! He eventually had to surrender his command to the coolie and admit his failure.

That evening, arrangements were made to attend an "underground" church that was actually located in a high-class high-rise! However, this stealth run could be carried out only in groups of two or three, and security remained uppermost in our words and actions as our rooms were bugged. Pam and I were sent to meet an unidentified escort at a previously disclosed destination. He easily spotted us and nodded, and we followed in silence down the secluded street to the high-rise, up an elevator to the twenty-second floor, and down the eerily quiet hallway.

Our guide gently pushed open the ornate door to reveal a plush apartment packed with about thirty worshipers of all ages. One young Chinese man sat on the floor and softly strummed his guitar, and the others sweetly filled the atmosphere with praise and worship. Some songs were sung in English; others were only familiar melodies: *Majesty; I Love You, Lord; All Hail King Jesus; Emmanuel; Give Thanks;* etc. There were representatives from five different countries present. Wes chose someone from each country to open with prayer. I was invited to lead for the Americans.

Wes shared a message on David and offered ministry for any who wanted personal prayer and hands laid on them. Almost all of them fell on their knees. He motioned for me to join him in praying for them. These precious people wept and wept. I don't know what God did exactly, but I know it was mighty to the pulling down of strongholds!

The following day was shopping day! I'll never forget the surreal sense of walking happily down the cobblestoned streets of Beijing, with the golden leaves falling from the tall trees and the wispy, warm breeze brushing over my being; the beauty of the Chinese people strolling past me; and their unique artistry being displayed along the way in sidewalk shops. There was such a sense of God's presence in what I considered to be an unexpected treasure—I was in CHINA!

We ate pizza and bananas on the bus that day, with more "Buford" jokes shared. Darrell told of trying to "help" me and getting left lugging Buford up a flight of steep stairs! The team decided they were going to empty Buford and lock him up—forever!

After freshening up at the hotel, we headed back out to the magnet factory to pick up our magnets and match up with the student-workers in an English class. I spent the hour teaching two eager young men some simple vocabulary. I have no idea if they learned the lesson, but they smiled a lot! We then crowded into a cold, barren, dirt-floor room to listen to Wes present a Gospel message. This was the first time many of them had heard the Good News. They responded so gratefully and expressed how encouraged they were by our visit.

Our last day in Beijing turned quite chilly—ironically cutting short our tour of the Summer Palace. Once back to the hotel, the hassle of packing Buford began—he had gained weight on this trip!

The team met at 6 p.m. in a private hotel dining room for our closing banquet. I wore my new, royal blue, floor-length Chinese gown and coolie hat. Ten workers from the factory joined us for the ten-course Chinese seafood feast. One of my students sat next to me, and a translator sat next to him, which made our conversation far more fluent than the conversation we had experienced the night before! I capped off our closing celebration by sharing my correlations of how each member of the team had predominantly demonstrated one of the Fruit of the Spirit:

Pam—Kindness: Ephesians 4:32 (NIV)
"Be kind to one another, tender-hearted, forgiving each other, just as God in Christ also has forgiven you."

Dana—Goodness: Romans 12:21 (NIV)
"Don't let evil conquer you, but conquer evil by doing good."

Theresa—Humility: Matthew 5:5 (NIV)
"God blesses those who are humble, for they will inherit the whole earth."

Mike—Faithfulness: 2 Timothy 2:2b
"Commit these to faithful men who will be able to teach others also."

Larry—Self-Control: Titus 1:7–8
"For a bishop must be blameless . . . just, holy, self-controlled."

Darrell—Love: John 15:12
"Love one another as I have loved you."

Wes—Joy: Nehemiah 8:10
"The joy of the LORD is your strength."

Emily—Peace: Isaiah 26:3 (NIV)
"You will keep in perfect peace all who trust in you."

Murray—Patience: 1 Thessalonians 1:2–3
"We give thanks to God always for you all, . . . remembering without ceasing your work of faith, labor of love, and patience of hope in our Lord Jesus Christ."

We were on the move by eight the next morning. At breakfast, I met an American lady who had come to meet her newly adopted Chinese child. I had noticed many new families dining there every morning. She informed me of Cascade International in Portland, Oregon, who partnered with The Women's Traveling Service around the corner from the hotel. It was such a joy to observe the hope in these eyes of expectation! Then it was off to the Beijing Capital International Airport, Seoul Incheon Airport, Chicago O'Hare International Airport, Raleigh/Durham International Airport, and home to Greensboro, North Carolina—twenty-two hours later.

Within days of my return, I received a letter from Pam and another from Emily. Pam wrote: "How are you and Buford doing? I had such a great trip, and I miss you guys so bad…"

Emily wrote: "Every time I think of you, I remember how you could part the waves (and find a place to sit miraculously on the subway) with your gracefulness. Your time with me was such a blessing! P.S. Poor Buford is probably under a bed or in a closet after all that excitement! I send him my love."

FAMILY EXPANSION

That year, 1998, proved to be a double-header for our expanding family! On the 18th of January our daughter, Kimberly, gave birth to our bodacious baby granddaughter, Gabrielle Alexis Wade. In June, when our daughter, Christi, married Alan Ford, our six-month-old sweetheart attended as the flower girl—carried down the aisle by her mother, the matron of honor! Her three-year-old brother, Nicholas (ring bearer), was coaxed down the aisle as well.

Chapter Ten

ASBURY THEOLOGICAL SEMINARY

Gate City Vineyard settled on a new senior pastor—Jim Snyder. Jim was a perfect fit following a transitional time of congregational healing. He was gentle, wise, compassionate, and anointed. I stayed on as support during his first year; then the Lord stirred the nest again as He unveiled my next steps.

I began hearing of the Spirit of God moving within the Methodist church at large and began reflecting over my strong Methodist roots. The Holy Spirit unmistakably whispered within my spirit as I sat with a parishioner during her husband's surgery. Cindy explained the operation in simplistic terms, enabling me to visualize the procedure: "The bone in Roger's hip is dying. So the doctor is taking a part of the healthy bone in his leg and transplanting it into his hip to bring new life." The Holy Spirit clarified, "That's what I am doing with you and John." God was removing us from a healthy part of His Body and transplanting us into a section that was dying, to breathe in new life.

That very next Sunday we welcomed to our pulpit a guest speaker who exhorted the congregation to steward their gifts wisely. He stressed the point that our spiritual gifts are not just for **this** church— "God might be calling you to the Methodist church down the street." The whole congregation, as if in a choreographed movement, strained their necks toward John and me to observe our reaction. Everyone knew it was God calling.

Within weeks we had joined a local Methodist church that welcomed us with open arms. An adult Sunday school class blessed me with opportunities to teach on a regular basis, the women's ministry overseers made room for me to teach and minister, and they even invited me to lead their annual women's retreat. I would be completing my Master of Theology degree in May, so when the pastor encouraged me to pursue Methodist ordination, it appeared to be the appropriate path. He also opened his pulpit for me to preach on the first Sunday of 2000.

It definitely felt as if I were being planted in a specific field of service; however, after only a year at Muir's Chapel, the Lord started stirring again! This time the nudges felt foreign to anything I had ever considered. A doctorate? Are you kidding me? That was absolutely not on my radar screen—never had been! I kept shaking it off. But everywhere I turned I heard, these words: "when you get your doctorate"—at the grocery store, a classroom, at church, and even at a garage sale! The message echoed across TV, radio, and a mosaic of magazine articles. But the loudest voice that volleyed for my attention was my husband's.

Okay, I reasoned that IF I were to get a doctorate it would be in ministry—that seemed to be my designated sphere of influence. Asbury Theological Seminary would be the logical venue since John and I, our daughters, and son-in-law all had graduated from Asbury University. Our daughters and their families live in the area, so naturally the possibility of retiring in Kentucky a few decades into the future was penciled in on our bucket list.

As I read over the Doctor of Ministry requirements in the ATS catalog, I felt a familiar peace, quite like being at home—preaching, teaching, prayer, spiritual formation. But then my eyes fell upon this strange arrangement of words: *Doctor of Missiology*. "What in the world is that?" I queried. I quickly scanned the paragraphs that followed the title. "This is a doctorate in missions that will prepare one for working in the field and the academy." There arose an excitement in my spirit because that addressed my heartbeat—missions and teaching. I originally aligned with that heartbeat on the day I allowed Jesus into my life.

However, as I continued reading the course description, I fumbled into what felt like a sudden foreign language fog as I read the words *contextualization*, *marginalization*, *indigenous*, and *missiological anthropology*! If I focused on each word by itself I could figure out what it meant, but when I tried to combine them into a coherent sentence my mind twisted in knots. Would I succumb to the comfort of the familiar ministry route or step up to the challenge of missiology?

We had already scheduled a trip north to celebrate my mother-in-law's eightieth birthday. While in the neighborhood, I made a commitment to check out Asbury Theological Seminary's doctoral program. The Dean of Ministry reviewed my resume in a rather matter-of-fact manner and suggested several options for fulfilling the requirements.

I then walked over to the E. Stanley Jones School of World Mission and Evangelism and met with Dean Whiteman. After he had scanned my resume, he responded: "You know you are not a sure shot for this. You do not speak another language, and you have not lived in another culture."

"I know," I replied. "I am just trying to follow what I believe to be the Lord's leading. If the door shuts that is fine with me." After an hour of discussion and deciphering my heart and my background, he looked me straight in the eye and said, "I think you should go for it." I was totally dumbfounded—I had not expected the door to swing wide open!

Dr. Whiteman requested that I write a paper on my short-term missions experiences, but after returning to my daughter's home and recounting the details of my day to the family, I dismissed it. They all thought it sounded like a perfect fit for me, but their assessment felt flawed. I lived in North Carolina, I was married, and I couldn't just drop everything and enroll in seminary!

The next morning, my husband and I left Kentucky on a business trip to Greenwood, South Carolina. He spent several days in meetings, while I read and relaxed poolside as I pondered my decisions. At the end of the week, John went into the hotel office to sign us out. I was casually waiting in the car when I noticed him excitedly waving for me to come in. It turned out that the hotel clerk's son-in-law had recently graduated from Asbury Theological Seminary with a doctorate in missiology! Five days earlier, we had never even heard of this degree.

As John drove down the road, I dropped my head in my hands, as I said, "O God, do You really want me to do this thing?" With those words still on my lips, I lifted my eyes to see a street sign that read "Missions Street." I screamed out to John, "Do you see that?" He laughingly shook his head and said, "Yes." We went home and I wrote the paper.

A few weeks later I returned from a retreat around 5 p.m. on a Thursday afternoon and routinely checked my mail. When I was at ATS, I had taken a Miller Analogies Test—an IQ test of sorts. You needed a score of at least 60 to enter a doctoral program. My stack of mail contained a letter from the testing center informing me that I had scored a 55. I thought, "Oh, well, that door is closed."

I immediately called the Dean's office, thinking that I would leave a voice message, but to my surprise Dean Whiteman answered the phone. I said, "I am so sorry, but I will not be coming to the seminary."

He asked, "Have you talked with admissions today?"

"No."

"Well, I sat down with the Director of Admissions last night, and we decided that God is doing something here, and we want to go with God. We admitted you."

I was stunned—speechless. I had three days to pack my personal belongings and drive to Kentucky for my orientation meetings on Monday morning. John and I were thrilled because we had such a sense that God was moving, but my emotions were aflutter! I cried all the way to Wytheville (about halfway to Kentucky).[14]

With the orientation meetings behind me, I sauntered over to the ESJ School and found Dean Whiteman's office door ajar. As I peeked in to greet him, I remembered him saying that a student who had been granted a half-scholarship had not been able to come at the last minute. I inquired if that scholarship was still available. He smiled and offered, "Just a minute; I'll check." He was back within a blink of an eye, announcing, "It is all yours." Half my tuition for the whole program was paid in full! I had never filled out an application, and I never signed my name to anything. "Whoa, God!" I did not realize until later that we had never considered how we were going to pay for this—we didn't have the money.

I believe God was making this call so crystal clear because He knew I would need to come back, and come back, and come back to **know** that He called me, and He called me to the ESJ School of World Mission and Evangelism. It was very specific, and my fingerprints were nowhere to be seen! There was no way I could have orchestrated this.

My next challenge was to decide on a topic for my dissertation. Remember, this was a totally unexpected paradigm shift for me. Everyone else in the program either had come from another country or had been a missionary in another country. Therefore, they obviously knew the foundations upon which their dissertations would be formed. I didn't have a clue. But God began to narrow my field of vision as I engaged with various students and professors.

When one enters the ESJ area at the seminary, he or she approaches a huge glass wall with "The E. Stanley Jones School of World Mission and Evangelism" engraved on it. I had no idea what made this man significant enough to have been given such a prominent memorial. I reasoned that since I was a student in this school, I should do some research on him. Thus, for my History of Christian Missions class with

Dr. Howard Snyder, I wrote my very first paper on E. Stanley Jones. I was duly impressed and delighted to learn about such an outstanding man. He was a Christian statesman of worldwide fame.

My curiosity concerning his wife, Mabel Lossing Jones, arose. I thought it odd that in all the volumes of information about E. Stanley Jones and by him, there was very little mention of Mabel. In his autobiography of 295 pages, there are only a couple of sketchy biographical paragraphs about her. This was one of the most intimate statements about her: "few women would have been equipped for such a sacrifice." Mabel Lossing Jones became the topic of my dissertation!

Dr. Whiteman granted me permission to pursue an independent study on "Women in Mission." To my delight, I was required to read a stack of biographies about these stellar women—captivating! I never dreamed of the adventures and contributions to the world that these women had achieved, women such as Phoebe Palmer, Catherine Booth, Mary Slessor, Pandita Ramabai, Amy Carmichael, and Kay Rader. The list goes on and on.

One of these outstanding women was Evangeline Booth. She should be extolled in every American History textbook for her tenacious leadership in our nation during the 1920s/30s.[15] When she returned from England to head the Salvation Army, Mayor LaGuardia and other dignitaries boated out to her ship. Once ashore, the police had to line the streets to block the cars back throughout the ticker-tape parade held in her honor. She spoke on the steps of the NYC town hall as thousands cheered her. You'll have to read the book to find out why!

I questioned why we had not heard of these women and others like them who had accomplished amazing acts of bravery, fortitude, and heroism and found that one of the main reasons is that most professionally written biographies have been written by men, about men. Logical, right? Therefore, we have a dearth of biographies of women. The result is that we have an incomplete account of history because we have only a one-sided view of that history—men's.

I love biographies. There is a power released when we hear or read real-life stories. That's why we, as Christians, are encouraged to share our testimonies—they convey the reality of God's unseen presence at work in the lives of ordinary people. There is encouragement and empowerment for women when they hear what other godly women have experienced and accomplished—especially in terms of handling leadership successfully and accomplishing ministry that is usually thought of as only a male's privilege. I wanted to share that encouragement and empowerment that emanates through women's biographies and help men to see the need to include women in leadership.

My objective in researching and writing a biography of Dr. Mabel Lossing Jones was to address in part an awareness of the historical missions of women, the potential impact of a biography and also to advocate gender equality in leadership.

ELLIOTT

That first year of classes challenged and expanded my vision of God's amazing handiwork in creating the various cultures of our world, but none compared to the awesome privilege of watching the birth of a baby for the first time—especially when that child was my very own granddaughter, Elliott Grace Ford!

DADDY'S TRANSITION

The second year of classes pulled me toward the opposite end of the spectrum of life and death. I received a phone call alerting me that my father was undergoing emergency surgery in Florida (my mother had died over a decade before).

I arrived at the hospital in the wee hours of the morning, traumatized by seeing him literally at death's door. His gallbladder had been taken out, and he was swollen beyond initial recognition. The staff said they did not know how he had lived through it. The doctor confided to me a few days later that his gallbladder was cancerous. His prognosis was six months to a year to live.

The Lord carried me through that week totally dependent on Him—causing me to call down heaven to earth on behalf of my dad, standing against the enemy and declaring daddy's healing through the Blood of the Lamb and the power of the Holy Spirit. When he was strong enough to travel, I drove him to our home in Kentucky—totally leaning on the Lord and singing His praises all the way.

When the oncologist in Kentucky examined Daddy and his records, he saw no reason to conclude that any cancer remained. Daddy still suffered with some breathing problems and bravely faced heart surgery the following month. He recovered wonderfully and insisted on driving back to Florida in the fall. It had been his custom for the previous ten years to stay with us from May until October and then spend the winter in Florida—always flying up in December for our Christmas celebrations.

When he flew back to Kentucky for Christmas, he had a routine checkup, and they found a growth the size of a lemon in his liver. He had surgery in January, but they could not capture it all. Even so, he recovered from the surgery remarkably well and flew back to Florida for about six weeks. He finished his business there, arriving back at our house on March 4—his eightieth birthday.

His strength was fading, but he felt fine until he caught a flu-type bug at the end of May. We set up a hospital bed in our living room, with hospice workers visiting regularly. I set up shop in my kitchen to work on Creative Memory Albums covering his life span. That kept me busy and near at the same time. I presented two large albums to him on Father's Day a few weeks before he died. He beamed with pleasure as he looked over precious memories.

Those last weeks were terribly hard. Trying to decide how much medication was needed and when to administer it became a daunting task. Watching him wane was painful. While he could still hold a conversation, he comforted me by saying I was the joy of his life. On another day, he expressed his anxiety that the Lord had not taken him yet: "I guess He doesn't want me."

I said, "No, Daddy, that's a lie."

He said: "I know. I know He loves me, and I love Him." Saying those words to me was a wonderful gift.

We decided to have Daddy cremated. When the coroner came to take his body from our home, I had the attendants dress him in his favorite pair of boxer shorts with ants printed all over them. He used to joke and say, "I've got ants in my pants" and then drop his drawers, revealing his ant-infested shorts!

We held his memorial service in Elyria, Ohio, at the Methodist chapel where he and my mother were lifetime members. I preached the message. John and our three children, their spouses, and our grandchildren each played a part. Kimberly sang "Holy, Holy, Holy" a cappella—breathtaking. I was so thankful I had already spoken before my son, dressed in his United States Air Force Uniform, arranged for "Taps" to be played as he saluted a picture of his grandfather. My son then knelt at my knee and presented me with Daddy's folded American flag from the Veterans Department—a precious moment, never to be forgotten.

Chapter Eleven

CHINA (OMS) 2003

The One Mission Society (OMS) had requested that the Gallahers and I lead a retreat for members of their leadership team, who were in need of spiritual refreshment. On September 25, 2003, I was scheduled to join Greg and Connie at Lexington Blue Grass Airport and depart at 11:25 a.m. for the first leg of our journey to Hong Kong. Yet, to my dismay, the plan seemed to implode when my passport became an issue. At 5:30 a.m. I phoned the post office inquiring as to its whereabouts and approximate time of its arrival. Thus, began a multi-state search via phone calls and checkpoints that culminated hours later with the notification that it had been located on a plane in Maryland at 4 a.m. that was due to land at the Louisville International Airport at 2:00 p.m.!

John and I toughed out the two-hour drive to and from Louisville to fetch it. We were then made aware of a $150 charge for changing the ticket—plus the difference in the cost of the two tickets ($1,500)! In shock, we swung by the Lexington airport on our way home, praying for a compassionate soul who would have mercy on me—and we found one! The extra charges were dropped due to the delay being caused by a blackout in the D.C. area over the weekend, which inadvertently had pushed the post office three days behind in deliveries.

The next day I arrived at Lexington Blue Grass Airport a couple of hours early only to hear that my flight had been delayed, which meant that once I landed at Detroit's Metropolitan Airport, I would have ten minutes to make it to my next connection. You guessed it! I missed the plane in

Detroit. They rebooked my flight, only to announce another hour's delay once again—thus compressing my connection in Tokyo down to a twenty-minute window.

In a heroic effort to help me meet my connection, I was escorted to the first-class seating area mid-flight, anticipating a quick exit. A young man who was holding a placard that prominently displayed my name greeted me, grabbed my carry-on, and led me—literally running through the behind-the-scenes turmoil of Tokyo's International Airport. He informed me that the plane they intended for me to catch was already airborne. We were scrambling to catch a second connecting plane on another airline. He assured me that this one would arrive in Hong Kong within minutes of the other; however, my luggage was still in the United States!

With a weary sigh of relief, I recognized the Gallahers and Longs on the other side of the baggage conveyor belt in Hong Kong. They whisked me off to Jack and Celeste Rae's amply appointed apartment overlooking the city. The Raes, members of the OMS team, were to be our hosts for a few days before we moved to the mountains for the weekend retreat.

Dealing with days of delays was a challenge, but adapting to another culture without my belongings, such as a fresh set of clothes and my curling iron, set me up for some emotional challenges. The next morning, we attended an evangelical English-speaking congregation that met in the YMCA. I showed up with swollen feet, looking shaggy and worn out. I missed John—especially when the Longs and Gallahers were walking together as couples. The air-conditioning periodically ramped up, so Greg wrapped his arm around Connie. Later Greg and David both collected their wives' empty communion cups for them—little gestures that I took for granted at home. Greg did take my cup after I spilled it on myself—not quite the same sentiment!

The jet lag lingered, although our second day slipped into a more natural stride. We visited the International High

School to watch Anna, the Longs' energetic sixteen-year-old daughter, engage in a series of volleyball matches. We ate lunch in a lavish Chinese restaurant embellished with pink tablecloths, and we soaked up the bright lights of Hong Kong atop a double-decker bus. But when Lori suggested prayer-walking in a nearby temple, Connie and I backed off—neither of us felt up to the spiritual warfare called for. We chose to sit on a bench near the side entrance and bless those bringing their offerings of fruit and cooked chicken—so sad to see them burning incense with their prayers to powerless idols.

On several occasions I was taken aback by the extensive use of bamboo scaffolding across the city—whole blocks of skyscrapers were encased in these woody grasses of jointed stems tied together at intermittent intersections. They appeared to be way too weak and unstable for such a massive undertaking. Later I learned how strong and sturdy they are! Wikipedia cites bamboo as having "a higher specific compressive strength than wood, brick, or concrete and a tensile strength that rivals steel."

The Lord revealed that the bamboo scaffolding represented my role in the Body of Christ: I may feel and appear to be way too weak for my calling, but God has positioned me to be a strength in supporting His work on the earth. Shortly thereafter, I spied a black and white drawing of Chinese bamboo and had it framed in gold-painted bamboo! It exhorts me every time I catch a glance at it. God uses the weak to confound the wise, and when I am weak, He is strong!

The focal point of our trip was the retreat with the OMS team in a tranquil mountainside resort overlooking Hong Kong. Greg opened with our theme of "Reflect. Receive. Renew." He challenged us to reflect on our callings to walk in His grace, which I desperately needed to grab hold of as I strived to finish preparations for speaking the next day. Looking back, I am convinced I was trying too hard. I had fasted the day before and was feeling faint. Plus, the physical and emotional struggles I previously alluded to had left me as feeble as the bamboo looked! But once I started sharing about the "prodigal son" in the morning session, the Holy Spirit began to move among us.

The Lord impressed me to offer a "mother's blessing" to any individuals who desired personal prayer. I'll always treasure praying over one young man who eventually became the president of OMS International—what a privilege to play a precious part in his journey. After my evening teaching, I led the team in a foot-washing service and asked Bill, an older gentleman, to sit in as a substitute for my father. The tears flowed and healing came as I washed his feet and asked forgiveness for both Daddy and me—for not sharing intimate heart expressions in his last hours.

My quiet-time hangout at the retreat was a huge rock shaped like an elephant and surrounded with bamboo trees and a slow-trickling stream. Several times, I shared that haven with a couple of the women who requested counsel.

Connie taught on prayer the next morning, followed by lunch, a much-needed nap, and a fun time playing Ping-Pong. Greg closed out the day with a teaching on sanctifying grace.

I started out our last morning on the mountain at my elephant rock, followed by hotdogs for breakfast, a team photo, and our final session. Greg spoke on "holy hands." I washed everyone's hands, and then he anointed them with oil. After serving communion, we huddled the participants into a small circle, where the Gallahers and I surrounded them and blessed them in prayer. There were lots of tears of thanksgiving and refreshment before returning to Hong Kong.

Most of the team met up the next morning in Shenzhen at the Three-Self Church.[16] The two-hour service was a bit of a trial since we could not understand much—actually nothing witnessed to our spirits. It was sad to see such a huge, Western-style building and service portraying freedom of worship, when in actuality it was merely a form of godliness but denying the power thereof—not unlike some services I've attended in the States!

That Monday morning, Celeste Rae left for the States to help her daughter's family move, and Jack departed for a men's retreat. Lori loaded up the Gallahers around 4:00 p.m. for a trip to the airport and their return to the States—alas, I had the house all to myself! I was so grateful for a day of alone-time with the Lord before departing for India to begin research on Dr. Mabel Lossing Jones!

Chapter Twelve

INDIA (RESEARCH) 2003

I arrived at the Indira Gandhi International Airport in New Delhi at 1:00 a.m. on October 8, 2003. It took an hour to claim my bags and shuffle my way through customs. The shuttle bus came an hour later to transport me to the domestic Sahara Air terminal. Armed military guards were stationed throughout the airport—one actually boarded the shuttle along with five Indian men and me. I felt safe enough until the shuttle stopped about forty-five minutes later at what I believed to be my destination.

As I attempted to step off the shuttle, an Indian shoved his handcart up against the bottom riser, thus blocking my way. "Your bags?" another man interjected.

"They are under the bus with the other luggage," I said. I thought they were trying to help me until I caught sight of my belongings being transferred into the trunk of a taxi! "No! No! No! I'm going into the terminal." The man taking charge countered, "They are not open."

"What?"

"The airport is not open."

I glanced back to discover that the shuttle bus had departed and the other passengers had disappeared! He continued: "They open at 6:00 a.m. We will bring you back after you've rested." This was surreal! I peered over the shoulder-high hedge to the one-story terminal building sitting silently in the dark. Sure enough, it seemed to be closed—there was not another soul to be seen. "I'll just wait here until they open."

He protested, "There is no place to sit."

"What? No place to sit?"

"No. We'll take you to a hotel—not far. You rest, and we'll return you in time for your plane."

I was literally at a loss. "Jesus, I need You." What was I to do? Where was I to turn? Who could come to my aid? Should I insist on retrieving my luggage and linger alone in this remote location? I got in the taxi.

I was thankful that the hotel was only about a mile away. The "boss" led me to the front desk and rang a bell, which startled a couple of sleeping bellhops to attention. The heavy-eyed night clerk insisted on charging me a fee of $40 for my three hours of R&R. I had been kidnapped, and now I was being hijacked! The two bellboys towed my suitcases about 20 feet to my "suite" and stood solemnly shaking their heads when I offered them a three-dollar tip. I shook my head too. "Sorry! That's all I have for you."

My security lock was a flimsy J-hook that I stuck into a small loop on the door jamb. It reminded me of the hook on the backdoor screen of my childhood home. Forty-five minutes of sleep with half an eye open was the extent of my endurance. After a feeble attempt to freshen up, I made an effort to quiet my soul. I prayed, read my Bible, and scribbled in my journal for a while, but I was too antsy to get the show on the road.

The second I began steering my suitcases across the textured tile floor, the twin bellhops awakened to their opportunity to swindle a few more bucks out of me and seized my belongings. The boss was waiting with the taxi. The four of them (two bellhops, taxi driver, and the boss) lined up, waiting for their tips! I handed the boss a ten-dollar bill and told him they would have to divvy it up amongst themselves. He was less than thrilled with me and gruffly motioned for me to get into the car.

My escorts deposited me on the sidewalk outside the airport entrance and took off. Until I entered the building, it looked as desolate as it had a few hours earlier. I about choked as I rounded the inside corner. A row of check-in counters with uniformed agents cheerfully assisting their clientele flanked my left, and a copious lobby of cushioned sofas and a snack bar was on my right!

I tentatively inquired as to their hours of operation and was told, "Oh, we are open 24/7." In stunned rage I related my ordeal to an airline agent who, although sympathetic, was powerless to facilitate a solution. She referred me to the armed policeman stationed across the room. As I began to spell out my kidnapping scenario to him, the loudspeaker announced that my flight was now boarding. Alas, no time to file charges!

Prior to leaving the United States, a casual conversation with Mike Adams had directed my path to Operation Mobilization's mission base in Lucknow, India. My plan had been simply to make a reservation in a Lucknow hotel and trust the Lord to lead me from there. At Mike's suggestion I contacted the base director, who invited me to stay with them—little did I know the extent to which the Lord was sovereignly caring for me.

When I arrived in Lucknow, Augustine and Saddu were waiting for me. Although we had never met, their kindred spirits showered me with much-needed solace! However, once we climbed into the van, culture shock set in immediately. As far as I can discern, there are no directions for operating a vehicle in India—except that one MUST have a hardy horn. The traffic is a free-for-all—summoning constant prayers for safety.

Cows are considered to be holy in India and must not be harmed. Killing a cow is a crime punishable by death. However, if you kill a person, you may walk away without penalty. These bovines control the ebb and flow of busy streets as they graze or lie down at will in the midst of the fray. Open sewers and "shops" (shacks) line the dirt-packed roads that are riddled with tuk-tuks,[17] bicycles, rickshaws, ox-drawn carts, cars, and pedestrians—a multitude of mankind pressed together in the dust-filled milieu.

The Operation Mobilization staff offered me a warm welcome and a sense of protection that I had not realized would be a prerequisite for an American woman traveling alone in India. They provided me with a private room and bath, a ceiling fan, a small desk, a low table, twin beds, and a sheet. It was not the Ritz, but it was safe. They anticipated my every need, providing a constant supply of bottled water, sanitary food, transportation, and a companion for every excursion outside the compound.

Moses, the OM director of the base, gathered my initial team together to introduce me and sketch out my schedule for the next two weeks. They set aside a corner for me in Jose's office with my own desk and access to a phone and then assisted me in placing phone calls to set up appointments and make other arrangements necessary for my research.

After an hour of rest, Ranjine drove Awon, Athriu, and me to Lucknow's primary marketplace in a sputtering speed mobile (what I would call a jalopy driven recklessly at high speeds). WILD! The girls diligently selected suitable material from the colorful stacks of carefully folded fabric to make me three *salwar kameezes* (Indian dresses with scarves and baggy pants). Our outing continued down another narrow, dusty path, not far from the city center, to the home of a seamstress/designer, who promised to complete the order within twenty-four hours!

Upon my return, Saddu was waiting to serve me supper: rice, bread, jelly, and a banana (I tried to taste a couple of other dishes—too spicy). He ushered me to my room and later reappeared offering fruit and water for the next day's breakfast since I had already decided to sleep in.

FIRST DAY-TRIP TO SITAPUR

October 9, 2003, was a fascinating day! My primary focus in flying to India was to visit the very site where Dr. Mabel Lossing Jones had poured out over forty years of her life for the Lord in mission—at the Boys' School in Sitapur.

OM arranged for a taxi to transport me and my new OM friend, Benjamine, to the now-named Mabel Lossing Jones Boys' School in Sitapur.

The two-and-a-half-hour drive proved to be yet another daredevil ride! Our driver adroitly zigzagged around cows, rickshaws, motorbikes, trucks, and colorfully adorned humanity. My jaw dropped over and over as we whizzed by little boxes on carts (presumed to be places of business) crammed together like a strip mall. Mild-mannered mendicants were mounted on bicycles and rickshaws with their spindly legs resting over handlebars, while they wistfully waited for customers. Doorless huts disclosed barber shops, basic underdeveloped businesses, and dust-covered snack shacks. Beautifully dressed women strolled the garbage-strewn paths as they balanced stacks of bricks on their heads. And did I mention the cows grazing, sleeping, or defecating in the middle of the action?

By the time the seeming merry-go-round romp had stopped at a cafe in Sitapur, I waxed woozy and was carsick! I fumbled through the foreign menu in hopes of finding something resembling "normal" to subdue my nausea. Aha! A tomato sandwich!

Do you ever wonder what happened to the lost people for whom you dictated directions? Hopefully they fared better than our driver's futile attempts to follow faulty guidance. After taking a confusing, circuitous route, we finally chanced upon our destination in the heat of the day. It proved to be a rather impressive entrance. The appropriate signage spanned two limestone pillars enclosing a concrete corridor lined with lavish flora that led to the closeted campus.

Mrs. Benjamine, the headmistress of the school, cordially invited us into her private, high-ceilinged quarters, where the simple-mannered lady served chai and shared what little knowledge of Mabel she had been privy to, as we sat under the steady breeze of the overhead fan. To my surprise, I learned that Mabel's daughter (Eunice Mathews), her granddaughters, and son-in-law were touring from the

United States and were scheduled to arrive in Sitapur the following Tuesday. What a wonderful coincidence! Perhaps I could connect with them! However, hopes of an invitation to join them were subtly silenced.

The Mathews supervised the control of Mabel's annuities that had sustained the school financially for the past five decades. Obviously, Mrs. Benjamine and her husband were industriously sprucing up the school in anticipation of the upcoming visit, and they were intently protective of their privacy.

The Benjamines courteously led me through the quadrangle of buildings that composed the center of the campus. The classrooms looked no different than the chapel; all were lined with long, splintered, wooden tables and benches painted in blue, pleading for replacement. The dormitory was a column of cot-like beds that were each covered with a single sheet, opposite a room-length ledge that supported the small, metal boxes that contained the boys' meager belongings. Most of the twenty boys in residence were shoeless, but there was a narrow ledge provided for a few paltry pairs of shoes.

It turned out to be a holiday of some sort in Sitapur, so many of the people and places I had hoped to see were inaccessible. The Benjamines suggested that I come back next week (after the Mathews had bid farewell). We left for Lucknow around 4:30 p.m. The scenery shifted up a bit—a slew of oxen pulling carts of all sizes and stuffed taxi cabs! (How many students can you cram into a phone booth?) I ate some chapati, vegetables, and fried potatoes for dinner.

BACK TO LUCKNOW

Friday morning started off with a miff. Athrui took one look at me in my new *salwar kameez* and determined it needed to be altered. She directed me to hop on a motorbike behind her and hang on. There was no time to settle myself—

off she buzzed to the seamstress's shanty. Athrui beckoned the seamstress out of bed and articulated the alterations to be done.

We were back at the OM compound by 9 a.m.! Jose was ready to take us to meet a Methodist pastor, Rev. Masih. It was another slightly slow-moving day—like everyone else so far, the elderly, rotund man knew next to nothing about Mabel. He hired a rickshaw to carry us to the church where Mabel's husband, ESJ, had experienced an encounter with God. We lingered around the grounds at the Lal Bagh School where Mabel had trained teachers, but it was closed for the holiday. We faced the same scenario with several other points of interest. My research was running into roadblocks at every turn.

Athrui and I pressed on to the Methodist Publishing House, where the staff half-heartedly agreed to search their archives for articles written by Mabel. We then backtracked to the Methodist parsonage, where we basked in a warm welcome from the pastor's wife, Angie Moses. She intently listened to my plans to research the records at Isabella Thoburn's College and cheerfully provided the principal's name and contact information, which were needed to secure permission to study there. She even enthusiastically offered to escort me on campus once I had set up an appointment!

Upon our return to the OM base, Athrui and I found the staff members lifting their voices in fervent prayer; the Spirit drew us into the flow of the Father's presence through the outpouring of our praise and worship. What an honor to join these humble servants who know how to seek the throne of grace with hearts fully surrendered to God alone—not defined by the delightful daily distractions that derail us in the States.

After this sacred time together as a team, the women slowly gathered in a smaller room for Bible study with Heidi, an American gal from Pioneer Ministries who weekly ministered the Word from a woman's perspective. She kindly invited me to initiate the teaching and prayer time. What a privilege to proclaim God's love and encouragement to sisters in the Lord who were desiring a deeper revelation of Him. His "word in due season" brought them healing of soul and hope for future success through spiritual warfare.

I got up on Saturday morning to take my mini-shower—the spout was clogged, and the two waist-high spigots were somewhat sluggish. One drizzled semi-warm water; the other dripped ice-cold water (I have yet to see a bathtub in India). Their "bathrooms" consist of shower spigots, sinks, and if you're lucky, toilets. The shower has no confines, so EVERYTHING gets completely soaked—mopping the floor marks the grand finale of the event!

Athrui made a hair appointment for me at 11:30 or 12:00 (time is rather insignificant in India). We left the base at one o'clock and arrived at the salon around 1:30 p.m. The tiny shop was owned and operated by an Oriental lady who at the time was teaching four Indian women how to style hair. Several other women in the narrow nook were having their faces wrapped in wax. A young girl shyly led me up the steep, narrow stairs to have my hair washed in a dilapidated reclining seat set in front of an ugly, old utility sink. The room appeared to double as a place to store discarded paraphernalia.

Downstairs they had just begun to blow-dry my hair when the electricity died out. Eight ladies in various stages of beautification sat in the eerie, darkened salon in silence. Now what? The owner evidently was not shaken as she steadily groped her way on hands and knees out into sunshine, with no instruction for her clueless clients. Within a few minutes, due to her neighbor's generosity and generator, the longing for a future life with air and light was fulfilled.

The ordeal continued as the cord of the blow dryer slid out of the loose socket with every twist of the stylist's wrist. My hope for a happy ending spiraled southward when I realized there was no curling iron in sight. Had I been aware of their limited cultural coiffure procedures, I gladly would have brought mine with me, but then again, it probably would have exploded in response to the extra wattage and the erratic electrical challenges.

The dazed woman dug out an old, rusty can of mousse from a rickety bottom drawer but could not seem to coax the substance out of the container. She tried pushing the spray tip, but only a thin, yellowish liquid dripped into her palm—no foam. However, she managed to massage it into my scalp anyway! Sorry, no photos to share!

On Sunday, Augustine struggled to start the stubborn old jeep, which sputtered and spewed before surrendering to our prayers. We eventually filed into the Methodist church where ESJ had first preached and where he ultimately had met Mabel Lossing. The caning of the chestnut-colored pews was in remarkable condition. The pews stretched out on either side of the aisle between elongated, vertical side windows, the shutters of which were flung open to usher in the soothing breeze. The lively leadership and sixty parishioners shared the life of Christ with us through communion, songs of praise, and prayers—an atmosphere of the Spirit that I have found worshiping in all of the other countries I have visited, validating a sense of oneness of the Body of Christ.

My afternoon by myself was restful, although I missed being able to discuss the day's activities with John; instead, I visited with thirty-five friends via penning postcards. The electricity cut off several times, so my tiny room overheated without the steady stirring of the overhead fan. Since it was the cook's day off, Saddu brought me Chinese food for lunch and chocolate-chip ice cream for dinner!

The next morning, my preaching on the prodigal son, with a major emphasis on forgiveness, was well received by the team. After a casual chai break, I taught on Deborah, from Judges chapters four and five, a rather delicate subject since women in India receive little encouragement or recognition of worth, even from Christian men. I ministered healing and hope to the girls—and dried their tears. Bless their hearts!

OVERNIGHT TRAIN TO JABALPUR

Joystna and I were able to carve out some rest time before catching the 4:00 p.m. train for Jabalpur and The Leonard Theological College, where I planned on pursuing my research. The train station itself was overwhelming—I never would have been able to navigate the throng of humanity on my own, let alone the massive maze of stairs, ramps, tracks, and platforms that were blanketed with moving bodies.

Our nourishment for the fifteen-hour, one-way challenge consisted of chips, cookies, and bananas. OM had reserved what I thought would be our own compartment since we were traveling overnight. It appeared to be sufficient on first sitting. Joystna and I sat across from each other, knee to knee, with a pull-down tray between us, and our bed shelves hovering over our heads. Across the open aisle were two single seats also facing each other, occupied by two men in military uniforms—could be worse—and it was! Enter stage right—a middle-aged couple who silently commanded we make space for them.

The husband, clad in military garb, received a robust greeting from the other two gentlemen. Joystna moved next to me, making room for the couple to be seated on what we thought was their side. The cozy nook soon felt quite claustrophobic. Joystna and I silently agreed to ascend to the bed shelves—just to secure some breathing space. We had no sooner scaled the metal rails than the woman broke out a bountiful basket of flavorful food, inviting the other military men to join the feast with loud conversation and laughter—standing eye-level with our reclining figures for several hours.

The din finally quieted down (not counting the captain's snoring about 5 feet from my face) when my bladder absolutely forced me to find a latrine. I will not paint the picture in detail, but it was a major maneuver! My baggy trousers were bound by a string tied around my waist, under my *salwar*. It was pitch dark. The train was jerking from side to side as it whizzed along the trembling tracks. I had to untie the trousers, tugging one leg of them and one leg of my underwear to the side of my body along with the hanging *salwar*, while holding onto a pole for balance and bending into a squat to release my waste into the narrow opening in the floor of the train—and no toilet paper!

That day, 6:00 a.m. did not come early enough! I prayed and read for a couple of hours on my bed shelf so as not to bother our new best friends. They finally started to stir around 8 a.m. Joystna and I freshened up as best we could after sleeping in our *salwar kameezes* all night.

Our 360-mile journey came to a close as our train chugged into Jabalpur at 9 a.m. A sweet sister of an OMer from the Assembly of God Bible School greeted us and guided us to the college. After an initial introduction to the principal, we left our bags in the girls' hostel and retained a rickshaw to the Hawabagh Girls Training College, where Mabel had been commissioned by the Indian government to institute in 1909. Unfortunately, the principal had no formal records of her founding history. She did, however, lead us on a tour of the now well-endowed and esteemed institution. As I entered the classrooms, the girls stood to attention, much as I surmise Mabel would have trained them to do.

Upon returning to the college, I received a key to the archives room—a rather small space with an old, narrow, wooden desk; a couple of four-drawer filing cabinets; and a wall of well-worn metal shelves. A dimly lit fluorescent fixture and low ceiling fan dangled overhead as I scanned through stacks of the Methodists' North India Conference material of the 1900s for five hours, finding tidbits of trivia that I hoped to insert into my dissertation.

Our train trip back to Lucknow was relatively low-key—I was so thankful to be "home"! I swiftly showered, donned clean clothes, and left for Nur Manzil, the Jones' psychiatric clinic, where Athrui and I were scheduled to meet Lillian Wallace, a longtime friend of their family—but no show. The bait of offense was ripe for the picking, but I chose to ignore the offer.

Angie promptly picked me up at 11:00 a.m. for my next appointment at the Isabella Thoburn College, where Mabel had once served as an instructor and later became a member of their Board of Governors. To my surprise, and to what I believe would be a shock to Mabel, out of the 2,500 girls in attendance, only 250 shared faith in Christ. The rest were split 50/50 between Islam and Hinduism—some even wearing slacks! One saving grace was that they were studying the *Jesus* film when I peeked into one of their classrooms!

Angie introduced me to Mrs. Russell, the matronly mannered principal, and led me to the library, where I foraged for the next four hours in research. Unfortunately, most of my findings could have been gleaned from resources in the States.

Sleep seemed elusive that night. Perhaps I was just snoozing lightly and thus easily startled every ninety minutes when the night watchman blew his whistle, which wooed me into a trancelike state of staring at lizards scurrying across my window screen.

SECOND DAY-TRIP TO SITAPUR

My taxi arrived at 8 a.m. sharp—unusually prompt according to standard Indian practice. Magdalene (another OM angel) agreed to accompany me on this trek back to Sitapur. We arrived at the boys' school in time for 10 a.m. chai, after which Mr. Benjamine offered his assistance in locating the Sitapur magistrate. However, our efforts proved to be fruitless. Let's just say the city official chose to withhold favor!

On my first visit to Sitapur, Mrs. Benjamine told me of an old man living in another village who had been a student at the boys' school in Mabel's day. Mrs. Benjamine intended to contact him and invite him to come and meet with me. Of course, my hopes of a delight-filled discussion were high but were dashed when he did not show up. These "dead ends" were beginning to discourage me. "Lord, I don't understand why it's so difficult to connect with people and to collect pertinent information needed for my dissertation. How am I to interpret so many interferences?" He directed me: "Don't get distracted. Just stay diligent on walking out your journey. Your assignment is to obey—the outcome is under My jurisdiction."

Mrs. Benjamine prepared a lavish lunch, shared some old pictures and memorabilia of the school's sacred story, and then presented me with a skillfully made, multicolored shawl and matching satchel. Mr. Benjamine and I continued with an in-depth chat concerning the Mathews family, which resulted in an insightful view of their recent visit. They shared the Mathews' email addresses with me and showed me their signatures, which were recorded directly below mine in the guest book! Mr. Benjamine quipped that they were quite curious about me and my mission. It was becoming crystal clear that my assignment encompassed encouraging the Benjamines.

Our life-threatening return ride to Lucknow lived up to its reputation—I almost screamed aloud a couple of times. Thank God for His protection and the precious intercessors who promised to pray over my itinerary! We arrived back at OM about 4:30 p.m., in plenty of time for Magdalene, Joystna, and me to mill around the markets.

All three of us tucked into a tight squeeze within the same rickshaw headed to the hub of merchandise mania. It was an adventure for sure—the sights, the sounds, the fun, the discomfort, and the frugal mindset of the OMers. HOWEVER, I could not help but observe how hard the slender man slaved to pull this overweight obligation in the

100-degree heat; over rough roadways; in the midst of massive, almost elbow-to-elbow humanity; for an exhausting twenty minutes!

When we dismounted, I was directed to pay this sweat-drenched man only 30 rupees (the equivalent of two dollars). I just couldn't comply—I handed him 100 rupees and notified the girls, "No change!" His facial expression and genuine gestures of thankfulness and joy are forever etched on my memory. He slowly trudged on through the crowd as I turned my back and wept. The awareness of his sacrifice for my comfort had humbled me. At my request, we rode home in two rickshaws.

CLOSING CONNECTIONS

On Sunday morning I was blessed with a surprise meeting with another OM guest who had just arrived from America! Debbie headed up an organization that helped women set up micro-businesses to sell their wares. She now resided in Palestine, and she shared how the recent earthquake there had helped bring unity in the region. Her church had adopted several families in crisis, resulting in many people receiving salvation because they saw how God protected and provided for the Christians!

Debbie photographed my batik[18] wall hanging that depicted Bible stories, which I had bought in Hong Kong from some industrious businesswomen. We discussed the possibilities of sharing the creativity we were seeing with the churches back home, which held the potential of opening sales among several countries. Our time together watered our souls—it had been weeks since either of us had enjoyed conversation with someone who spoke the same language—so relaxing and refreshing.

Busy, busy day! Athrui arrived before 9 a.m. to drape me in my new sari—spinning yards of finely fashioned fabric across my left shoulder, fabric that was then gathered, pleated, tucked, and pinned around my waist, thus blanketing a basic skirt and blouse. I felt regal as I inspected my image in the mirror. Upon entering the base chapel, even the men affirmed my appearance.

Lunch with Bishop Thomas and his family was rather formal. His daughter, Rohina, expressed her desire to become a Christian counselor and was intrigued with my explanation of the ministry of David Seamands, who had grown up in India as the son of missionaries and then became a pastor and a much-sought-out seminary counselor/author in the United States. I promised to send her some of his books.

Athrui diligently dressed me once again for little Lydia Moses' birthday bash. Several divine appointments delighted my heart at the party. I had taken a series of Graham Cooke's teaching tapes with the hopes of finding the perfect person with whom to share them. Graham is a powerful prophetic teacher who would be a great encouragement to someone ready to grow in that dimension. When I met Alison, I discerned that her spirit had been seeking prophetic teaching, and when I prayed over her, the Spirit confirmed she was the one He had chosen to be blessed by the tapes.

I ventured out on the veranda, where I met a lady who happened to have known Mabel! She offered a few sketchy scenarios and names of some others who knew Mabel and might still be alive. Angie and Moses then shared their testimony concerning the miraculous circumstances surrounding Lydia's birth. There is such a sense of expectancy that God is doing something special here.

As this trip to India was coming to a close, I was reminded of a promise to Paul Collins, a colleague of mine from Asbury, who asked me to contact his sister-in-law, Vanita, and her family in Lucknow. Vanita's daughter, Smitta, had already applied to attend the University of Kentucky, and they were eager to meet me.

Dr. Joel and Smitta picked me up (in a car) and chauffeured me to their house for lunch—quite a spread! Chinese rice, chapati, chicken, potatoes, green beans, tomatoes, curd, dairy cakes, and butterscotch ice cream! Dr. Joel, Smitta, and I ate first, and then Vanita and their other daughter dined. I thought it rather strange at first and then realized that these humble, gracious people owned only three matching plates with which to honor me. They also gifted me with a lovely chicken-weave shirt (a Lucknow specialty) and a necklace/earrings set. How could I decline their request that I pack a stack of clothes for Paul's family? Unfortunately, Vanita and Smitta stopped by the next morning with another huge stack for me to transport to the United States!

On my last morning in Lucknow, I shared chai with my OM sisters and Saddu. They had saved my life and served me in so many ways—I would never be able to express my gratitude entirely or compensate for their tender loving care. I presented them each with personal gifts, laid hands on their heads and prayed for them, and then washed their feet—tearful, heartfelt moments. At lunch, the whole team blessed me with a beautiful brass plate bedecked with a blue peacock in the center—an ancient Christian symbol of eternal life. As I write these words sixteen years later, I gaze solemnly upon its beauty, remembering the precious people who took care of me and the promise we hold of a grand reunion someday.

Jose provided a daredevil drive to the airport—NO HORN. It is almost impossible to arrive anywhere safely in India without a horn! (When I returned home, I sent him one for Christmas!) Joystna, Athrui, and Jose sat with me in strained silence at the airport. We were all too sad to say good-bye. My eyes had already been aching all day. It was a relief when the call to board came and brought some closure to our time together.

OM arranged for Denish to meet my flight in Delhi, escort me to my hotel that evening, and then accompany me back to the airport in the morning. They were not taking any chances on me being abducted again! However, my Indian challenges had not come to a conclusion just yet. Their culture hit me hard again at the baggage check-in—OVERWEIGHT because of the stacks of stuff Vanita had saddled me with! It cost me $120 AND took me about twenty-five minutes to deal with it.

Then the customs officer spent an exorbitant amount of time scrutinizing the couple standing in line ahead of me—he eventually sent them scurrying away for a security check! Lo and behold, I had been aboard the plane hardly two seconds before they had to slam-shut the hatch. Relief and resentment jockeyed for my focus as I fumbled down the aisle to find my seat. I finally settled down and by the grace of God repented.

It felt like downright deliverance to deplane in Hong Kong. I was FINALLY free to navigate safely on my own! I checked into the impeccably CLEAN airport hotel, ate at McDonald's, strolled through their sophisticated mall, sank into a HOT bubble bath and then indulged in an hour-long body massage!

I awoke from a deep, eight-hour sleep before 7 a.m. and promptly summoned the bellhop, but it still took almost two hours to transition through all the steps—baggage check-in and customs search. My newly purchased Chinese letter opener was confiscated! Oh, well. I lost my passport—turned out that I had placed it on top of my purse while they were checking my bags, and it had fallen onto the floor. Three times, I left behind my India map cylinder—in Hong Kong, Japan, and Detroit. I was so relieved when the efficient airline attendants retrieved it for me at each location!

When I landed in Lexington, Christi and Elliott were waiting for me at the foot of the escalator. El ran into my arms all smiles, with her sweet little voice of welcome warming my heart. John and Alan (Christi's husband) hovered over the baggage conveyor belt area after a couple of quick hugs, and my friends, Gail and Jim Wilkes, presented me with a bountiful bouquet of flowers arrayed in a classical crystal vase. They relayed Greg's regrets for missing my homecoming, but he was wrestling with issues in his back. Unbeknownst to us, Julie, our missions pastor, had planned on joining the party, but my flight had landed early, and we were long gone before she showed up. Nevertheless, the outpouring of love from all these caring people filled my soul to overflowing.

It was so good to be home after an AWESOME trip in God's GRACE. "Thank You, Lord. May it bear much eternal fruit for the Kingdom—BIG GRAPES! In Jesus' Name. Amen!"

We stopped by the Fords' house for a few more minutes of storytelling before continuing on to 612 Ridge View Drive, Nicholasville, Kentucky—our BRAND-NEW HOME! John and I had signed the deed before I left, and he had us moved in by the time I arrived home. John's mother had died in June and my father had died on July 1. Our inheritance covered the complete cost of our house as well as an upgrade in furnishings. This spoke to me of God's message of salvation—we did nothing to earn it or deserve it; it was simply a gift of grace, our inheritance, PAID IN FULL!

USA MABEL RESEARCH

Once over the inevitable jet lag, I jumped into my Stateside research on Mabel in February of 2004, beginning with a review of E. Stanley Jones' biography, *A Song of Ascents,* followed by a rigorous inspection of his papers (twenty boxes) in the archives in the B.L. Fisher Library at Asbury Theological Seminary in Wilmore, Kentucky. From there, my journey continued on to Drew University in Madison, New Jersey, to scan their archives, which proved to be merely a collaboration of information already gathered. From there, I went to Baltimore, Maryland, to peruse personal correspondence at Lovely Lane United Methodist Church and visit Mt. Olivet Cemetery, where both ESJ and Mabel are buried. Next was a short trip to Bethesda, Maryland, to interview the Jones' daughter, Eunice Mathews, and her husband, Bishop James Mathews. My final stop was at Gaithersburg, Maryland, at the Asbury Nursing Home, where Mabel lived out the last of her one hundred years.

The following March, my travelogue continued when I went to Upper Iowa University and the local public library in Fayette, Iowa. Then I traveled to the Clayton County Courthouse and public library in Elkader, Iowa. The current and former mayors of Clayton, Iowa, consented to an interview and offered news clippings, pictures, and valuable information regarding Mabel's formative years, as well as her furlough visits and retirement activities in Clayton. That night I stayed at The Claytonian Inn (*circa* 1940) in the "Jones Suite"—no phone, no TV, with nothing to do but enjoy the front-yard view edging the Mississippi. The next day I garnered tidbits in the Garnavillo Public Library and visited with Irene Frese, whom Mabel had mentored when Irene was a young mother. Next stop—the Guttenberg Public Library for more newspaper clippings.

In Dubuque, I attended a Sunday service at the church Mabel had attended during childhood. The church historian, Clara Burchett, provided copies of letters from Mabel's early missionary work, and Ruth Clarke, a member of the church who had been a little girl when Mabel left for India, shared her memories as she conducted a personal tour for me, pointing out relevant landmarks remaining from Mabel's young adult life. The Dubuque County Courthouse and Loras College also provided pictures of the area consistent with the time when Mabel was a resident in that area.

Several interviews with Mabel's acquaintances in Cedar Rapids and Des Moines provided more stories and priceless personal letters from Mabel. The Iowa Commission on Women also added their archival data. Of course, there were myriads of emails and phone interviews, the most important and illuminating being those from Eunice Mathews.

TATUM

Our new baby granddaughter, Tatum Elise, entered our lives on March 29, 2005. Her name connotes "joyful meadows," and she has lived up to every nuance of her calling. She seemed to have a cheerful tune constantly flowing from her little cherub lips throughout her younger years. Her bubbly personality and easy-going manner continue to encourage our hearts with contentment and satisfaction in the simple rhythm of life. Tatum was only six weeks old when she slept through my Asbury Theological Seminary doctoral graduation ceremony!

DOCTORATE OF MISSIOLOGY

I titled my dissertation "E. Stanley Jones Had a Wife: The Life of Mabel Lossing Jones, 1878–1978."[19] Mabel mentored me posthumously, as I pondered her navigation of life. I had forever felt a call to stand beside men in leadership, but even when God graced me with an opportunity, I would feel "less than" and quietly step aside, but Mabel modeled the Spirit-led courage to accept her calling in spite of the mores of her day.

As I shared earlier, God had sternly communicated that when I stand before Him, I have to answer for my own actions. I cannot hide behind my skirts or justify myself with "but John didn't." God painted a clear picture of John and me that settled my spirit: Jesus is the boat. John is the mast. I am the sail. I can't be the sail without John's support—and of course, neither of us can stand without Jesus holding us up and the Holy Spirit blowing His breath upon us! We are a team.

God used the ESJ School to widen my worldview and enable me to embrace world missions and ministry holistically. The faculty modeled gender equality and made me feel that my calling, giftings, and insights were valuable—that I held something worthy to be added to what I previously thought to be the masculine-only mix. They affirmed me, validated me, and provided a safe environment for me to understand and embrace God's call upon my life. The ESJ faculty taught me how to let God out of the box. And when I did—He took me with Him!

Chapter Thirteen

KENYA (CENTENARY) 2005

It was July 4, 2005, when our whole family unpacked our respective lawn chairs and lined them up on the curb in front of the B.L. Fisher Library in anticipation of the legendary Fourth of July parade. By far, the lawnmower brigade had been our favorite entry through the years, although this year our grandson's marching with his Cub Scout troop took first place.

The whole community had congregated, full of patriotic support for our country. One young man in the crowd singled me out and excitedly exclaimed: "Kathryn! I just read your book!"

I replied, "Oh, I didn't know it was available already" (thinking he was alluding to my dissertation).

"No, I bought it at a yard sale!"

Oh, my, he was referring to a self-published testimony of God's guidance in our early marriage and ministry that I had written twenty years ago! This conversation sparked the thought that my daughter-in-law knew nothing of those early years—perhaps she would enjoy reading some of our colorful family history secreted in those pages!

A few weeks later, the little book on a shelf in my office caught my eye again, so on the spur of the moment I stuffed it into my carry-on as I left for the airport—anticipating the refreshment of my memory en route to Kenya. I had prepared to teach on the Book of Ruth at a women's assembly; however, upon arrival, another invitation arose for me to speak at the African Pentecostal Church's Sunday service. The Lord quickened to my spirit that my "recently revived testimony" was to be the subject of my sermon. If I had known in advance, I probably would not have considered it to be an appropriate choice—little did I know what God was conceiving. He intended for this congregation to hear a firsthand account of how He moves to bring healing in the context of delicate marital difficulties.

There were twelve of us making the trip to Mwimutoni, a small village about an hour north of Nairobi, which our New Covenant Sunday school class supported. One of our classmates, Rebecca Kihihu, actually grew up there. When the class had studied *The Prayer of Jabez* and sincerely prayed that the Lord would expand their borders, Rebecca spoke up and suggested that her needy native village was possibly the place for the class to broaden their outreach, and thus our ministry to Mwimutoni was set into motion.

Nancy Hern and I were traveling without our husbands, along with two single gals, Ellen Marmon and Arvella Humes, plus four couples: Patrick and Deborah Kihihu, Gordon and Joyce Patterson, Phil and Mary Puddington, and Doug and Brenda Dean. During the previous months, we had met periodically in preparation for the trip and had already bonded in prayer and class participation, so we enjoyed a solid foundation of camaraderie to begin with, which made for a pleasant ebb and flow of our mission.

We arrived at the Methodist guesthouse in Nairobi on July 15, 2005, the night before my fifty-ninth birthday. I shared a sparse but adequate room with Arvella, an amiable woman about my age whose childlike anticipation of our opportunity to experience the Kenyan culture was contagious. The late hour of our arrival combined with drowsiness from jet lag quickened our ability to wind down into sweet dreams in record time!

We awoke refreshed before the alarm went off the next morning. After breakfast the team congregated in the Deans' room for devotions. I led, citing 2 Corinthians, Chapter 9, where God exhorted us to give of ourselves wholeheartedly, resulting in His promised overflow of blessing—manifesting

Himself beyond our natural expectations. It was going to be a good day!

Our first stop was the Sarit Centre to exchange currency and pick up supplies. I secured twenty-six postcards and stamps, hoping to mail them in the next day or two so that family and friends in the States would receive them before my return. The trip to Mwimutoni mirrored the traffic previously described in the chapter on India—driving rules were pretty much made up on the run. The scenery was similar as well: stretches of poverty and beautiful flowers and trees, but instead of cows rummaging along the garbage-strewn roads and roaming whithersoever they chose, the donkeys took dominion. As usual, I sat shotgun because of motion sickness; however, I believe everyone was eligible to claim that seat by the time Danson, our driver, had navigated the narrow, dirt paths down to the village.

It was customary to visit Rebecca's parents' home first since they were our initial contacts. Their dirt floors were walled and roofed by sheets of corrugated aluminum. A cow stall, a sheep stall, and a chicken coop were part of the property. Priscilla, Rebecca's mother, served enough food to feed the proverbial army: potatoes, peas, beans, rice, cabbage, chapati, and goat! I became quite adept at covering my mouth with a napkin and discreetly depositing said delicacy into my pocket until further opportunity for permanent discarding. Following the meal, we took charge of the cleanup, which consisted of washing dishes while bent over a low tub in the yard—pretty much at a 45-degree angle!

We then toured the new Hope Center, which had been supported by our Sunday school class. A year ago it had been merely a piece of property, but now two good-sized, corrugated tin-roofed and cement buildings provided tangible evidence of progress being made. One accommodated space that was designated for cooking and serving hot lunches for more than sixty orphans, and the second one served as an office, plus living space for Paul and

Dorcus, who had moved in with their own four children to oversee the activities at the Center.

Other new additions included two cows, a coop full of chickens, and a large-scale garden where irrigation techniques were being taught and where the food was being grown to feed the orphans a hot lunch (literally their only meal of the day). Our team was privileged to prepare and serve these meals several times during our stay.

By the time we approached the Hope Center, we had acquired quite a number of young "escorts" who were fascinated by Arvella's bubble-blowing skills. We experienced great enjoyment just observing their enthusiasm for such a simple activity.

We continued down the path to the primary school, which consisted of a row of six cement-block rooms adjoining one another. The students sat on rough, wooden benches wide enough for three to sit at a time, with matching wooden tables. The teacher's "aide" was a single slab of slate mounted on the wall in front of the students. Our class had covered the school fees and uniforms for the orphaned students in the first through eighth grades, as well as for the high school students, who met in another area. We ended our tour at the old, abandoned, 1936 brown-bricked train station that mission teams were renovating into a two-room clinic, complete with a new cobalt-blue corrugated tin roof.

Once back at the guesthouse, the team gathered again for a rather short debriefing of the day's events before they energetically pulled out *Lion King* masks and graced me with flowers, cards, and the singing of "Happy Birthday"! It was quite a lot to take in on this uniquely unforgettable day!

The following morning, our first Sunday in Kenya, we attended the Nairobi Chapel on Mombasa Road. The Westernized worship proved to be a wonderful, Spirit-filled service that was easy to understand and engage in. The theme was "Remember to Remember." The pastor exhorted us:

- Remember your story.

- Remember that God is God.
- Remember the mountains He has taken you through.
- Remember why you are here—we are not here for ourselves.
- Remember our covenant with God— "I have a Father."

The pastor exhorted the congregation, saying that "testimonies are the focus, not preaching—make it personal." (Remember that Rebecca had invited me to speak from my heart when I was to speak at the African Pentecostal Church on the next Sunday.) The Lord's voice and direction could not have been clearer: "Tell what the Lord has done for you. A lighthouse draws attention to itself." He then read from 2 Corinthians 2:10: "Boast in the Lord"—lessons He has taught you along the way. Remember God's faithfulness.

A sentence at the bottom of the bulletin stated: "In the next two weeks you will be entering into a new phase of your history, one that will present opportunities for new challenges. You would be remiss to move forward without first taking some time to remember your past and thank God for His blessings." There could be absolutely no doubt that the Lord was faithfully leading me in the way I should go!

After church we caravanned to Patrick's parents' home in a nearby village for more Kenyan hospitality and another feast! While listening in on several candid after-dinner conversations regarding marital distress, I received the Lord's further confirmation to share my testimony on the following Sunday.

Arvella and I had just returned to our rooms around four o'clock, hoping to squeeze in an afternoon nap, when the phone rang. It was Rebecca; she was asking me if I would like to accompany her and Patrick to a crusade taking place in the middle of a slum district in Nairobi.

We arrived shortly thereafter, at the edge of a sea of people surrounding a stage, as singers were ending their praise time. I never heard if they suspected something dangerous was about to happen, but I was troubled when someone started up the van before Patrick had finished praying. However, I felt completely at peace while giving a brief testimony from the platform and afterward spotted a graceful bird soar across the sunset while the preacher spoke about the Holy Spirit being "sacred air." The moment he finished his message, our escorts shuttled us off to the guesthouse, saying it was not safe for us to be outside the compound after dark. Praise the Lord for hiding us under the shadow of His wing and returning us safely!

FIRST ASSIGNMENTS

Danson drove our van back to Mwimutoni on Monday morning. We enjoyed getting to know each other, even though we struggled at times to understand certain cultural expressions. For example, when Danson stated, "God has no cabin," he meant "He is everywhere!"

One of our first assignments of the day was to assist a team of seven from Dover, Ohio, and Somerset, Kentucky, in unloading medical supplies delivered to the clinic—a common task. Then Nancy, Mary, and I wandered over to where Agnes was winnowing beans. I had read about winnowing in the Bible (Matthew 3:12) but had never really thought about it being a reality of everyday life in today's world. For those who may not know, winnowing is the process by which chaff, dirt, etc. are freed from grain by tossing it in the air by hand, shovel, fork, etc. and allowing the wind to blow away the impurities. In our modern world, this is carried out via mechanical combines. In Agnes's world, this was done by filling a relatively flat basket with beans, and then, after a spirited shake, tossing them up into the air and catching the falling beans in the basket, minus the debris.

After a couple of hours of winnowing, my "first-world"" arms began to ache. I was thankful when the water committee summoned us for a tour that showed us where the pipes had been laid up to the well's holding tank. Each section stretched for 20 feet. It had taken 350 men of the village to dig the ditches for the one-and-a-half-mile length of pipe—mostly up a steep hill. This was an amazing accomplishment, because the men of the village usually do not do ANY work! Previously, the women and children had been obliged to walk several miles daily to scoop up dirty water from puddles via old plastic containers and haul them home. But now . . . they have their own well.

Simply climbing to the top of the holding tank was a challenge, but Patrick and I conquered it before trudging on a little farther to view the Great Rift Valley. The Valley is a series of continuous geographic trenches that run approximately 3,700 miles from Lebanon in South Asia to Mozambique in Southeastern Africa, with its deepest area around Mwimutoni.

After a meal of hard-mashed potatoes and kale at Pricilla's house, we returned to Hope Center as the children were winding up their lunch period. Several of us jumped in and started washing and drying the dishes. Nancy and I then joined Agnes in sorting pans of beans, although I kept throwing them into the wrong bowl. I tactfully excused myself to spend time with a small group of children ranging from around eight years old to twelve years old who eagerly asked questions about our families, enjoyed looking at our pictures, and elatedly tousled my hair—salt and pepper in appearance and a different texture than theirs. They were so sweet and well-behaved and easily entertained!

A more moving experience for me ensued on Tuesday, as we helped the Ohio Team hand out new shoes and socks to the orphans. We showed them individually how to pull on the stylish socks and made sure their shoes fit and were laced properly. Their gracious grins and squeals of delight were reward enough, however; they responded with repeated words of thanksgiving and even sang to us!

Rebecca pulled aside a few of us ladies to present eight foam-and-gauze-stuffed mattresses (we transported them in our van) to an old woman who was raising her eight grandchildren because their parents had all died of AIDS. As we carried these mattresses into her home, which was made of mud and sticks with a dirt floor, she wept with joy and thanksgiving. The eight children had been sleeping in four single beds, with holey rags (loosely referred to as "blankets") crumpled in a small heap between them.

We then returned to Nairobi, and after grocery shopping for a special meal to share with the high school students the next day, we joined the Ohio Team at Java's for some American food and fellowship. All went well as we relaxed in an hour or so of "down time" together; however, as we prepared to leave, Joyce discovered that her purse, which had been strapped over the back of her chair, had been stolen. It held credit cards, a good amount of money, and her cell phone. Rebecca immediately called the police but to no avail. We were thankful that Joyce's passport had remained in the guesthouse, safe.

We arrived at Mwimutoni a little later the next day, due to several issues of import: the Pattersons were dealing with precautions and the ramifications of Joyce's stolen purse; Phil was catching us up on his negotiations with the government officials and a vocational school in Nairobi—pursuing electricity for the primary school; and Ellen was reporting on her side-trip to encourage a small church in Mombasa. Nevertheless, we persevered in our plan to make peanut butter and jelly sandwiches, pack them up, walk the path to the secondary school, and set up shop on wooden benches outside the high school in time to serve lunch to 125 students!

We provided diluted pineapple juice too, which was probably too sweet for them—they are not used to a lot of sugar. They expressed gratitude since they usually do not even get water to drink all day. After they ate, we paired off with the fifteen students whom our class sponsors (pays their educational fees) to socialize more personally with them—asking questions, filling out information forms, sharing photos of our families, and taking snapshots of them, which we then printed out for them. They were THRILLED! They had never seen pictures of themselves before.

The young men I interviewed were extremely interactive, eagerly sharing experiences and opinions and asking all kinds of questions. I talked quite some time with a young man named John who yearns to come to the States and play "football" (our soccer). In preparation, he suggested that my son-in-law, Alan, come to Mwimutoni and coach him. Paul, another good student, knows a lot about history and the Bible and aspires to become an architect. Lazarus and John were both intensely interested in the United States. I drew them a map freehand that even surprised me with its accuracy! It opened up a whole slew of serious inquiry.

Once back to the Hope Center, we linked up with the Somerset Medical Team to unload their supplies, count pills, and fill and label bottles of liquid medicine. Over the next three days, eight hundred men, women, and children lined up to receive free medical care at the Hope Center.

On Wednesday morning, our whole team rolled up their sleeves to help paint the new clinic (the old railroad station). About fifteen people were waving paint onto the stucco walls all at the same time. It was a sight to see: some were standing in wheelbarrows to reach higher, and some were on their hands and knees to reach lower—all singing, laughing, and getting the job done!

As Patrick and I sauntered down the well-worn path to wash brushes, Rebecca came rushing toward us aflutter with an account of the clinic being overwhelmed with people requesting medical attention, but Rebecca discerned that much of the turnout stemmed from psychosomatic symptoms due to the availability of free pharmaceuticals. She proceeded to gather a group of fifty people who were willing to believe God for their healing and herded them behind the clinic. We exhorted them with healing scriptures, and several of us gave testimony to previous personal healings, which Rebecca followed up with a powerful prayer. Then she instructed some of us to lay hands on them and pray for them individually.

A handful of expectant hearts received immediate healing—aches and pains left in the name of Jesus! One woman who was doubled over with severe abdominal pain rejoiced that she could return to her field for another full day's work. Another lady could see only black and white forms; she received her full sight. The crowd raised shouts of joy and thanksgiving before I closed our time with prayer, recognizing God's loving provision.

After we fed the orphans lunch, we scuttled off to the primary school to present a Bible lesson whose theme was "Jesus Is the Light of the World." We passed out glow-in-the-dark stickers on tongue depressors and taught them to sing "This Little Light of Mine." Passing out small packs of crayons and sheets of stickers to the six hundred children brought great pleasure to us as well as them—almost every one of them received these gifts with bright smiles and "Thank you!" or "God bless you!"

SIDE-TRIPS & CLOSING CEREMONIES

The next day we made a side-trip to Rafiki Village, a couple hours' ride from Nairobi. It is a first-class orphanage with a Pre-K–12th grade Christian school that is also attended by children from the community who are in poverty. This outreach is supported by Bible Study Fellowship, a soft spot for Brenda, who had served as part of the Lexington leadership for many years and eagerly looked forward to observing the facility firsthand. The three-storied mansion originally belonged to the family of Jomo Kenyatta, the first president of Kenya. It did not disappoint. From the spacious gated grounds to the well-equipped kitchen to the spotless dining hall, the well-kept children obviously were receiving the nurture of body, soul, and spirit.

Back at Hope Center, Agnes anxiously waited for me to meet her daughter, Margie. Agnes has five children and has taken in other orphans who are receiving educational assistance from our Sunday school class, but the class has a policy to help only orphans. Agnes had approached me earlier in the week, asking me to help her daughter enter high school. I discussed the situation with Brenda and Ellen, who were well aware of the extenuating circumstances and the class policy—they graciously left it up to me. I decided to sponsor Margie myself. Of course, she and Agnes were thrilled—Agnes made me a necklace out of corn and beans!

Regretfully, I did not realize my error until much later. The class could not afford to sponsor all the children and therefore had set up parameters. Now, my rogue behavior would put pressure on others down the road to do the same—when that is not the mission.

The team spent our last free day at Nairobi National Park—basically on a mini-safari! We rode in special vans with the roof lifted up so that we could stand, with nothing between us and wild animals roaming freely across the tall grasses. We observed giraffes, zebras, ostriches, klipspringers, rock hyraxes (rock rabbits), gazelles (running), water bucks, Ruppell's griffon vultures, and cobras (real close)!

Lunch evolved into quite an event carried out at a restaurant called The Carnivore. The decor, accented with upholstered zebra-skin chairs, heightened one's anticipation of an unusual cuisine! Straw-hatted Kenyan waiters circled our table with the carcasses of various animals skewed on long swords, from which your choice would be carved off—and cooked! I feasted on fresh helpings of lamb, beef, turkey, chicken, crocodile, ostrich (sweet and tender), and camel (tough).

On our last Sunday in Kenya, we left the guesthouse at 9 a.m. The service at the African Pentecostal Church started at 10:30, but my turn to preach did not come to pass until 12:30 p.m.! Africans do church as a celebration ceremony, and they are not in a hurry! My first surprise came as the priest strode down the center aisle flinging incense—I didn't see him coming until after the "sprinkling" of oil landed on my forehead. Two children's groups sang and danced, accompanied by hand-crafted drums; a couple of youth groups performed; and a visiting trio performed. The pastor preached a mini-sermon followed by exuberant congregational singing, while the women danced their baskets of "first fruits" to the altar for a blessing.

By this time I was worn out and didn't expect much of a response from the congregants—especially when my testimony would be a stretch for them—translation and content that they did not normally address in church. But assured by God's previous confirmations and Rebecca's ability to translate, I testified about marital challenges, unfaithfulness, God's miraculous intervention, and forgiveness.[20] The intense faces of the men and women alike let me know that they were receiving ministry from the Holy Spirit the whole hour. Rebecca later confirmed that they needed to hear that powerful, clear, and direct message on marriage, fidelity, and forgiveness.

Priscilla prepared lunch, but I lingered in the van by myself as I tried to rest and regroup for the women's meeting that was to start at 3:30 p.m. Women from eight other churches joined us, and of course each group sang and danced for the others. Rebecca gave a mini-talk on sex education, emphasizing the need for mothers to instruct their daughters on the power of purity. By the time I started to teach on Ruth (5 p.m.), I was worn out again, and to make matters worse, my interpreter didn't understand what I was saying—she did not have a Bible with her and could not find the Book of Ruth in the Bible that was handed to her! This threw me off several times. I did not sense any anointing, and I was freezing. The sun was going down, and Patrick was pacing outside—antsy about leaving before dark. Bummer. Nevertheless, we took time to pray with a line of women who desperately needed it and received the hope that only Christ can give.

On our last morning in Mwimutoni, we went room to room in the primary school and passed out pencils to the children—two each, and they were thrilled. We went back to Hope Center to prepare and serve the orphans lunch. Then I delivered a few gifts to Agnes's house, where I met her husband, her other four children, and her niece and nephew, whom she had taken in when their parents had died of AIDS. Sweet family. They excitedly received pencils, some hats, a couple of shirts, a sweater, and a hand towel for Agnes—it was like Christmas morning for them!

I'm not sure what time we left Nairobi, but we arrived in Amsterdam at 4:30 a.m. I wandered through the airport, searching for an isolated spot to focus on the Lord. I found a quiet corner, seemingly overlooked by other travelers. However, after a while, a familiar praise song softly drew my attention to a middle-aged black man who was seated in the row behind me, humming. I started singing the words along with his melody, and my heart soared! There we sat, back to back—total strangers, opposite sexes, opposite skin color—praising God together in the midst of our crazy world! It was glorious! We experienced a touch of heaven as our voices and hearts blended perfectly in worship—we never spoke, and shortly thereafter he disappeared (he may have been an angel).

Arrived in Newark around noon. Departed at 5:30 p.m. Landed in Lexington at 7:00 p.m. John, Christi, and the girls were waiting for me. Ellen took pictures of us as we came down the escalator and then passed out homemade brownies (she had returned a day earlier).

Going to Kenya with this group was a really great experience. The Deans did an excellent job of leading. The team exhibited graciousness and flexibility toward one another as well as to the Kenyans, and the village of Mwimutoni received great encouragement on many levels. Most importantly, God was glorified.

Gathering of young female students. Higiami Chapel, Japan, July 1996

Prison Warden and U.S. Team. Archangels, Russia 1996

International Institute Leadership Conference.
Jos, Nigeria 2007

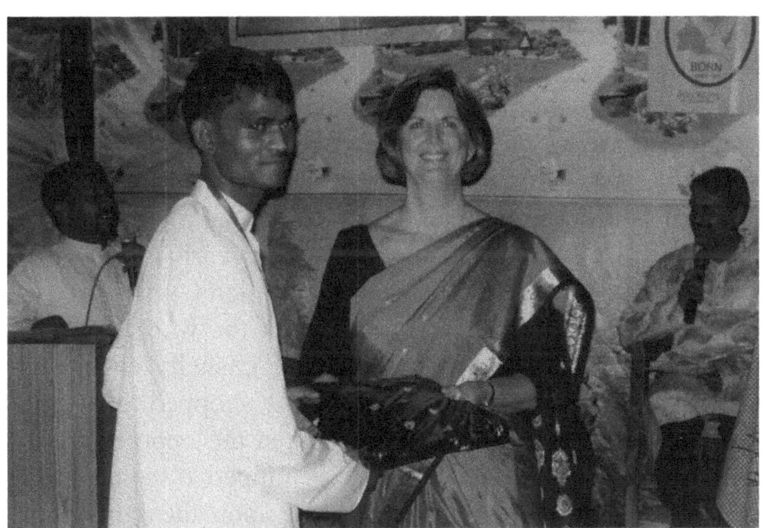

Bible Institute Graduation. Patna, India 2008

Chapter Fourteen

UNITED ARAB EMIRATES (CRESCENT PROJECT) 2006

PRE-FLIGHT TRAINING

The United Arab Emirates (UAE) is a federal absolute monarchy sovereign state in Western Asia at the southeast tip of the Arabian Peninsula, situated on the Persian Gulf, bordering Oman to the east and Saudi Arabia to the south, with the maritime neighbors of Iran to the north and Qatar to the west.

The UAE, in essence, embodies seven emirates, Dubai being the largest and most populous—a truly global conglomerate of international aviation and maritime trade. Everywhere we turned, we faced dozens of the five thousand high-rises being built all at the same time, commanding 16% of the world's cranes in this, "The World's Richest City," and a hub of the wealthy Middle East, which previously could boast of nothing more than desert sand. One of the lures of their business and tourism advertising is a yearly ladies' two-week shopping extravaganza that elicits millions of primarily Muslim women from all over the world. What a unique setting for Christian women to casually engage in conversation with Muslim women as we shopped together!

When the Crescent Project presented the opportunity to "Journey Behind the Veil," my spirit jumped at the prospect of being a vessel of love poured out upon these precious souls—even after the project suffered a snafu of sorts a couple of weeks before showtime, when their beloved Sheikh Maktoum bin Rashid Al Maktoum died and the country entered a month of mourning. Many of the festivities were canceled and a number of would-be shoppers stowed their allowances away for another year, but our airline reservations and lodging accommodations required us to proceed as planned. Of course, God remained on His throne, and His divine appointments were not to be dismissed.

Nine handmaidens (four in their twenties, two in their thirties, and three in their fifties) from various regions of the United States flew to Dallas, Texas, for three days of intense training on the Muslim woman's worldview. While waiting for the hotel van to arrive, I struck up a conversation with the young woman who cautiously had joined me on the black mesh bench. Sure enough, twenty-seven-year-old Christina was to become my new roommate! She is the single mother of five-year-old Cora, serves as a dispatcher for the fire and police departments in her hometown, and works with her mom, who is a naturopathic doctor.

At the hotel we found four other teammates: Janet, Sharon, Mary, and Joan. Our six-pack decided to share introductory life stories over dinner at the Olive Garden. Once back at the hotel, we met up with Betty Jo (not her real name) and Julie, our youthful facilitators, who filled us in on some fundamental logistics. Rachel, our remaining compatriot of the younger generation, whizzed in just as we were finishing up—all aboard and accounted for!

The next morning, our prayer journey began with what was to become our standard method of operation throughout our seventeen days on assignment: prayer, worship, and time spent devotionally in the Word of God together. After our initial training session and lunch, we prayer-walked and toured the Islamic Center of Irving during their scheduled Friday afternoon prayer service.

We were warmly welcomed into this two-storied, immaculately maintained facility, constructed to accommodate more than three thousand worshipers at a time beneath an exquisite, golden chandelier that hung higher than the second-story gallery. Two attractive, young, American women, duly attired in their hijabs (head scarves) and abayas (long cloaks), ushered us upstairs to a large U-shaped corridor that extended around three sides of the sanctuary, with glass walls that provided a clear view of the men on their knees and the Imam teaching them from a pulpit. These glass walls were lined with Muslim women who also were kneeling, bowing, reciting their prayers, and listening to the Imam.

The Imam spoke for about a half-hour in Arabic, after which we engaged in conversation with the two American women. Jennifer, an energetic teacher, eagerly related her story. Post-9/11 she had searched for a deeper spirituality. Unfortunately, her husband had no spiritual hunger, and thus they had divorced. She is now married to a Palestinian. She believes that her attire serves as a strong statement of her spiritual depth in Islam.

Elizabeth was not quite as exuberant; she came to the service "to be lifted up." This physician's wife was raised in a small Southern town and had attended both Baptist and Methodist churches but never "bought into" Jesus being the Son of God. She met her husband on a blind date and shortly thereafter received her conversion into Islam through reading a book—although she has never read the Koran or the Injil (another sacred Islamic text). She "loves to listen to the Koran on tape"—even though she doesn't understand the Arabic language! Her family, of course, is heartbroken and has no desire to tolerate her turning away from Christianity, which is obviously quite grievous for all.

Several of the other women were adamant about their faith, even angry when invited to share. They talked in circles, and when they came to a dead end, they would coolly close down the conversation with "I would have to talk with the Imam." Everything they knew came through the Imam. They appeared to be confused, hurting, lost little girls hiding behind veils and robes. BUT Jesus walked among them that day, and we trust that His Spirit of love is at work within their hearts.

It turned out to be a long afternoon session: debriefing, lectures, and lifting prayers for the Muslim women. Faud, one of our instructors, voiced his disdain for the Imam's unkind discourse about non-Muslims not worshiping God—of course Jennifer and Elizabeth had no idea what the Imam had said, since they don't know Arabic!

Here are a couple of insights I found to be helpful: It is not the name of Allah with which we disagree; it is the character of Allah in Islam, which is demonic. Also, when sharing with a Muslim, it is of utmost importance to stress that the Sonship of Christ is a spiritual Sonship, not a physical one.

Dinner was served at a Mediterranean restaurant where the menu was Greek to me (funny)! I tasted something so hot I felt that my tongue was literally on fire! Once I had regained my sense of adventure and "can-do" spirit, I enjoyed a lamb kabob and other unidentifiable offerings.

The prayer tea was the highlight of our last afternoon of preparation. We relaxed on rugs (towels) with scarves and veils wrapped around our heads, while Katelyn, a Crescent Project administrator, explained:

- Muslim women know nothing of the intimacy of prayer with "Abba Father." Allah is far off and inaccessible to them. They face their struggles alone.
- Sharing a cup of Arabic coffee (*ahweh*) or a cup of tea (*chi*) helps us to identify with our Muslim sisters and to better understand how much they value hospitality. Friendships are developed via this time-honored Bedouin tradition.
- We can join them through prayer and identify with their burdens as we intercede for them to know God's love expressed through their prophet Isa.
- God is calling us to pray for the daughters of Ishmael, through whom God can build His kingdom families, and nurture future leaders from Muslim peoples for His glory.

"After this I looked, and there before me was a great multitude that no one could count, from every nation, tribe, people and language, standing before the throne and before the Lamb. . . ."
Revelation 7:9 (NIV)

The evening commissioning service drew our time of knitting our hearts and minds together to a close as we locked arms and received the laying on of hands by the Crescent Project Leadership.

"Oh, give thanks to the LORD! Call upon His name; make known His deeds among the peoples! Sing to Him, sing psalms to Him; talk of all His wondrous works!"
Psalm 105:1–2

MALL MINISTRY

About eight hours after departing Dallas, we arrived at the Gatwick Airport in England and then took a bus to Heathrow Airport to board for the last leg of our route to Dubai. My Swedish seatmate spent most of his time reading *The Da Vinci Code*; however, we did engage in brief conversations about his interest in videography and his visit with his aunt in Bangladesh!

We landed in Dubai at 11 p.m.—somehow we had lost a day en route! It was 1:30 a.m. by the time we had dragged our luggage and our languishing bodies through the doors of our palatial lodgings and up the grand staircase into our luxurious quarters. Even though I would be rooming with the four "young uns," we each were afforded ample space to spread out and still have some privacy. In true Dubai over-the-top fashion, this guesthouse provided an oasis for missionaries in the Middle East to enjoy R&R on occasion and even have family from the States join them for a few days. Becky and her husband had served as the hosts of the house for more than thirty years—their two daughters were now attending college in the States.

Our befuddled leader, Betty Jo, ran into challenge number one right away—her passport had passed through the wash at home, and the Dubai officials did not want to accept it! She was forced to spend our first morning getting her picture taken and skirting stumbling blocks at the American Embassy. The rest of us were redirected to one of the world's largest shopping malls, City Centre Deira, a multilevel shopper's paradise that is designated in tour pamphlets as a destination in itself!

Known for moving in the fast lane, I lived up to my M.O. and in record time acquired several veils, small rugs for my granddaughters' dollhouses, and a stuffed giraffe before setting up shop in a Starbucks for a couple of hours with Julie as we waited for the others to trickle in!

Like a magnet, the young American mother caught my attention—her homesick, overwhelmed, lonesome look betrayed her "I've-got-it-all-together" appearance, as she navigated the baby buggy between tables. Her countenance lifted spontaneously in response to our comforting smiles, and shortly after introducing ourselves she began pouring her heart out. Oliver was the baby, and Elliott (from observation) was enjoying her "terrible twos"! Her husband, an airline executive, was swamped under the stress of learning the protocol of his new promotion. They had moved to Dubai only two weeks ago, and their initial adjustment had suffered the further complications of the family fighting illnesses the whole time—this was their first outing.

I cradled the baby, and Julie entertained Elliott while their mama enjoyed the freedom of a few minutes of rest. All went well until Janet joined us and spilled her hot coffee, which went streaming over the entire table. The commotion scared Oliver, who let out a scream—drawing the disdainful stares of passersby. His mother panicked as well and quickly ushered her little family out of the restaurant. We continued to support her in prayer throughout the week—

understanding that even this was a divine appointment; she was part of our assignment.

We continued watching the women dressed in black abayas in fascination as they seemed to float through the mall—we couldn't see their feet. At one point Christina asked a couple of the Muslim ladies for permission to take their picture, but when she stepped outside the café, a Muslim man who had been staring at us approached me aggressively with hostility, demanding an explanation of her actions. "We are just visiting and want to remember the people and the culture of Dubai." He backed off but clearly indicated his suspicion of a sinister plot afoot. I later discovered that some Muslims believe that a person's soul can be stolen by taking their picture!

"My heart is steadfast, O God; I will sing, I will sing praises, even with my soul. . .. Oh give us help against the adversary. . .. Through God we will do valiantly, and it is He who shall tread down our adversaries."
Psalm 108:1, 12–13 (NASB)

New day—new mall! It looked like we were entering an exotic pyramid with towering ionic pillars lining the WAFI Mall entrance, which were etched in what appeared to be Egyptian-type figures and symbols. We ordered lunch at an outside cafe with a waterfront view of the Burj Al Arab, an all-duplex-suites hotel, which is Dubai's most identifiable landmark. It is frequented by the world's wealthiest inhabitants, who are whisked to and from the airport via the Burj's fleet of Rolls-Royce Silver Seraphs. We're told its interior is reminiscent of *The Thousand and One Nights*.

Joan voiced what we all were sensing—the secular spirit of Babylon breathing through every sight and structure, eliciting an awe of the biggest, the highest, and the best in the most man-made utopia in modern history. Dubai boasts of an indoor ski slope at the Mall of the Emirates, underwater restaurants that are approached via submarines launched from the Burj, the largest underwater resort, the largest airport terminal, the world's tallest buildings, the world's richest horse race, the greatest champion horses, performances at the world's largest musical fountain, camel races, the world's largest swimming pools, magnificent golf courses (Dubai is known as "The Sporting Capital of the Middle East"), and the list goes on and on and on. If a luxury condo is on your shopping list, you are eligible for a free Jaguar if you sign up while they last!

OASIS HOSPITAL

One of our out-of-the-city excursions entailed a two-hour bus trip to Al Ain, where we were to tour the Oasis Hospital (now known as Kanad Hospital). The hospital came into existence in 1960 when Sheikh Zayed bin Sultan Al Nahyan endowed a piece of property to pioneering American medical doctors Pat and Marian Kennedy. "Those first patients and Bedouin families experienced the blessings of God through the love and sacrificial care of the Kennedys and the medical team. They brought the healing touch to diminish the high infant and maternal mortality. Over the first five years, more than 1,200 babies were born, increasing the population of Al Ain by 50%."[21]

The countryside panorama consisted primarily of desert, with occasional walled villages encompassing one and two-storied, palatial, white or sand-colored compounds. It had been a hectic day of "hurry up and wait" caused by sparse communication and scanty directions! But God faithfully intervened, and we arrived at the guesthouse in Al Ain around 11:30 p.m.

The outreach morale was waning, as Betty Jo declared our daily prayer meeting would begin at 10 a.m. the next morning and yet left us in limbo for half an hour, as we waited on her. All in all, Betty Jo exhibited how NOT to lead a mission trip! Once we focused on the Lord, our praise and worship changed the atmosphere—repentance and forgiveness released His presence and made it a safe place to open hearts. Rachel then burst into tears, telling of being fondled on the bus trip the night before. We encircled her, laid hands on her, and prayed for healing and cleansing, followed with reassuring hugs for her well-being.

Samira, a Christian nurse from the hospital, joined us just before I led the devotional and then shared her testimony of God's grace turning her life around. Christina spontaneously responded with a soul-soothing chorus. Unfortunately, our two-hour encounter ended with Samira's abrupt announcement that we were required to wear skirts at the hospital. Mary melted into tears—she had not packed a skirt, since Betty Jo had told her she would not need one. In fact, several of us were left skirtless!

It was grievous that Betty Jo had neglected to do her homework, thus creating needless hassles for the rest of us. We were thankful that we were able to improvise with a wardrobe made up of trench coats and long scarves! On the other hand, the efforts on the part of our Oasis Hospital hostesses to provide a positive experience were disrespectfully overlooked—a lot of time and energy wasted.

Janet and I kept each other laughing throughout the whole two weeks! We shared the same age, life-experience, and faith to rise above the seemingly endless chaos—this was only one more opportunity to bond as we took pictures of each other in our Darth Vader trench coats in the hospital nursery!

At 5:00 p.m. a newborn's family extended an invitation for us to visit with them. They had been assigned the traditional separate rooms adjoining the mother's room, where the family lived for the duration of the delivery and post-delivery days. We mingled with the mother, grandmother, brother, sisters, and aunts—what a spread of celebration!

A huge, 3-foot-wide basket of fruit and another 3-foot-wide basket of various individually wrapped chocolates amid four teddy bears—all wrapped in cellophane, silver trays of other sweets, huge arrays of flowers, and much more were lined up on a cloth covering the center of the floor. Also on display were the mother's gifts to her daughter: a silver and diamond necklace, earrings, and bracelets. We sat on the floor along one side of the feast and smiled in awe of their gracious gestures to entice us to eat.

After serving us coffee and dates, they ushered us into another room to graze on goat and veggies. We accepted "no-thank-you" portions along with a delicious pomegranate drink. THEN they perfumed us! They brought forth an incense candle in a silver urn and one by one, they lifted the hems of our shirts and sprayed sweet aromas under them, while perfuming us on the outside with other expensive fragrances (Elixir being one).

We experienced great joy sharing our journey with this family. We showed them pictures of our husbands, children, grandchildren, etc. and showered more heart-to-heart smiles and hugs upon them before returning to the Al Ain guesthouse. It is so heart-stirring to observe how God is at work in the lives of His children on the other side of the world.

Betty Jo could not remember the address of the guesthouse, so an angel guided the taxi "on a wing and a prayer"! Upon arrival at the guesthouse, we went straight to the quiet rooftop and soaked in the peaceful vistas of the setting sun until our next scheduled meeting, which ended up starting an hour late. I filled our time with testimonies of prior ministry opportunities and filed my nails! Our meeting was not a profitable one—Rachel left in tears. I followed her out and listened to her heart while the Holy Spirit hovered over her with His peace.

We attended the Evangelical Church of Al Ain the next morning and met four visiting missionaries from Operation Mobilization. Alexandria, from Russia, knew my friend Awon who had taken care of me in India, so we bonded immediately. Small world.

BACK TO DUBAI

It felt good to be headed home (back to Dubai) and away from Bob, the dog who peed all over the floor in Al Ain. I was struggling to be sweet by this time! Rachel and I made appointments at a nearby beauty salon—she needed a pedicure and I needed a professional hair stylist. Mariam, my hairdresser, who moved to Dubai from India, handled the request for a wash and dry just fine but left me in the lurch when she revealed that she did not have a curling iron! I prayed for the Lord to love her through me anyway.

Mariam had come to Dubai with her husband to earn enough money to support their three children, ages 8, 10, and 12, who were growing up back in India under her mother's care. She had not even seen them for two years but was looking forward to visiting them for a month in May. She gave Rachel permission to take our picture together without her covering on—a big deal! I told her I would be praying for her, and she replied, "I will carry your picture in my heart." As we left her shop, she tearfully and softly whispered, "I am going to miss you."

Betty Jo and I spent some alone time together after dinner. I trust that God gave me the words she needed to hear and gave to her the grace she needed to receive them.

The Lord's presence was palpable during our devotional time the next morning as I spoke on the power of unity and spiritual warfare—for we surely had pressed through much of it in the preceding week. We locked arms and prayed, and then I anointed each one with oil and declared prophetic blessings over them.

Rachel, Christina, Julie, and I arranged to meet with Rachel's red-headed expat friend, Serina, at the Starbucks in WAFI Mall. After courteous introductions and chocolate cream frappes, she drove us to the Dubai Gold Souk in her jet-black Jaguar. The Gold Souk is one of Dubai's most impressive sights, with shop window after shop window displaying miles of glittering gold jewelry. We also visited other souks that were dedicated to textiles, spices, and diverse souvenirs—I purchased lovely gifts of silk scarves and shawls.

We stopped at a sidewalk cafe to catch our breath and sip on mango juice before boarding a water taxi (*abra*) to transport us across the Dubai Creek, which winds down the center of the city, separating the new from the old. The water was rather choppy that day, but the mile-wide crossing managed to come to an end—only a few moments shy of severe motion sickness manifesting!

Near the mouth of the creek, Heritage Village highlights traditional arts, crafts, food, and lifestyles—a campsite gathering of nomads, a house made of palm fronds to let the air circulate, and wind towers were common sights. Rachel and I engaged with a few Muslim women in a tent, watching them cook over an open fire and trying to communicate love and respect. As best I could tell, they were receptive, but their expressions were concealed behind black leather face masks *(niqab)* that ringed around their eyes. One of them motioned emphatically that we follow her into the neighboring tent, where she patiently applied henna patterns on Rachel's left leg and left arm!

I declined the decorating of my skin but later bought a *niqab* in the gift shop. I can't imagine living encompassed within this contraption! I also attempted to purchase a couple of pictorial books about the area from a male Muslim manning a souk; he brashly bartered for the best price. Gratefully, a friendly Muslim woman (fully garbed) whom I had befriended earlier intervened on my behalf—I basked in the comfort of our female camaraderie that crossed the cultural divide!

I took a water taxi across the Dubai Creek again the next day to prayer-walk the peaceful promenade for a couple of hours. At one point I sat on a bench facing the glamorous, bustling city with a heavy heart for these people God loves—people who do not know about the peace and beauty of a personal relationship with Jesus. Joan and I met three Muslim women to converse with, bless, and add to our prayer list, along with our "pro-America" cab driver from Afghanistan, who shouted our praises as he wove through the stately streets back to the "Edge of the Woods."

After the scorching sun slid below the horizon, we ventured out to the carnival-type atmosphere of the Global Village, where individual countries each housed an assortment of bazaars in their buildings. My team's meager expenditures amounted to three rugs and a ring, but it was fascinating to observe the Muslim women in their milieu—they hardly come out during the day because it is so hot but fervently take to festivities after dark.

Dr. Susan Brown greeted us and presented an hour of orientation to the Dubai Women's College the next day, prior to our personal tour of their finest technological and most relevant academic programs—as well as their extensive library facility, exercise equipment, and T.V. production studio! We were thrilled with the opportunity to interact with twelve Muslim women in a communications classroom. I was blessed to have one-on-one time with Abeer, a sweet, young, twenty-five-year-old woman who was married and had a five-year-old daughter. She was the editor of their excellent, high-quality, monthly magazine, *Desert Dawn*.

We discussed morals in media—she showed me a CD by Josh Groban that she had incorporated into a music video she was producing (I did not know who he was). Then she pointed to one song on the album, "You Raise Me Up," and said, "This is good church music." She insisted that I take the CD home with me! We exchanged email addresses and posed for photos together. What a beautiful bonding of hearts!

IMTINAN

Another divine appointment arose through Betty Jo's friend Imtinan. They had become acquainted at a Starbucks the year before, and Imtinan had accompanied her around various venues of interest to tourists. Betty Jo called Imtinan and arranged for Rachel and me to meet her. We were told that her sister Manal had recently returned from the Hajj, where she had been trampled. The Hajj is a pilgrimage Muslims take to Mecca, where they circle the Ka'aba (a black, stone cube about 50 ft. high, with a 35 ft. x 40 ft. base) seven times. That year, three hundred Muslims had died in the stampede. I pictured the three of us mounting a dreary staircase, stepping into a dark room, and devotedly praying for poor Manal's recovery.

At 7 p.m. Betty Jo handed the cab driver the address Imtinan had provided. At 7:30 the cab came to a stop in front of what looked like a Ritz-Carlton Hotel—lighted palms, luxuriant fountains, and a red-carpeted staircase awed our senses as we gazed upon the breathtaking scenery inside the electronic gates. Imtinan and Manal, both impeccably dressed and coiffed, appeared in the doorway like models poised at the end of a runway. Could this possibly be the poor girl I had envisioned whom we were going to pray back to life? Indeed, it was. She still gently protected her side but impressively kept her composure.

Just inside the colossal double doors, on either side, were white, marble pedestals topped with silver trays of world-class chocolates, individually wrapped in gold foil with red ribbon and red miniature roses! Four baskets of wrapped fruit were also lined up on pedestals between the trays of chocolate.

As we entered the massive foyer, the elegant, round table with an abounding flower arrangement and the winged staircases ascending to the second floor assailed my attention. On either side, doubled pillars bordered a sitting room—each with furnishings uniquely suited for high-society gatherings. The one to the right was walled at the far end with a glass wall overlooking the indoor swimming pool—that was the direction Imtinan led us toward.

Imtinan and her four sisters all live here with their father. Mr. Balfaqih owns an international accounting firm with offices in London and Montreal. Hiba was too shy to visit with us but listened from an upper balcony, as evidenced by Manal periodically calling out to her to come down. Jihan came in from work in her father's office dressed in her stylish abaya shortly after our arrival and quickly changed into bell-bottom jeans and a T-shirt (she has very progressive views and is setting her own pace). She is engaged and considering adopting a boy, but she would have to wear her abaya at home once he turned twelve, so she has not decided yet as to whether she wants to make that sacrifice. She wears makeup, has amassed a collection of designer abayas, and wears a wardrobe of the latest fashions under them. On weekends she wears jeans with colorful scarves the way she wants to—much to Imtinan's distress!

The strained conversation suffered at first due to the distance between seating arrangements. One felt like you had to yell to be heard, and conversely one was not able to hear well. After Jihan retired for the evening, we eventually paired up: Rachel and Manal, Betty Jo and Nana, Imtinan and me—distracted only when the maid wheeled in carts of cold/hot drinks, sweet pastries, and gourmet hors d'oeuvres throughout our five-hour sojourn.

As Imtinan shared her story, I heard, saw, and felt her fear-based existence—she was a prisoner of her own soul and spirit. Her fear of men, fear of travel, fear of interviewing for a job outside her father's company, and fear of ending up an old maid (she was already 30 and considered a spinster) were the tips of an iceberg consisting of pain and shame. Layers at deeper relational levels began to rise as she shared about abuse by a preschool teacher. That was the root of her fear of being attacked and unprotected. In the remaining few minutes of privacy that we had, I briefly shared God's love for her, and she gave me permission to pray with her before Nana ushered us home at 12:30 a.m.

I couldn't help but compare Imtinan with Mephibosheth (2 Samuel 9) as I led our team devotions the next morning—both of them living like lonesome, fearful, hiding people when in fact they had access to healing and happiness! After prayer we headed out to the Blue Souks, which seemed boring except for finding a couple of Barbie dolls dressed in abayas for Elliott and Gabi. Sharon bought a rug for $19,000 that supposedly would have cost her $25,000 in the States.

Operation Mobilization's ship, the *Doulas*, docked nearby, offering an opportunity to connect with Awon (one of the OM gals who took such good care of me in India). Our time was short-lived due to my bout with seasickness, but I was able to tour their famous floating bookstore that beckons thousands of visitors in every port.

Second Chronicles 20:15 was the scripture I spoke from on the morning before we visited the Jumeirah Mosque:

> *"Do not be afraid nor dismayed because of this great multitude, for the battle is not yours, but God's."*

It prepared our hearts to sit on the floor and listen to their pitch to promote understanding of Islam for an hour. From there, we proceeded to an even hotter venue—the Jumeirah Beach!

We wore slacks or long skirts with long-sleeved tops because Betty Jo wanted us to model an example of the modest American woman! To be fair, we did espy several Muslim women robed in their long, black abayas on the sandy shores, while their husbands and children romped around in swim attire. So disconcerting!

Neeroo, a new Christian, asked us to join her and Mubeena, a new friend she had introduced to the Lord, at a coffee shop. They are both Organization & Change Development Consultants and just beginning their journey with Jesus. We read some Psalms of encouragement aloud and prayed with them—excited about their newfound faith. We shared hugs and tears and email addresses!

We lunched at TGIF in the lovely air-conditioned Emirates Mall while watching the skiers slalom on the other side of the glass wall that separated us. Imtinan had called and asked us to meet briefly at the mall before we left for the States—she and Manal gave us picture frames, silver bracelets with the letter *D* (for *Dubai*) dangling, and a book: *What Is Islam?*

The Lord had impressed Isaiah 61:1–3 on my heart that morning as I prayed for her, so I shared that with her and promised I would write it out and send it via email when I got home. Betty Jo had previously written out Psalm 103:1–5 on a card accompanying a gift we had given them. I was so relieved to have had this awesome time together, with the assurance that we would continue communicating.

"The Spirit of the Lord GOD is upon Me, because the LORD has anointed Me to preach good tidings to the poor; He has sent Me to heal the brokenhearted, to proclaim liberty to the captives and the opening of the prison to those who are bound; to proclaim the acceptable year of the LORD, and the day of vengeance of our God; to comfort all who mourn, to console those who mourn in Zion, to give them beauty for ashes, the oil of joy for mourning, the garment of praise for the spirit of heaviness; that they may be called treess of righteousness, the planting of the LORD, that He may be glorified." Isaiah 61:1–3

"Bless the LORD, O my soul, and all that is within me, bless His holy name. Bless the LORD, O my soul, and forget none of His benefits; Who pardons all your iniquities, Who heals all your diseases; Who redeems your life from the pit, Who crowns you with lovingkindness and compassion; Who

satisfies your years with good things, so that your youth is renewed like the eagle." Psalm 103:1–5 (NASB)

At 11:30 p.m. on Friday, February 10, we left the guesthouse in Dubai en route to the airport for our 3 a.m. flight to London. I slept for about three of the six and a half hours in the air next to Collen (her husband had surprised her with a trip to Dubai for her fortieth birthday). Our team hustled from Heathrow to Gatwick, just making it in the door before our flight to Dallas departed. I spent the next nine and a half hours squished between two middle-aged men. Julie sat in front of me, so we had fun passing notes and poking each other! Mary strolled the aisle several times with tears in her eyes—we were all going to miss each other, but it was a relief to finally get to my motel room and soak in the silence of being alone for a few hours.

The flight to Detroit finished off the last leg of my "Journey Behind the Veil," and I arrived in Lexington around 4 p.m. on Sunday, February 12. John was waiting for me at the foot of the escalator—I covered my head and face with a black veil just to tease him. I may have looked the same on the outside, but my heart had been stretched with a love for my Muslim sisters forever.

Seventeen days of practically praying without ceasing, planting seeds of hope, watering them, and declaring victory in Jesus' name impacts your life. We came up with a list of 104 names or descriptions of Muslim women with whom we had experienced personal conversations—and they are all recorded in heaven! Thank You, Lord.

BAN & OHA

When John and I were introduced to the International Hospitality Program, we jumped at the opportunity to host a couple of female students, beginning in the fall of 2006. The goal was to create a fantastic cross-cultural learning experience for both the students and their "first friends"—their host family. Our intent was to encourage them through phone calls and various social interactions—some were scheduled by the Office of International Affairs, such as a potluck chili supper, ice cream social, or an initial shopping spree. We were also encouraged to spend more time with them over coffee, movies, concerts, and the like, according to our mutual interests.

It was with great anticipation that I attended the reception to meet and greet our new arrivals at the University of Kentucky. Ban had just flown in from Iraq and Oha from China. I was drawn to both these dear ones immediately and introduced them to each other—it turned out that over the years, they were to be our guests, together, on special occasions such as Thanksgiving, Christmas, and Easter. They even graced us by attending our youngest granddaughter's baptismal service and on another occasion spent a day at The Ark with us! They had won our family's hearts within minutes and naturally became integral participants in all our festivities.

A few of our myriad special memories with them were when I met with Oha for Bible study before her classes became intense. It just so happened that I had bought a Chinese Bible on my trip to China in 2003, and we were both delighted when I delivered it into her keeping. Ban was moved to tears many times as God met her during church services with us. She also joined John and me for a three-day trip to Missouri to visit Anna, our eldest granddaughter. And then . . . there were the times John taught both Ban and Oha to drive!

Once they had graduated with their master's degrees in 2009, Oha moved out of state but stays in contact with us. Ban remained in Lexington and now works in the pharmacy at UK. We do not see her as often as we would like to, but when we are able to spend some time together, it's like a family reunion.

John and I are eternally grateful for this unique blessing that God orchestrated in order for us to share life with these precious young women. We trust that He will continue to draw them unto Himself and reveal His love for them in even greater ways.

FIRST DECADE OF JUBILEE ENDED & SECOND DECADE OF JUBILEE BEGAN!

My Decade of Jubilee had come to a close, and the Lord's fulfillment of His promise had beautifully and powerfully exceeded anything I could have envisioned: travel in ten countries, pastoral ministry for three years, name change, new house, a Doctorate in Missiology—PLUS a new son-in-love and four more grandchildren! Talk about BLESSED! God truly created a decade of celebration—BUT surprise, surprise! The next decade would be a "double portion"! It would look different but build on the adventures of the previous decade as I engaged with new encounters both at home and abroad.

CALL TO CHAPLAINCY

At 6 a.m. on Saturday, August 27, 2006, Comair Flight 5191 (a Delta connector) crashed at Lexington's Blue Grass Airport upon take-off, killing forty-nine of the fifty passengers on board. While Lexington sat in a state of shock, my heart yearned to comfort the families gathered at the Campbell House Inn, but the plastic, yellow police tape strewn around the parking lot prevented my entrance. Of course I prayed for them, but I wanted to come alongside them; after all, I had experience as a pastor and as a counselor (although I was not actively engaged at that point).

Within days I connected with the International Fellowship of Chaplains, a professional chaplaincy that required stringent educational and extensive ministry experience, letters of recommendation, and fulfillment of specific crisis intervention courses. For me, the major attraction to this organization was their governmental clearance. Following Hurricane Katrina, they had been given immediate access to cross the yellow tape and administer aid to those who were traumatized. Thus began my course for ordination as a disaster relief chaplain.

In the midst of these studies, I attended a women's conference where we each were presented with a notebook with a one-of-a kind collage on the cover. The organizing team had prayed over these for hours while they were being assembled, trusting that each woman would receive just the right one to speak specific significance to her heart's cry. Outstanding on mine were large, white letters spelling out "BOLD IS BEAUTIFUL" and two red strips of tape that intersected in the center. I immediately heard in my spirit, "You are at a crossroads." I believed this confirmed that I was to continue with the chaplaincy.

A large cluster of white hydrangeas took up about a fourth of the cover, and though I questioned the Lord as to their meaning, I did not receive an answer—UNTIL I approached the chapel of Heidelberg College a month later on the way to my ordination service. I asked, "Lord, am I really supposed to do this?" I looked up and there, across the entire front of the building, were bushes of white hydrangeas!

Chapter Fifteen

INDIA (CBE) 2007

It amazes me how small this world shrinks at times—like when I spotted Celeste Rae, my hostess during my Hong Kong trip in 2003, descending the escalator in the Newark International Airport on the way to her mother's funeral in Indiana, while I was ascending the opposite escalator en route to a Christians for Biblical Equality Conference[22] in Bangalore, India. We briefly caught up, enjoying the edifying comfort of someone in the vicinity embracing our personhood, before continuing our individual journeys in the world at large.

I intended to leisurely spend my 7.5-hour stopover contentedly browsing through a copy of my latest book, *E. Stanley Jones Had a Wife,* only to become deeply distressed by the excessive amount of typos that I observed. I knew it was my fault; I was under contract to present a camera-ready copy to the publisher, and I had blown it!

The seminary printer and my laptop lacked compatibility, putting me in a tailspin. I had worked for years researching and preparing this book in its dissertation form, which went well and can be accessed online,[23] but the technological demons to be fought in transforming it into a format for a general reading audience had worn me down. Being computer-challenged in the first place, plus the fact that patience was my short suit, I felt like I could not face another day of fighting this monster and stuck it in the mail—MAJOR mistake, MAJOR lack of judgment, MAJOR sin, MAJOR ruining of future impact this book could have had. I did not ask the Lord for help, nor did I consult Him before making my decision. And here I was on my way to mingle with people who would have valued the content and opened doors to profess it on an international scale at conferences and via other media venues—but I was too embarrassed to promote it, and rightly so.

Regretfully, I could not deplane in Paris during the 1.5-hour layover there before leaving for Mumbai, but I enjoyed an exit-row seat on the aisle with plenty of legroom and additional elbow room due to an empty middle seat. Karauthic, a pleasant young man who had worked for Merrill Lynch in the States for three months and was returning to Mumbai, occupied the third seat. We chatted for hours about marriage and writing, which excited him enough to read a few chapters of my book.

On the flight to Bangalore, I met a friendly woman about my age from London; she was headed to the same conference, so we shared a cab to SAIACS (South Asia Institute of Advanced Christian Studies), which was a godsend, since I had previously experienced such an unpleasant ordeal at that same airport.

There were twelve of us who arrived a couple days early in order to take a side trip to Mysore. Beuliah, a New Zealander who is teaching at SAIACS, served as our hostess. Our group also included Mimi and Julia from the CBE offices, Arbutus Sider from Philadelphia, Kathy and Barry Phelps, Cori from San Diego, Mary from Arizona, Kevin and Lilian Giles from Australia, Helen from London, and me.

MYSORE TRIP POSTPONED

Our trip to Mysore was postponed for a day because of a Bunt uprising—the people were protesting over water rights; therefore, traffic would be dangerous, and the situation may even have become a violent one. SAIACS was well out of town, so we thought we would be safe if we stayed there. The delay afforded an opportunity to audit Dr. Kevin Giles's[24] class on the Biblical interpretation (hermeneutics) of house churches—comparing the first-century and the twenty-first-century approach. For three hundred years the church met in homes, the largest congregation being about fifty people, but most hovering closer to twenty.

"How is it then brethren? Whenever you come together, each of you has a psalm, has a teaching, has a tongue, has a revelation, has an interpretation. Let all things be done for edification."
1 Corinthians 14:26

There were 480 synagogues in Jerusalem when it was destroyed, and most of them consisted of interactive home circles, with the host being the person who owned the home—often women! Kevin further postulated that in the United States we remain as children and expect the pastors to do everything for us, but that is coming to an end—trending toward the realization of the need of the *ecclesia*, i.e., a gathering, a coming together, a community portrayed by Paul's itinerant ministry as he proceeded from house church to house church.

Later in the afternoon, we met with Antonia, a lovely young Indian woman who joined our circle quietly and who seemed apprehensive. Her demeanor became quite understandable as she shared her story. It was difficult for her to get away that day—she was not sure her husband would allow it, since she does not enjoy the freedom that married American women have to go where they please, when they please.

Antonia works for a social service agency that ministers to women in crisis. She cautiously shared about a recent incident of a woman running to the agency seeking shelter from her husband. It was a well-known fact that her husband had been unfaithful for years, and there was nothing she could do about it. She had remained faithful to him, but when he found out that she had spoken to another man, he beat her mercilessly. The agency was her only hope of escaping this terrifying treatment. Her husband had pounded on their door in a fit of fury—fortunately, they were able to temporarily dissipate his temper.

A few days later, he came to the agency, fervently begging for her to return to him. He solemnly promised things would be different and signed an agreement saying that if anything happened to her, he would take full responsibility. The young wife succumbed to his wishes.

Two days after that, he was back banging on the agency's door with a large, bloodied knife in one hand and his wife's head in the other! He brazenly mocked them, saying he was going to the police station to turn himself in, knowing full well there would be no punishment—the wife is considered to be her husband's property, and he may do what he darn well pleases with her! In India, he could go to jail for killing a cow, but there would be no consequence for killing his wife.

Many in the West hold a "soft" hierarchical doctrine that they defend as God's ordained plan, when in fact, if they could grasp how this cultural interpretation lays the foundation for the abuse of women around the world, they would shiver at the injustice.

Antonia continued to enlighten us on the unequivocal abuse of the Brahman ideology, even among Christians. Christians do not understand how the culture is influencing the church—they try to uplift, NOT EMPOWER. One pastor had sent a woman in his congregation to a Hindu leader for counsel, although there are many other churches with counseling ministries in Bangalore.

Brahman systems rule. During the previous election, only 18% were Hindu, but 40% were told they were Hindu at voting time. *Dalits* (the lower class) are egalitarian, but they are told they are Hindus so the percentage of Hindus will be higher for the World Bank statistics, and if they become Christians, they lose their rights to education, health benefits, etc. They have been socialized to accept the Brahman ways, and the church is not trying to understand.

Some believe that HIV is a judgment of God; therefore, they are either not responding or slowly responding. Some NGOs are giving medical assistance, but nothing is really changing.

In the Brahman ideology of hierarchy and patriarchy rule, Brahman men are the authors, journalists, computer technicians, doctors, lawyers—the elite. The visions Antonia and others are espousing elicit evangelical Christians to begin understanding equality and their role in bringing it about. CBE is at the forefront of this ideological warfare.

India is a shame-based culture, which is used to control people, and there is a serious lack of churches and Christian counselors to help them break through this stronghold. The girls marry at a young age to avoid being shamed as "not good enough," but the family is shamed if they can't fork over a decent dowry.[25] Christians are making decisions on marriage based on status and money. Some ministries are teaching young men to turn down dowries, yet in other churches the pastor pockets a tithe of the dowry!

More women are choosing not to marry in order to avoid being mistreated, and if a woman dares to speak out for equality, she often finds herself shamed and isolated. But the bold injustices remain. For example, midwives receive fifty rupees for delivering boys, thirty rupees for delivering girls; however, if the female baby dies before she leaves the house, the midwife receives fifty rupees. Sixty-four percent of third pregnancies that are girls are aborted. A girl under five years of age will not be taken to a doctor and will not be educated or fed.

It appears that men are the answer. Antonia's cry is to the Christian fathers, husbands, brothers, and pastors—they are the answer; they are the keys through Christ to educate the church and turn this travesty around. It will take Christian men who have received the biblical truth of equality for all to have the vision and the courage to stand for the oppressed women and *dalits*, much as William Wilberforce took a stand on behalf of the slaves. Certainly, called women have a crucial role of leadership alongside these called men, voicing the truth of equality and courageously leading as doors open. It was a delight to witness this very image at the Bangalore Symposium. Numerically, the genders were balanced in leadership as well as in attendance.

The divine delay that we experienced in Bangalore that morning brought the reality of God's passionate mission in India to our doorstep with an impacting challenge. He desires us to be as passionate in this pursuit as He is. The degree to which we do not respond to this injustice is the degree of injustice that will not get met.

FROM MOSQUITOES TO MYSORE!

I awoke the next morning with a gazillion mosquito bites. I looked like I had chickenpox blisters ALL OVER, and a cover-up was impossible. I attempted to turn my head discreetly when anyone approached me—embarrassed to embark on our trip to Mysore appearing as such an eyesore! Oh, well! We slipped through two protest demonstrations on our way and were thankful that the protesters didn't detain us or force us to take a detour.

Once we had arrived at Mysore, "The City of Palaces," we finished our day touring the Tipu Palace (others didn't seem distraught over my speckled skin—there were plenty of ornate art pieces and sculptures to occupy their attention). Vanity! Vanity!

John had stuffed cards of encouragement into my suitcase, to be opened every other day—they always brought a feeling of comfort from home, especially as I read one on Valentine's Day! Helen and I headed out to the market on foot after a hearty breakfast of pineapple, papaya, and an Indian sweet pastry. It is always hard for me to find something special for my eleven-year-old grandson, so I was delighted when my eyes lit upon a miniature wooden wagon. I gladly handed over my rupees and received a box for it as well. A few steps down the street, I noticed the small sticker that read "Made in China"! We laughed for several blocks, and I decided to take it out of the box and just tell Nicholas that I had "bought" it for him in India!

We continued down to Maharaja's Palace and strolled the stunning tour shoeless (required). Next on our agenda was an hour-and-a-half ride to a national park for a jarring safari jeep excursion through some jungle for another hour and a half. This safari was not nearly as breathtaking as my Kenyan experience—some domesticated elephants were actually chained around their ankles, and the deer and monkeys were as common-looking as the ones that reside in the Cincinnati Zoo.

St. Philomena's Cathedral was our last stop of the day. It was erected in Mysore *circa* 1936. The Maharaja had donated the land for the future Catholic church to be built upon so that the Christian people of Mysore would pray for him! The 175-foot spires of this Neo-Gothic architecture were inspired by the Cologne Cathedral in Germany. It is one of the tallest cathedrals in Asia.

The next morning, we turned toward the bird sanctuary before leaving for Bangalore but had second thoughts because of the Bunt situation, which turned out to be true discernment—we were stopped twice on our way back, once for forty-five minutes and then for ninety minutes. The Bunts had blocked the road with logs and tires they had set afire; at the second stop, they lined up school children across the road—sitting on the hot pavement! They spray-painted the front of our bus with some obscenity in a slimy green-glow color, then encircled the bus with glaring faces and raised fists, but no harm came to us, and we arrived back at SAIACS in time for tea and the first two sessions of our conference.

LET THE CONFERENCE BEGIN!

Carolyn Pappy, a colleague from Asbury, greeted me, and what a great surprise to see Joystna (my OM friend from Lucknow who had ridden on the overnight train with me to Jabalpur). I had no idea our paths would cross here! She recognized my red salwar kameez (one of the three outfits the gals at OM Lucknow had made for me).

The plenary speakers for the conference came from Australia, Bangladesh, England, Egypt, India, Korea, Philippines, and the United States. While it is not my intention to share about the entire three-day event at this point, I will allude to the egalitarian issues addressed that quickened my spirit—those nuggets or nudges that spoke to my current walk with the Lord.

Each day commenced with a couple of hours of corporate prayer and praise. This set the tone for imparting and receiving the insight that the Holy Spirit was teaching, which transcended religious and cultural warp. All eight of the speakers were established authors who held doctoral-level degrees and possessed a sensitivity to the Spirit.

Dr. Richard Howell[26] focused our attention upon understanding gender roles in both the Old and the New Testament, stating that the Bible is a product of a patriarchal culture and presenting the Gospel as a reversal of culture and social hierarchy—emphasizing that any power is to be used to serve.

Robin Claydon[27] reminded us that both Mary and Joseph received their calling directly from God. When we are called to do something other than the norm, there will be misunderstanding and ridicule. That's when we need someone of like mind to walk alongside us. Joseph was called to carry out a supporting role to his wife and her Son.

Dr. Kuruvilla Chandy[28] clearly stated the fact that God is not a male—God is Spirit. Yes, we use male pronouns to describe Him because God chose to make Himself known in a patriarchal society and sent His Son, Who obviously came as a male, but maleness reflects only half of God's image. Being "a man's man" does not represent God's image:

"And God said, Let US [the Trinity] make man in Our image; according to Our likeness."
Genesis 1:26

"So God created man in His own image, in the image of God He created he him; male and female He created he them."
Genesis 1:27

He created us in His image—His image is an integration of male and female.

Dr. Chae Ok Chun[29] confirms that the major contemporary challenges for women in mission include the identification of issues and the documentation of their work. Women have traditionally stifled any expressions of their sufferings, acts of heroism, and missions of mercy—thus, their stories have remained hidden. The role of women in mission holds a wealth of blessing begging to be brought to light.

All change begins on the inside, within a secure relationship. One primary avenue for this to become a reality is for men to make room for women leaders to serve as examples of hope and power—women leading alongside men. Also, women are in need of assertiveness training—how to open their mouths and give voice to the voiceless, and women also need venues in which to express a woman's perspective.

Between sessions, I usually retired to my room for a brief respite. My roommate, Manjula, and I made use of that time to trade tales from our unique ministry tours of duty. She and her husband work for a missions organization near Jabalpur—as matchmakers! I found that to be fascinating—

never thought of that being a specific field of ministry, but it is a growing, greatly needed calling to facilitate Christian singles in finding suitable mates in India.

My friend Joystna from the OM base in Lucknow joined us during breaks as well; her countenance conveyed a struggle with deep depression. Although the three of us spent time in prayer together, I felt relief when Manjula offered to meet with her separately—she is much more in tune with the cultural issues that Joystna is confronting. I trust that seeds of hope and the ministry of the Holy Spirit will continue to carry her through this challenging chapter of her life.

The conference concluded with communion and closing thoughts by Ellen Alexander, one of the original organizers of the event. She talked with us about two kinds of bread: leavened and unleavened—one we eat whole; the other remains worthless until it's been broken.

She spoke of chapati, the daily leavened bread, the buying and selling of which determines the basic economy of the Indian nation, and is an essential part of their diets. In the Old Testament, a portion of the dough of leavened bread was saved to start another batch. If it was not handled properly, it became hard, cold, cut off, dead. In 1 Corinthians 5:8 it tells us to get rid of old leaven—the old ways we relied on for life. Jesus said, "I am the Bread of Life." Our daily walk is dependent upon receiving Him as our nourishment and strength.

"Behold, I will do a new thing, now it shall spring forth; shall you not know it? I will even make a road in the wilderness and rivers in the desert."
Isaiah 43:19

The Passover bread was unleavened bread, representing a breaking away from the past and moving on to something new. Bread in Jesus' hand was always broken. This brought to mind several teachings from the conference that shed fresh light on my understanding of the "new" that Jesus is speaking into my life and the need to break away from old limitations.

Leviticus 7:12 instructs the priests to bring the bread as a thank offering, not only in the physical act of taking communion but also in the living out of life in oneness with Him—offering thanks for the most common blessings of His daily provisions. Father, I thank You for Your daily provision—spirit, soul, body, finances, relationships, freedom, favor, and deliverance through Jesus' body broken for me, and His blood poured out for me.

"The steadfast love of the L*ORD never ceases, his mercies never come to an end; they are new every morning; great is your faithfulness."*
Lamentations 3:22–23 (KJV)

Before leaving for the flight home, I distributed copies of my hefty dissertation to Joystna (to take back to OM in Lucknow), Kuruvilla Chandy (to carry back to Isabella Thoburn College), and to George (a SAICAS administrator, to place in their library). This was a major labor of love on their part, due to the fact that each one measured 11.5" x 8" x 2" and weighed 5 pounds!

Mary, Arbutrus, and I left SAIACS for the airport at 11:30 p.m. Their plane was to leave at 3 a.m. and mine at 4:30 a.m. I had a stopover in Mumbai, another in Frankfurt, and another in Chicago before culminating the thirty-six-hour-trip in Lexington at 11:30 p.m. My steadfast, loving husband was standing there at the foot of the escalator to welcome me home and eagerly listen to my lengthy account of all God had shown me, taught me, done through me and for me—the diversity, the faithfulness, and the beauty I experienced walking in His grace.

Chapter Sixteen

NIGERIA (ILI) 2007

Doctors Wes and Joy Griffin cofounded the International Leadership Institute[30] more than nineteen years ago and are now training, mobilizing, and multiplying leaders empowered by the Holy Spirit to transform nations through the Gospel in more than fifty-five countries. The Institute is basically making seminary-level preparation available in strategic areas around the world, where those who do not otherwise have access to these studies are taught Eight Core Values[31] of leadership principles.

Julie Broderson[32] and I were privileged to receive invitations to teach at their Nigerian National Conference in Jos. Dr. Bauta Motty, a friend and colleague from Asbury Seminary, served as the leader of the conference. Bauta is a renowned national leader of his ECWA[33] denomination, the largest in Africa, and serves as provost at ECWA Theological Seminary, the largest theological institution in Africa.

My daily devotional time for this trip began with Psalm 63 and the first chapter of *The Red Sea Rules* by Robert J. Morgan and continued "chapter and verse" each day. It is so encouraging to sense God speaking through His Word and through the written words He has inspired in His children—it brings me great peace and sets the pace for my day. Each morning He focuses my attention on a specific area where the Holy Spirit is adjusting my walk. So I started my trip to Nigeria with the assurance that it was God Who had called me to go, prepared me, and would be glorified through me.

I'll spare you the details of our initial itinerary: Lexington, Detroit, Amsterdam, Abuja, except to say I enjoyed my time with a lovely couple who was en route to

Italy. Bauta's wife, Deborah, and her brother, Aruba, received us with a warm welcome and escorted each of us to our own air-conditioned room in the ECWA guesthouse. This was an unexpected accommodation—a luxury actually—that allowed us to recoup from our transatlantic trip and fortified us for the long day ahead.

We started out worshiping with a large, colorfully dressed ECWA congregation. The men's choir was clothed in long, pastel, cotton shirts, and they sounded as pristine as they looked! The lively praise band led us in a joyful Spirit-filled service. The pastor preached in English with a strong Nigerian accent, which made it a challenge to grasp every word, but I was able to catch the general content.

The two-and-a-half-hour ride to Jos reminded me of Kenya—not only the panoramic scenery but also the potholes that appeared sporadically as we drove along the dirt-filled roads! The conference took place at ECWA's Miango Rest Home—not to be confused with the American image of an old folks home. We would probably refer to it as a retreat facility, although it reminded me of American housing in the 1950s. The Kent School, a Christian boarding school, shared the property, although I never saw the children.

Bauta greeted us enthusiastically and eagerly guided us to our surprisingly spacious living quarters. We each had our own side of a duplex—sitting room, bathroom (with a tub), two bedrooms, dining area, and kitchen (which I would not be using)! I had not expected such exclusive lodgings! After nesting in, I napped for an hour and then dined with Bauta and Julie, after which we collaborated on our participation in the conference proceedings.

Bubble burst! I left home planning on teaching two sessions, but Bauta took the prerogative of assigning me two more areas for which I had not prepared! I was thankful that the Lord had already assured me during my morning devotions that His hand was upon my partnering with ILI: "Realize that God means for you to be where you are. . .. He has placed you here for reasons perhaps known only to Himself." I was leaning on the Lord BIG-TIME! But then again, He had been pouring out His blessings all day—our luggage landed when we did, we slept in air-conditioning, I successfully skirted car sickness, and now I could retreat to my own private rooms!

I passed the rest of the evening studying between panic attacks and pity parties (overwhelmed by Bauta's seemingly random distribution of responsibility, disappointed that he did not gather us together in prayer, and offended by what felt like a lack of consideration). After the release of a few tears, I repented, forgave him, and rendered my burden into God's hands. I am weak, but He is strong!

The next morning, the Lord's sweet presence swept over my world—like the fragrance of freshness after the rain. He assured me once again that He would never put me where His presence could not sustain me, and He will keep me here in His love and give me grace to behave as His child. He who carried me this far was not going to drop me now.

I studied until noon, then joined several women pastors/leaders at lunch. Bauta blessed both Julie and me with a gift of two authentic African dresses. Wow! They are so comfortable and much cooler than our American clothing. Before I taught on "Intimacy with God," I sat in on Bauta's class in which he explained the vision of the ILI.

I began my lecture by laying the Biblical foundation for having intimacy with God, based on Exodus 33:9-11 and John 17:21b–22 (NIV):

"As Moses went into the tent, the pillar of cloud would come down and stay at the entrance, while the LORD spoke with Moses. . .. The LORD would speak to Moses face to face, as one speaks to a friend."

". . . Father, just as you are in me and I am in you. May they also be in us . . .."

Then I took a look at barriers to intimacy: superficiality, failure to prioritize, and focusing on information instead of intimacy.

The next morning, the Lord brought to my attention the fact that He weaves everything together to advance His purposes. Shortly thereafter, Julie stopped by on her way to breakfast and Bauta on his way back—we were beginning to function as a team. Thank You, Lord!

I taught the first session of the day: "Biblical/Spiritual Leadership," in which I defined leadership, discussed the importance of leadership, and looked at leadership in history and in the Bible: *God changes the course of history through the selection of men and women who will act on His behalf.*[34] Bauta culminated the teaching with a discussion focused on current Nigerian leadership, which helped the students understand the concepts by applying them to concrete situations.

Julie led the afternoon session on "Passion for Mission," during which we were allowed to spend fifteen minutes alone with God to ask Him to show us His vision for our future. A map of China, India, Africa, and other coastal countries that bordered them came alive before me. I saw myself laying hands on people and the Holy Spirit being poured out for healing of spirits, souls, and bodies—like drops of water from a faucet, the Holy Spirit was being imparted. It brought back memories of the visions of earlier years—the pink float being pulled around the China Sea, Indian Ocean, Atlantic Ocean; the word LANGUAGES sliding down a chalkboard; waking to the sound of African drums. My vision was being refreshed. I had not previously received the connection of the pink float with that of women's ministry—a new nudging of the Spirit.

Next, I was back up to bat for the afternoon, teaching on "Servant Leadership." Of course, Jesus is the Biblical model of servant leadership, and His motivation is love—the love of 1 Corinthians 13. As we focused on specific passages that documented Jesus' modeling of servant leadership, the Holy

Spirit showed up in a gentle but powerful way. After about twenty minutes of teaching, I requested that the forty leaders rearrange their chairs into one large circle.

One of Jesus' heartfelt demonstrations of servant leadership occurred when He knelt and washed the disciples' feet. I asked, "Are you willing to follow suit and participate in a foot-washing?" In unanimous agreement, they shed their shoes, and a basin of water and some towels were placed in the center of the circle. I led them in a declaration of surrender: "Lord, I am willing to be a servant."

We sat in silence as the Holy Spirit touched one after another. With tears brimming over their eyelids, each one humbly embraced the basin and towel, then reverently knelt to wash and wipe dry another's feet. Some of these leaders were heads of large denominations, some were seminary professors, and some were principals of schools, but most were small village pastors. They all submitted one to another in a sacred flow of the Spirit's ministry.

I then returned to my "Nigerian nest" to prepare for my next opportunity to teach. Julie dropped in after dinner, and in the midst of our conversation the lights went out. Bauta came to our rescue and lit a candle for us. Since I had no light to study by (I don't know how Lincoln did it!), I left my books and attended the evening session—the auditorium generators were running at full speed, but eventually even they started kicking off and on. I stumbled my way back to my nest and found my lights shining once again—allowing a few more hours of study before bedtime.

In the morning, my devotional time ministered encouragement to my heart from Psalm 68:11, 35 (NASB):

"The Lord gives the command [to take Canaan]; the women who proclaim the good news are a great host (army)...God ... gives strength and power to His people. Blessed be God!"

With His truth tucked away in my spirit, I offered my fourth teaching, titled "Overcoming Obstacles." Obstacles are anything that stands in the way of accomplishing God's plans and purposes. These stumbling blocks are rooted in personal issues, external struggles, and/or spiritual warfare. Our primary personal obstacles relate to our sense of self-esteem—how we see and feel about ourselves.

"For as he thinks in his heart, so is he."
Proverbs 23:7a

Low self-esteem springs open the soul to a host of negative attitudes and behaviors: fear, anger, pride, anxiety, bitterness, resentment, and immorality to name a few. The bottom line: it is not spiritual to feel bad about ourselves or to take on rejection. "Where the mind leads, the man follows."

I shared a personal testimony of overcoming obstacles of verbal abuse (I was told: "I could kill you," "I am ashamed of you," and I was called "your royal high-ass"), emotional abuse (I was constantly criticized, never affirmed), and physical abuse (I was chased and hit, and my privacy was invaded). BUT GOD brought a great degree of healing through a counselor who had me picture a barrel marked "resentment" at the foot of the Cross, where one by one I surrendered those hurts and forgave.[35] I have found that forgiveness is a major factor in receiving freedom from pain. Jesus set me free from the snare of the enemy!

"Our soul is escaped as a bird out of the snare of the fowlers; the snare is broken, and we are escaped. Our help is in the name of the LORD, who made heaven and earth."
Psalm 124:7–8

I continued teaching on the external obstacles of false brothers, difficult Christians, opposition, criticism, and daily pressure to perform. I emphasized that conflict is unavoidable. One must pray for wisdom and discernment, and explore options for win-win solutions. Recognizing that the battlefield of spiritual warfare is the mind, a lifelong scripture I have employed is found in 2 Corinthians 10:3–5:

"For though we walk in the flesh, we do not war according to the flesh. For the weapons of our warfare are not carnal, but mighty in God for pulling down strongholds, casting down arguments and every high thing that exalts itself against the knowledge of God, bringing every thought into captivity to the obedience of Christ."

Think about what you think about!

"Therefore submit to God. Resist the devil, and he will flee from you."
James 4:7

Relief and thanksgiving for God's faithfulness in guiding me through all four of my assigned teachings saturated my soul with a sense that His will had been accomplished. Now I could sit back, relax, and enjoy the remainder of the conference. My readings in *The Red Sea Rules* the next morning confirmed my perspective: "If He is glorified, I am content. Jesus did not ask 'How can I get out of this?' He will gain honor for Himself over our adversarial situations...He will make burdens melt like wax in the sunshine."

THEN, about forty-five minutes before the first session of the day, Bauta asked me to teach it—material I had never laid eyes on! The pastor assigned to lead that session had a death in his congregation and had to leave the conference ASAP. I immediately bowed my heart, and Jesus began filling me with the hope of my calling—He and I could do this! So I taught on "Transformational Leadership" with LOTS of interaction!

We focused on leaders as change agents and Jesus' admonition on how to bring this about—expressed in the Sermon on the Mount: a set of beatitudes that reversed normal expectations, higher moral standards, grounding in unchanging truth, and a challenge to live like salt and light (change agents).

I asked them to pull out a sheet of paper and identify people in their congregations who were innovators, early adopters, early majority, late majority, and laggards.[36] They then shared their assessments within small groups.

We also discussed the ILI's description of a transformational leader and gave them opportunity to share their strengths and weaknesses accordingly:

- Leads by example
- Inspires people
- Encourages people to "think outside the box"
- Works personally with individual subordinates

This teaching completed ILI's vision of leadership as an equilateral triangle: Servant/Spiritual/Transformational.

The conference continued for another couple of days, so I sat in on several more of Julie's teachings but for the most part reveled in the freedom to roam about at my leisure. One afternoon, Julie made arrangements for us to be driven into the Miango market—a very different feel from our isolated compound. The colorful crowd seemed to swarm along the dirt paths lined with lean-to-type shops. Some wares were spread out on the ground atop burlap-looking cloth—lots of assorted vegetables, lots of children running in circles, lots of roaring motorcycles and rust-eaten automobiles. And lots of yellow wildflowers, which flagged that the rainy season was ending.

On another afternoon, I went for a walk and talked with the Lord through the Kent School grounds and came upon a charming little white chapel but strolled on—embracing the strong sense of serenity filling the atmosphere. I found a wooden swing hung from the limb of a strong, sprawling tree, overlooking rolling hills opposite a field covered with yellow flowers and a large pond. The tranquil breeze seemed to be swaying the swing back and forth in a soothing arc—it felt like the rocking of a cradle. Just Jesus and me, together in the middle of an Eden, content to BE—enjoying one another's company.

The conference ended with a simple graduation ceremony; I was honored to offer the closing prayer. When Bauta publicly thanked Julie and me for coming, he told of my original concern about being culturally offensive, i.e., that they would not be receptive to what an American woman had to teach. One of the men stood and shouted out, "She is a Nigerian in white skin!" And they all cheered! What a blessing! I will cherish that confirmation forever.

We ended our time together by taking an "official" conference photograph, plus photographs of several small groupings, and they each wanted a personal photo with Julie and me. It took a while, but it was such a joy to share hugs and smiles with them.

"O God, You have taught me from my youth; and to this day I declare Your wondrous works. Now also when I am old and grayheaded, O God, do not forsake me, until I declare Your strength to this generation, Your power to everyone who is to come."

Psalm 71:17–18

ON TO JOS

As we rode the bumpy roads to Jos, we came upon a couple of young boys working diligently to fill potholes with dirt—they were hoping for a fee to secure our safe passage! Julie accommodated them with what amounted to about 40 cents (it seems they had created the potholes, hoping to earn payment for filling them). We made a brief stop at Rikivi (an orphanage supported by Bible Study Fellowship) to greet and encourage Tom, the director. This Christian orphanage resembles the one I reported on while visiting in Kenya—the front gate even featured the same metal longitude and latitude lines forming a globe with silhouettes of children and adults holding hands arched over the top.

We continued on to the Baptist guesthouse and dropped off our belongings before visiting Bauta's daughter, Iya, at college. This beauty radiated the peace of God in her crisp blue and white school uniform. She gave us a guided tour that included the room she shared with nineteen other girls. Their line of bunk beds left little room to move around, but we were able to squeeze between one set and sit on her bed for a delightful chat. I had brought her a "High School Musical" calendar and nail kit, which she received with a grateful hug and beautiful smile.

Our next stop was the ECWA Seminary, where Bauta works. I'm not sure if it was due to extreme car sickness or not, but suddenly I felt like I was experiencing a heart attack. After a couple of hours of rest, most of the symptoms began to diminish, so I proceeded to dinner with Immanuel (a pastor at the seminary) and his wife, Lydia. They took us to a nearby restaurant called Benelyas. I don't remember a lot about it except that I let Julie eat half of my spicy fried rice!

Since I didn't die that night, I agreed to attend the ten o'clock service at ECWA the next morning. They have two services, held a couple of hours apart with about three hundred parishioners participating in each one. Before Emmanuel began preaching, he asked Julie and me to stand, proceed to the front of the church, and face the congregation. Then the congregation broke out in song as they ALL came parading past us in a single file, with hearty handshakes of welcome!

Emmanuel's sermon exhorted us to not quit—just keep it simple. "People will turn their backs on truth and chase mirages, but you keep your eye on what you are doing—

accept hard times as well as good. Keep the message of salvation alive, and do a thorough job as God's servant."

From there, we headed to Bauta and Deborah's home for lunch. Their village is quite rural, but they live in a walled, gated home equipped with a generator, a garden, and chickens as well as a watchdog! Deborah set a lovely table and served us a delicious fresh chicken dinner—she works miracles in her kitchen. Later, when several of their friends stopped by to meet us, I offered one of the ladies some of Deborah's homemade delights, and she replied, "No thank you; I am watching my height!" I laughed and decided to echo her response from now on—it's such a fun perspective on dieting!

I had met their village pastor, Samuel, at the conference, and he had told me about his children, so I had come prepared with presents for them: nine-year-old daughter, a hair bow; seven-year-old boy, a rubber snake; four-year-old boy, a wind-up toy; two-year-old girl, a doll; towels and lotion for his wife; and a wallet for Samuel, plus some snacks. They all showed appreciation, but I will never forget the face of that little two-year-old girl—she was beyond thrilled with her simple, handmade cloth doll dressed in Nigerian garb—this was the first time she had ever held a doll, and it was like Christmas morning in the States for her—and for me!

Emmanuel came for us around 6 p.m. to take us to his house for dinner. We told him we could stay only a short time, since we needed to pack for our departure in the morning, which turned out to be a blessing because their electricity had been off for three days! We ate our candlelight dinner under very hot and very dark circumstances—we met his two little girls but could hardly see their faces.

I held up fairly well in strength and health until the last day, when I awoke with intestinal rumblings and explosions that lasted most of the morning. Bauta and Aruba, his nephew, were supposed to pick us up at the guesthouse at 10:30 a.m. I was thankful that they were an hour late. I took four Cipro pills, and as they were loading my luggage, I cautioned, "Just a minute!" and ran to the restroom one last time. We were headed to the Abuja airport—about five hours away. After two and a half hours, we stopped at the village where Bauta grew up and were blessed to meet his precious ninety-five-year-old father. His mother was working in the bush, so we missed getting to meet her.

We stopped by Aruba's house briefly and met his wife and son, and then we shuffled off to a restaurant for lunch. Of course I did not eat anything! I sipped on a soda. We found out later that Aruba is living in Abuja without his family. He was working for a bank, but they went belly-up. Bauta said Aruba's wife started cooking for us the second her son told her we were coming down the road, but Aruba hardly spoke to her! I was so angry with him when Bauta told me about it! Aruba should have at least eaten a meal with her. However, this is not an uncommon scenario in Africa—men leave their families for the big city supposedly to earn money to support them but end up abandoning them.

We rode through miles of vast countryside and small villages along the way to Abuja, arriving at the airport around 6 p.m. Once we had checked in, we sent Bauta and Aruba on their way. Bauta would be staying at the ECWA guesthouse, because as is true in Kenya, it is not safe to travel in Nigeria at night.

Our layover in Amsterdam was only for two hours. I purchased a bottle of water for $3.91 so I could take my pills, but they confiscated it at the gate, so I swallowed my Ambien a little early, hence I "weaved" my way to my seat with some help from Julie! I slept for about eight hours and then got drawn into a movie that they abruptly turned off twenty minutes before we landed in Detroit, where customs took my tweezers and hair pick and broke off part of my toenail clippers! The layover lasted a couple of hours—time enough to walk off my discontent.

My daughter Kimberly greeted me in Lexington with a dozen red carnations! It was fun to share a few highlights of the trip with her as she drove me home. John was at a retreat that weekend but had left me a vase of flowers on the kitchen counter. Good to be home.

Great is Thy faithfulness, O God my Father,
There is no shadow of turning with Thee;
All I have needed Thy hand hath provided—
"Great is Thy faithfulness," Lord, unto me!

My heart is full of thanksgiving for all those who faithfully prayed for me. Your investment was the key for a successful kingdom mission. James 5:16 in the Amplified version says it best:

"The earnest (heartfelt, continued) prayer of a righteous man makes tremendous power available (dynamic in its working)."

Your seeds of faithful prayer shall bring you great reward. You will share in the fruitfulness in the Kingdom of God that transpires through the transformed lives of those who attended this conference.

"For as his share is who goes down to the battle, so shall his share be who stays by the baggage [stays at home and prays]; they shall share alike."
1 Samuel 30:24b (NASB)

Chapter Seventeen

INDIA (CENTENARY) 2008

Welcome to Bihar in Northeast India—at one time perceived as "the graveyard of missions"![37] Patna, one of the continuously inhabited places in the world, has prevailed as its capital city since 490 B.C. but has been the seat of power for more than one thousand years. From 500 B.C. to 500 A.D., the ancients considered it to be one of the most important, prosperous cities in India, housing an important military base and celebrated cultural centers.

Patna stretches along the sacred Ganges River, which is worshiped by Hindus as the Goddess Ganga. Seventy-five percent of Patna's population is Hindu, and they believe that a holy bath and various other rituals in the Ganges wash away their sin. Others burn the dead bodies of family members on its riverbanks and spread the ashes in the water.

The Bihar state boasts of Prince Gautam, who is believed to have attained enlightenment and become the acclaimed Buddha. King Ashoka, who ruled from Patna, sent Buddhist monks to spread their religion throughout the neighboring southeastern countries. One can easily see why Bihar has been an especially difficult terrain for spreading the gospel!

This once honorary state has more than two hundred years of mission history—hundreds of missionaries representing several agencies toiled, sweat, and died trying to share Christ with these people, under unprecedented opposition and persecution at the hands of militant Hindus. When the discouraged missionaries departed after their schools, hospitals, orphanages, and other development projects had failed, the remainder died and were buried in the compounds, creating graveyards with no one to tend them.

By the time Bihar broke loose from British colonial control,[38] which had threatened to destroy their culture and make them British, most foreign missionaries had been forced out of the country, leaving no strong, indigenous church leadership to supervise the mission activities. Most mission facilities had been shut down, sold, or seized by local scavengers.

In the early 1970s, some of the Bible colleges of South India challenged their graduates to consider North India as their mission ground. This resulted in the pioneering missionary work of two major organizations: Gospel Echoing Missionary Society (GEMS) and Friends Missionary Prayer Band (FMPB).

- 1992: The First Bihar Statewide Consultation on Unreached Peoples commenced in Patna and was attended by 350 church and mission leaders—they were learning the need for partnership and networking.
- 1995: BORN was officially launched: **B**ihar **O**ut-**R**each **N**etwork! During the ensuing years they:
- Strengthened partnerships and networks
- Registered with the government
- Established schools of evangelism
- Trained the grassroots founders for church planting
- Developed oral communication methods
- 2006: The BORN missionary movement opened a new department (Church Administration) to strengthen the newly formed independent churches in their pastoral care and church structure:
- 30,86 new churches were reported
- 35,144 baptisms were reported

This historical background establishes the premise of our excursion to Patna in 2008. Centenary United Methodist Church in Lexington, Kentucky, had been investing financially and prayerfully into the BORN movement and thus requested to participate in their fifteen-year celebration ceremonies on April 26–27, 2008. Jennifer Kane and I joined our missions pastor, Julie Broderson, to represent Centenary on this joyous occasion. We prepared to teach in their Bible school, attend their Esther Fellowship's Women's Conference, and participate in baptisms and graduations, along with other opportunities to learn and share.

It was later revealed to us (a few days prior to the event) that we were the designated speakers of the two-day Women's Conference for approximately sixty women who would be traveling from all over the state of Bihar to sit at our feet! As I began to pray in preparation for our time in Patna, the Lord showed me a picture of a three-legged stool and spoke Ecclesiastes 4:12 into my heart:

"Though one may be overpowered by another, two can withstand him. And a threefold cord is not quickly broken."

The Lord was assuring me that our three-legged stool (Jennifer, Julie, and I) would stand strong. It was the picture of balance: spirit, soul, and body—our ministry would manifest as a perfect balance of our personalities, callings, and giftings. As I meditated on this, the Lord brought to mind the account of Moses, Aaron, and Hur defeating the Amalekites in Exodus 17:11–13:

"And so it was, when Moses held up his hand, that Israel prevailed: and when he let down his hand, Amalek prevailed. But Moses' hands became weary; so they took a stone, and put it under him, and he sat on it; and Aaron and Hur supported his hands, one on the one side, and the other on the other side; and his hands were steady until the going

down of the sun. So Joshua discomfited Amalek and his people with the edge of the sword."

We literally lived this scripture out! Even though we were there for each other the whole trip, on the last day I was so weary and weak that I wasn't sure I would make it through my teaching. Then I suddenly felt a chair touching the back of my leg—Jenn and Julie were backing me up. Just the feel of that chair and their expression of love empowered me.

Another time, Julie was teaching and the translator could not understand her—he called for someone else to come, but that individual was clueless as well. Julie looked my way with tear-filled eyes, and I was at her side with my arm around her waist in a split second, praying in the Spirit. Once she had regained her composure, Jenn and I commandeered (from another ministry) the help she needed. Julie's husband sent us an encouraging email with our new slogan: "Glad to Bi'har with my Patnas!"

We flew out of Lexington's Blue Grass Airport at 2:30 p.m. on April 18 and then spent about five hours in O'Hare International Airport before flying off to Delhi. Reverend Ponraj presented each of us with a fresh bouquet of flowers in Delhi before driving us to a hotel for the night—our domestic flight to Patna would leave at 7:30 a.m. Barely two hours later, we had an orientation lecture at BORN Headquarters and were introduced to another team from California: Pam, Leslie, David, and Cody.

The afternoon entailed an excursion to the Ganges River to observe the baptismal service of sixteen new female Christians. The girls looked glorious as they approached the water's edge in a single file, but we struggled to focus on the sacred scene, because a short distance down the riverbank, dogs were chewing on a dead body!

On Sunday morning our trio sang and shared our testimonies of God's goodness. The sweet atmosphere was conducive to lingering conversations and fulfilling fellowship after lunch with Myrna and Jack Klassen from

San Francisco, who had now joined in the celebration. It turned out to be a much appreciated, slow-moving day. We squeezed in naps in our room (we three shared a room in which the air-conditioning worked on a random cycle, and our restroom consisted of a sink, a high water spigot, and an "in-floor" potty). That evening, I had the privilege of passing out awards at the Bible school graduation ceremony and preparing communion.

During my quiet time on Monday morning, the Lord exhorted me to help refresh the people with a revelation of God and His love for them. God has different plans for different people—different callings, different points of emphasis. I was to serve faithfully in the functions He gave me and be ready to partner with others.

Julie's alarm sounded at 4:45 a.m.; she would be traveling with part of the California team to a small village six hours away. Jenn and I couldn't get back to sleep, so we aligned our hearts with the Lord's and had a great prayer time together. We dressed "American" for breakfast—planning on spending the day studying and scheduling our responsibilities for the rest of the week; however, our planning period ended when David announced that the leadership had scheduled us to leave for the school in thirty minutes!

We had changed clothes and were prepared to walk out the door when I was petitioned to edit a couple of pages of Ponraj's book ASAP! Pam came alongside to help me deal with the unexpected demand—the Lord had already designed a way to combine our efforts and complete the assignment in record time.

We had a glorious afternoon with these twenty-five eager-to-learn, young girls ranging in ages from fifteen to twenty-five years old. Jenn and I began by teaching them the song titled "This Is the Day." Myrna shared her testimony in such a beautiful, gentle way that the girls were encouraged to speak up and tell their stories as well. This mutual sharing was inspiring to all of us—it was obvious that the Holy Spirit was on the move! After a short break, Jack even felt comfortable enough to bless us with his testimony. I then responded to the Lord's leading: "Tell them I love them."

When Christi, our third baby, was born, I wanted to be sure Kimberly, our four-year-old, and Kevin, our two-year-old, knew I loved them just as much as this new baby. So I lined up three small, white candles—each representing one of them. Then I proceeded to light a large, white candle and make it plain that this flame was ***all*** *my love and said: "When Kimberly was born, I gave her* ***all*** *my love (I lit her candle); when Kevin was born, I gave him* ***all*** *my love (I lit his candle); and when Christi was born, I gave her* ***all*** *my love (I lit her candle). So* ***each*** *one of them held* ***all*** *my love."*

Myrna, Jack, and one of the girls acted out this analogy—each representing one of my children. I doubt that my babies realized what I was so desperately wanting them to understand thirty-six years ago, but it was a dynamic demonstration of God's love for these young girls in the Bihar Bible school—they got it! We prayed with them and loved on them individually before departing for the day.

There was lively discussion around the lunch table—everyone was eager to share how God had moved that morning in the girls' school. After an hour of rest, Jenn and I buckled down and began working on the basic logistics for carrying out our assignments and studied until 9:30 p.m. We later received word that our teammates would not make it back until the next morning.

The field workers (those who minister in the villages) and Bible school students congregated in the conference room at 10 a.m. Jenn and I co-led with the cooperation of an interpreter. We sang. They sang. Several field workers shared updates, testifying about how God was moving in their midst. I didn't know why, but all at once I felt disconnected—from them and from the Lord. I opened my mouth and taught on Deborah but felt as anointed as if I had memorized my message from a telephone book. I was not bringing fresh manna—I was presenting a message more appropriate for passive American women!

Here I was, presumptuously trying to teach these "Deborahs" of the faith who were already fostering others with the Word and wisdom of God. They were serving on the frontlines as dedicated leaders in their communities and standing focused—listening to the Spirit for direction and shattering cultural standards! This was clearly not the message meant for them.

Julie's special ops team returned around 12:30 p.m. and reported on their successful mission. After lunch, Julie, Jenn, Pam, and I chatted in our room until the air-conditioner conked out and the temperature climbed to well over 100 degrees. We sauntered over to the celebration tent to help Leslie, who had flown in from California. She was recording interviews for a public relations video being shot to promote BORN. Our expert assistance entailed passing out candy to the children on this extremely hot and sticky afternoon![39]

We returned to our room in an effort to find some relief as best we could. I had rather quickly slid into a half-dozing state when Serbita (the cook) pounded on our door to announce that dinner was ready. Jenn answered and went with her. A few minutes later, Serbita came barging back in, switching on the light and bellowing out, "Dinner is ready." Julie was in the restroom with the door open and kindly replied, "Thank you." I squinted and got up, gruffly grumbling at her, "Turn off the light!" Julie went on to dinner, but I remained in the room trying to repent—grieving over my temperamental outburst.

Earlier that day Jenn had pointed out to me the need to cover my head when we pray—the others were already courteously complying with this cultural custom. I had hoped that my fasting, prayer, and study would prepare my heart for this trip, but to my deep disappointment the worst in me was popping up. By the time Julie and Jenn walked back from dinner, I was in tears—totally ashamed, I confessed my selfish attitude and failure to represent Christ and asked for their forgiveness.

They heard me out and hugged me with arms of compassion while they prayed over me. The burden of my shame lifted, and great peace began to light up my soul once again. I continued on to Myrna and Jack's room, where I repeated my confession. They, too, wrapped me in a warm embrace as they prayed blessings over me. There is nothing like a clean heart to help you sleep in the hottest of circumstances!

"Confess your sins to each other and pray for each other so that you may be healed. The earnest prayer of a righteous person has great power and produces wonderful results."
James 5:16 (NLT)

"If we confess our sins, He is faithful and just to forgive us our sins and to cleanse us from all unrighteousness."
1 John 1:9

The Lord assured me the next morning that our walks with Him are progressive: "Do not be discouraged with yourself. You are called to a life of absolute surrender, complete dependence, and unquestioning submission. Do not carry burdens—let Me guide, lead, and empower you."

GREAT IS HIS FAITHFULNESS

More new team members arrived on the scene: Norma, Dixie Lee, Nancy, and Patty flew in from Colorado Springs to teach on dehydration methods. While they were settling in, Jenn, Julie, and I headed for the girls' school. In the morning session, I taught on taking our thoughts captive.

"For though we walk in the flesh, we do not war according to the flesh. For

the weapons of our warfare are not carnal but mighty in God for pulling down strongholds, casting down arguments and every high thing that exalts itself against the knowledge of God, ***bringing every thought into captivity*** *to the obedience of Christ."*
2 Corinthians 10:3–5 (*emphasis mine*)

We cannot just let our thoughts roll around in our heads; we must think about what we are thinking about! If they are not godly thoughts, we must capture them and cast them down in the Name of Jesus. I picture myself raising up my hand and grabbing hold of them and throwing them down as an act of obedience. The lies that our enemy plants in our heads can't stay around if we resist them!

"Therefore submit to God. Resist the devil and he will flee from you."
James 4:7

Most of the time you will find that those thoughts are fear-based—don't listen to them! Take hold of those thoughts and resist them.

"For God has not given us the spirit of fear; but of power, and of love, and of a sound mind."
2 Timothy 1:7

Jesus said:
"Peace I leave with you, My peace I give to you: not as the world gives do I give to you. Let not your heart be troubled, neither let it be afraid."
John 14:27

"Be careful for nothing; but in every thing by prayer and supplication with thanksgiving let your requests be made known to God; And the peace of God, which surpasses all understanding, shall grant your hearts and minds through

*Christ Jesus. Finally, brethren, whatever things are **true**, whatever things are **noble**, whatever things are **just**, whatever things are **pure**, whatever things are **lovely**, whatever things are of **good report**; if there is any **virtue**, and if there is anything **praiseworthy**; meditate on these things."*

Philippians 4:6–8 (*emphasis mine*)

"You will keep him in perfect peace, whose mind is stayed on You."

Isaiah 26:3a

"Casting all your care upon him; for he cares for you."

1 Peter 5:7

Julie brought the twelfth chapter of 1 Corinthians alive in her teaching on the Body of Christ, focusing on verses 14–21:

"

"For in fact the body is not one member but many.
If the foot should say, 'Because I am not a hand, I am not of the body,' is it therefore not of the body?
And if the ear should say, 'Because I am not an eye, I am not of the body,' is it therefore not of the body?
If the whole body were an eye, where would be the hearing? If the whole were hearing, where would be the smelling?
But now God has set the members, each one of them, in the body just as He pleased.
And if they were all one member, where would the body be?
But now indeed there are many members, yet one body.
And the eye cannot say to the hand, 'I have no need of you'; nor again the head to the feet, 'I have no need of you."

Next, we taught the girls the children's song titled "Head and Shoulders, Knees, and Toes," and they giggled with delight! The fun continued with a short skit dramatized by the dynamic duo—Julie and Jenn. Julie stood with her arms tucked behind her back, and Jenn stood behind her (Jenn is much shorter—couldn't see her). She stuck her arms through Julie's arms and started putting makeup on Julie's face—hilarious!

Julie then demonstrated the difference between healthy self-esteem and poor self-esteem by using two water bottles cut in half—one remaining pure and the other being filled with dirt, stones, dead leaves, etc.

"Or do you not know that your body is the temple of the Holy Spirit who is in you, whom you have from God, and you are not your own?
For you were bought with a price; therefore glorify God in your body, and in your spirit, which are God's."
1 Corinthians 6:19–20

I ended our time with the girls by illustrating the necessity of women serving alongside the men, using a quarter as a visual aid. If someone from another country came into the room and I showed her a quarter with Washington's head on it and explained: "This is what a quarter looks like. It is worth 25¢," and she proceeded down the street and purchased something requiring a quarter in change but received a coin that had an eagle on it instead—she would think she was being cheated. But in fact, she just didn't realize that the eagle (or perhaps a state emblem nowadays) was on the other side of her Washington coin. The world has majored on the male side of the coin, but it takes both sides to make the coin valuable. It takes both the male and the female engagement to balance society and secure its value.

That night, we finally found some peace and quiet and were able to make plans for the Esther Fellowship's Women's Conference that would start the next day! I stayed up until 11:30 p.m. trying to get my brain to concentrate, correlate, and cooperate! The Lord gave me warning early on for the upcoming day: "Draw for yourselves water necessary for a long siege. Make strong your fortress." It did turn out to be a very hot, very difficult day due to heat exhaustion.

I taught two sessions on the first day of the conference: "Overcoming Obstacles"[40] and "Esther." I will share only a few highlights from "Esther," to help you get a gist of what God wanted to say to them:

- The timing and place of your birth were not accidental.
- Even though you are only one person, you can make a difference.
- To fulfill a great calling, you need great preparation.
- Whatever God has called you to do is extremely significant.
- Obtain grace and favor through seeking and heeding counsel.

"When a man's ways please the LORD, He makes even his enemies to be at peace with him."
Proverbs 16: 7

- Be courageous, even when led in a different direction than you have planned.

"Trust in the LORD with all your heart; and lean not on on your own understanding; in all thy ways acknowledge Him, and He shall direct your paths."
Proverbs 3:5–6

- When God's timing is right, no person or devil can stop Him.

"Yet in all these things we are more than conquerors."
Romans 8:37a

"...being confident of this very thing, that He who has begun a good work in you will complete it until the day of Jesus Christ..."
Philippians 1:6

I taught on the Book of Esther, explaining how after she had endured a whole year of rigorous oil treatments, instruction on royal etiquette, and teachings on how to please the king. She was eventually prepared to enter into his chambers. I eased slowly through the aisles and anointed each woman with jasmine oil, symbolic of Jesus sealing their hearts with the promise of one day seeing Him face-to-face. I invited Lal, my interpreter, to sing some quiet songs of worship as the Holy Spirit fell upon us in a warm embrace, filling the room with His sweet presence.

SHINE, JESUS, SHINE
Fill the land with the Father's glory.
BLAZE, SPIRIT, BLAZE
Set our hearts on fire.
FLOW, RIVER, FLOW!
Flood the nations with grace and mercy.
Send forth Your Word, and let there be Light![41]

On Friday morning, we began the conference with a foot-washing ceremony. The women serving on the other teams came alongside us, so we were able to set up several "stations" that consisted of a plastic chair, a tub of water, and towels, which were switched out periodically. Ten American women tenderheartedly serving sixty Indian women in this fashion was a vision of true beauty—very touching. After we washed their feet, they insisted on washing ours. It was quite humbling—a glimpse of the Kingdom of God.

Julie taught them about what it means to be a disciple—following Jesus and doing what He says to do. In her interactive, creative way, she had them playing Aunty

Says—a take-off on Simon Says. She has such a gift for making learning fun and memorable!

That afternoon I taught on Ruth, focusing on the power of faithfulness and sacrifice and the wise choices she made. She demonstrated the fruit of determination and steadfastness.

- Loss does not mean everything in your life is over.
- One season has passed; another can now begin.
- Do not passively sit around and wait.
- Pray and then step out.
- Go make new friends.

"Return to your rest, O my soul, for the LORD has dealt bountifully with you."
Psalm 116:7

Jenn did an outstanding job of narrating the story of Ruth, while our "drama team" (Julie as Boaz, Dixie Lee as Naomi, Norma as Ruth, and Myrna as the other guy!) acted it out. We were in stitches—American and Indians alike! We finished the conference with a processional. We four taller team members held two scarves as a canopy of blessing as our Indian sisters walked single-file under it while we prayed for them. As they exited the canopy, each woman was handed a red rose and given hugs. Hugging is foreign to their culture, but they caught on really quickly and hugged us back, then turned to their Indian sisters and hugged them as well! God's love and His joy just couldn't be contained.

"This is My commandment, that you love one another as I have loved you."
John 15:12

"Now thanks be to God, who always leads us in triumph in Christ, and through us diffuses the fragrance of His knowledge in every place. For we are to God the fragrance

of Christ among those who are being saved and among those who are perishing."
2 Corinthians 2:14–15

Our three-legged stool had become a place of rest and refreshment for the girls and women with whom we crossed paths in Patna. They were able to find a place to "take a load off," to "prop up their feet and relax," to "let their hair down," to "catch their breath," to enjoy receiving God's love—and expressing it freely!

Ponraj spoke to us for a few minutes after dinner about the official celebration that was to take place on Saturday and Sunday. Later, in our room, Julie, Jenn, and I kind of huddled together as we sat across our beds, leaning into each other, holding hands and thanking God for His faithfulness. The Lord's presence was tangible once again. We each prayed aloud. I verbalized that in my heart I was singing "Great Is Thy Faithfulness," but my throat was parched and my voice so weak that I couldn't get it out. They began to sing it—strengthening my voice to sing along.

After we had made it through several verses, Julie told us that this was the Broderson Family Song, that they had always sung it with Beth (Julie's lively, mission-minded sister-in-law who had recently died of cancer). We knew in that moment that we were to dedicate this whole mission to Beth, to honor her memory with the fragrance of Christ that permeated this weak and weary three-legged stool.

God had promised us before we left Lexington:

"The one who calls you is faithful and he will do it."
1 Thessalonians 5:24 (NIV)

AND HE DID!

Great is Thy faithfulness, O God my Father;
There is no shadow of turning with Thee;
Thou changest not, Thy compassions they fail not;

As Thou hast been Thou forever wilt be.

Summer and winter and springtime and harvest,
Sun, moon, and stars in their courses above
Join with all nature in manifold witness
To Thy great faithfulness, mercy, and love.

Pardon for sin and a peace that endureth,
Thine own dear presence to cheer and to guide,
Strength for today and bright hope for tomorrow,
Blessings all mine, with ten thousand beside!

Great is Thy faithfulness!
Great is Thy faithfulness!
Morning by morning new mercies I see:
All I have needed Thy hand hath provided—
Great is Thy faithfulness, Lord, unto me![42]

BORN CELEBRATION

Saturday and Sunday brought us to the climax of the celebration for BORN, as more than five hundred pastors and leaders gathered in an auditorium on the other side of Patna, which meant a long, hot ride through the crowded, noisy, business district in the center of town. I was thankful that the festivities did not begin until around 10:30 a.m. The auditorium's cooling system consisted of a few overhead fans and small, open windows along the top sides of the building.

Most of the orators spoke in their native tongues, thus making it a physical feat to stay alert, let alone appear awake! They served a lunch buffet full of foreign-looking items. I settled for rice, cucumbers, a piece of bony fish, and a cup of ice cream before returning to BORN headquarters for an hour's rest. Myrna helped me dress in my sari, which was a major production with all the twists and tucks! We returned to the auditorium about thirty minutes late but just in time to be ushered up on stage and presented with flowers and a copy of Ponraj's new book. He then brought the service to a close after another long message.

I heard the Lord's admonition during my quiet time on Sunday morning: "There is a time to speak and a time to be silent, a time to wait and a time to act." Only He knows the right time for the fulfillment of His purposes. When God opens the door for you, seize the moment. When He gives you opportunity—sow! Well, as is often the case for me, I hear what He is saying but don't administer the application correctly . . .

When we arrived at the auditorium, communion was being served. Shortly thereafter, Ponraj invited the ordained pastors to join him on the stage. Julie kept motioning to me to go forward, but I hesitated, because although I was an ordained chaplain and had served as a pastor, I was not actively functioning in either role at the time. Later, when I spoke to Sheila, Ponraj's wife, I found out that she, too, was an ordained chaplain but did not go up because Ponraj did not want women in that capacity on the platform! I am sure that is what I had sensed earlier but was not sure if I should have gone up or not. Culturally, I submitted, but as Julie pointed out to me later, it would have been a great encouragement to the women who were present to see another woman participate.

Interestingly enough, my scripture reading for the day included Galatians 3:28–29:

"There is neither Jew nor Greek, there is neither slave nor free, there is neither male nor female: for you are all one in Christ Jesus.
For you are all one in Christ Jesus. And if you are Christ's, you are Abraham's seed, and heirs according to the promise."

To this day, I don't know if I did the right thing, but for several days after that I did hear the Lord repeat, "Kathryn, hand Me the whip you have beating yourself up with!" And every time I handed it over, I enjoyed just being me. "Thank You, Lord!"

We bid farewell to our newfound friends from California and Colorado Springs early the next morning as we left for the Patna flight to Delhi. It was going to be a long day of walking around the capital city of India for twelve hours. We deposited our luggage at the local YMCA and meandered around the shops and sights in a kind of zombie-like mode. The highlights of our meandering were the Imperial Hotel and McDonald's!

A palm-lined drive leads up to the awe-inspiring, luxurious, pink and white facade of the Imperial Hotel. Inside, you step onto marble floors shining under vast chandeliers, showcasing imposing portraits of maharajahs and their five thousand-piece art collection. For me, the best part was sitting in a soft, overstuffed chair in their air-conditioned hallway!

Our flight to Chicago departed at midnight, and I immediately dug into reading *The Shack*. I couldn't pull away from this unique portrayal of the Trinity. God is so much bigger, wider, deeper, higher than we have ever begun to grasp! I long to know Him better.

We landed at O'Hare International Airport at 5:15 a.m. Seeing an egg-shaped clock that rocked back and forth was the only memorable moment on my stopover. When I spotted it, I gave a sigh of relief because I had found something of interest as a gift for Nicholas; it is so much harder to find a gift for my grandson than my granddaughters! I exchanged my currency. I finished reading *The Shack*.

"Let us press on to know the Lord. His going forth is as certain as the dawn, and He will come to us as spring rain watering the earth."
Hosea 6:3 (NASB)

Christi and Tatum met me at the Blue Grass Airport this time and gave me a wonderful welcome home! While we were running a few errands, I became nauseated and took advantage of every "potty stop." I was already missing my 100° temperatures—the frigid 57° inside my house was quite a shock. I slept for about six hours, awoke at 10 p.m., and then took a bath, after which the big *D* set in and would not stop! Christi came out the next day to care for me and clean all my soiled laundry and bathroom facilities. She spent the next night with me—what an angel! By morning, my gut was still gurgling, but the worst was over, and John would be home later to watch over me.

The following Sunday, Julie, Jenn, and I hosted a special service in the chapel at Centenary United Methodist Church to share with those faithful prayer warriors who had strengthened and protected us. It was a precious and powerful time of recounting God's sustaining grace in the various scenarios of our three-legged-stool mission. We spoke for an hour and officially ended our presentation on time, but when we had finished speaking, the people just sat there; no one moved—they were so touched by the presence of the Spirit.

God blessed us to be a blessing, and we were blessed in return!

HIS TIME MINISTRIES

Feeling the nudge of the Holy Spirit to step out of my latest nest, I began organizing His Time Ministries, which was basically my heart to expand my ministry.

HIS TIME MINISTRIES

HOPE-FILLED
ITINERANT
SERVANT

"He makes all things beautiful in His time."
Ecclesiastes 3:11

TEACHING
INTERCEDING
MINISTERING
ENCOURAGING

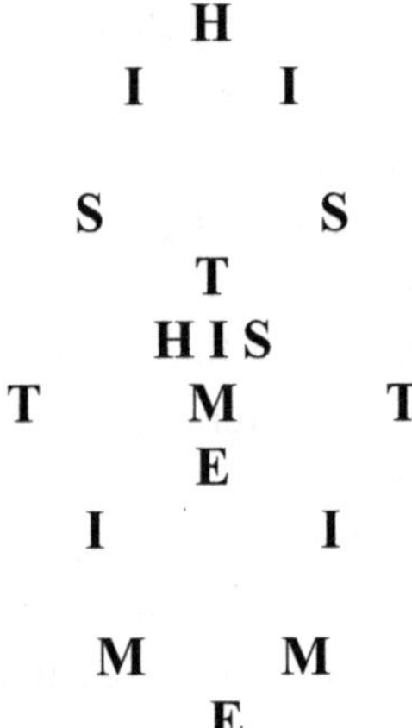

I invited five mature, Spirit-filled women to pray and speak into my life any wisdom, discernment, or red flags that the Lord may reveal to them about my ministry plans. We coordinated our calendars to meet in my home on January 18th. Monkey wrench: after I had solidified the agenda for our afternoon together, an unexpected circumstance arose.

I had spoken at an Asbury Seminary event earlier in the month and then attended a late luncheon with former colleagues and my husband. When one of the women mentioned that Asbury University was searching for a Cross-Cultural Director, everyone at the whole table had turned to me and voiced their agreement that I should apply. They thought I was the "perfect fit" for the position. It hit me cold-turkey—I was counting on introducing His Time Ministries soon, not sitting behind a desk! I smiled and shrugged it off.

But John became quite adamant about me at least applying. So I did.

Within the week, I was scheduled for an interview—only going through the motions to please John and the others who were prodding me along. There were twenty-some applicants, so I felt fairly certain that I would be filtered out, but I willingly added it to the prayer list for our His Timing meeting.

The Lord confirmed to me that *"my times are in His hands"* (Psalm 31:15) and that my cloud would move *"at the appointed time"* (Numbers 9). This was a stepping-through-the-gate time for me—saying "yes" to God. I read Joyce Meyer's words: "In finding your destiny, God leads you through your natural skills and abilities—unique talents . . .. do what ministers life to others." It was a time of humbling myself before Him and others in order to move into my destiny. I was so eager to serve.

We opened our prayer time on January 18th by inviting the Holy Spirit to come and have His way. Donna Hicks drew us deeper into God's presence through praise and worship with her heavenly voice, guiding us to His very Throne of Grace. I then briefly reviewed my ministry and mission experiences and related some present opportunities, including Asbury and my vision for His Time Ministries. We spent another considerable amount of time in prayer and silently listening for the Lord's direction.

Donna spoke of her singing—that it was a talent but a gift only when anointed by the Holy Spirit. My ministry gifts were not something new—they had always been anointed and released for others, only now they are more visible. Laura Beach exhorted me: "Don't be a teenager. Step up." She seemed to address the possible position at Asbury, saying that the wheels of academia run slow and my personality would morph the position. She had a vision of a blooming amaryllis plant—with many blossoms (usually only one at a time), deep roots, fragrant, also called the resurrection lily. I later researched the name *amaryllis* and found that the botanical name referenced a shepherdess, and it meant "to sparkle."

The ladies anointed me with oil and laid hands on me in prayer. We took communion together and lingered in the joy of the Lord's presence. Two weeks later, I was offered the position at Asbury and knew I was to accept it.

DIRECTOR OF CROSS-CULTURAL EXPERIENCE

In the fall of 2007, the Cross-Cultural Experience Component of the General Education Core Curriculum was initiated at Asbury University. However, procedures, policy, and oversight were not established until 2009, when they hired me.

My first couple of years focused primarily on the paperwork and public relations elements necessary to enable the students, parents, faculty, administration, and mission organizations to function on the same page—the majority of whom were not aware that the Cross-Cultural Experience was required for graduation, let alone the guidelines for fulfilling it. Hence, a line of action was needed ASAP! This would include the intention of the requirement, a basic description of an immersion in another culture, criteria for approval, options for satisfying the requirement, and post-experience mandates. An equally essential item on my initial agenda was to draft decisive, legal emergency and liability forms.

Of course, there was a long list of policy and procedural clarifications to include related to potential challenges: cancellations, refunds, behavioral discipline and consequences, sexual harassment, etc. Faculty essentials were also extensive. These policies and guidelines, plus much more, were eventually made available in an eighty-seven-page manual.

For the most part, it was energizing to work on campus, attend chapels, and engage with the students and faculty on a daily basis; however, the discord that would inevitably arise with any new project was disconcerting to say the least. Someone was always unhappy with me! But then again, I wasn't always happy with them either. There were many godly, sweet, earnest Christians who made it all worthwhile, and I believe my efforts were in keeping with what the Lord expected of me.

My spacious office was situated in an ideal corner location, with two windows facing out over the middle of campus, along a promenade that almost everyone had to pass through at some point during the week. I would open both windows every spring and offer free doughnuts to seniors, or sometimes I would stick large flyers taped on poles to catch the attention of passersby for some upcoming event or due date for Reflection Papers.[43] My windows and bulletin board were always drawing attention to something seasonal or informational.

I mentored a couple of students each semester for almost seven years—what a joy to follow their journeys and watch them grow in their walk with the Lord. Karen Kohen, the Administrative Assistant for the Provost, and I would meet on Wednesdays and have a precious time praying for the students and faculty. Shannon Montgomery was my Administrative Assistant for almost the whole time—she was truly my right arm and sounding board. She made my job look easy—I helped raise her kids!

Trudi Goodrich was on the custodial staff while her husband studied at the seminary—nothing was ever too much for this sweet grandma who looked like one of the students. I loved our oneness of spirit. Bonnie Banker was the registrar for a goodly part of my time there—she had been one of my professors when I was a student, and then she was my boss, but she is forever my friend! Greg Haseloff, the chaplain, was always good for a cheery "hello" or an encouraging chat. There were numerous others who blessed my days as CCE Director, each a gift from God.

It was also during this time period that my third book, *Trophies of God's Grace,* was published. The book contained interviews with forty Christian women who had impacted my life and gave a brief synopsis of their victories in overcoming life challenges, thus creating a forty-day devotional. The meaning of each woman's first name was researched, along with an appropriate life scripture, and each entry ended with a prayer.

Chapter Eighteen

ENGLAND (CELEBRATION) 2012

The outstanding occasion for our traveling across the pond was to attend the celebration ceremonies for our son's promotion to Chief Master Sergeant in the United States Air Force. He and Melissa were stationed at the Royal Air Force Base in Lakenheath, England, where he was currently the Superintendent, 48th Munitions Squadron, 48th Fighter Wing, and she was the Master Sergeant supervising the Wing Commander's Support Staff.

It was especially exciting to have John traveling with me—it is so much easier and makes for a much more pleasant plane ride when not running down the yellow brick road alone! An added bonus was when we were bumped up to business class, seated across the aisle from Mark Mellinger, a friend from our Sunday school class at Centenary.

Another amenity I had not been accustomed to was having family greet me at a foreign airport. Kevin and Melissa were there talking with Mark when we deplaned. Kevin whisked us off on a sightseeing route that went by Windsor Palace—so much more expansive and imposing than I had imagined from seeing photos of it! The quaint town of Windsor surrounds the palace with gift shops, restaurants, and other touristy fare.

I found England's signage most engaging. One of the first signs that caught my fancy was a warning triangle like the yellow yield traffic signs we see in the United States, but this one was white with red trim, and in the middle were black silhouettes of an old woman and an old man with a cane.

Immediately beneath the sign was another white one with "Elderly People" written in black!

We made a quick stop at a little farm store to indulge in their delicious Loseley Dairy Ice Cream— "Truly Toffee" and a Brown Bag of Crisps cooked in oil.

The English drove in the same crazy, big-city, chaotic fashion that I had encountered in other countries, but their roundabouts made driving a bit more nerve-racking. The old country roads were terrifying as well—the narrow, seemingly one-lane roads were often lined with high hedges or stone fences on both sides. I could not imagine there being two-way traffic and speeding at 60 mph at that! If the road ran through a village, it was seamed with sidewalks. One might tend to entertain second thoughts before taking an evening stroll, but seeing people walking or biking on the sidewalks was a common sight.

Kevin and Melissa were renting a three-story, brick, new home on Chestnut Grange on the Green in Barrow, England; it dominated the landscape of the little village. It was flanked by two other houses that were about the same size. Across the Green (a park-like, grassy field on either side of the lane often frequented by ducks) were houses that looked like those I'd seen from the miniature antique dollhouse vintage.

A small, one-story market faced the Green. It seemed about the size of a gas station "get 'n' go" at home and was packed with fresh produce, baked goods, and everything else you could think of. About a half-block down the lane was a little stony-sided Baptist church. A little further down you could drop your mail into a slot a foot lower than the top of a 5-foot-high and 2-foot-wide red cylinder situated near the sidewalk for convenience, since the Barrow Post Office was a narrow section of a brick building set back behind a high hedge. On the way out of the sleepy little village, we passed an Anglican church and cemetery. This would pretty much describe the average village: "quaint" with the presence of an old, boarded-up Anglican church.

Kevin woke us up at 10:00 a.m. the next morning by singing the song I used to sing to wake him up when he and his siblings were kids—FUN!

Good morning! Good morning! Good morning!
It's time to rise and shine.
Good morning! Good morning! Good morning!
I hope you're feeling fine.
The sun is just above the hill, another day for us to fill with all things we love to do.
Oh can't you hear it calling you?
Doodooly do, doodooly do!

Melissa drew us to the table with the aroma of bacon, eggs, and biscuits beckoning us downstairs!

We drove through vast, rolling green countryside with more quaint little villages, and large Anglican churches all along the way to Cambridge. The humongous, stately, ancient buildings of King's College and Jesus College were awesome sights—so strange to see red, double-decker buses on Jesus Street! On our way home, we stopped at Gog Magog Hills, an organic farm that sold fresh produce, spices, and cheese. I bought some to-die-for toffee waffles that disappeared in the wink of my eye. Kevin also took us on a sightseeing trip around the military base, where he bought tickets for us to take a bus tour in London on Monday.

We drove to the coast along the English Channel the next day to Great Yarmouth, a picturesque little seaside town with narrow streets nestled against a small castle and harbor. WINDY! Lord Nelson's Monument is a point of interest there; he served as a flag officer in the Royal Navy and was known for his inspirational leadership and unconventional tactics during the Napoleonic Wars.

The 144-foot-high commemorative monument is a fluted, Greek, Doric column erected upon a square pedestal that is set upon a raised base. At the top, "six priestesses of Artemis support a statue of Britannia standing on a globe, holding an olive leaf in her outstretched right hand, and a trident[44] in her left."[45] Britannia is portrayed as the national personification of the United Kingdom. Her name means "island," and although never a real person, she is the symbol of England's spirit—power and unity.

There were multicolored, tiny-house-type cabins for rent lined up along the shore and opposite them a fascinating row of row houses with several chimney stacks over each one—I counted twenty rooftops, looking in only one direction. It made me think of Mary Poppins!

We traveled back through New Market, England, an equestrian town, which is also the Sister City of Lexington, Kentucky! It emanated the same sophisticated atmosphere and spacious horse-farm elegance, reflecting obvious societal and commercial ties. We stopped at a castle in Farmington, but it was closed, so Melissa and I used "the loo" in the pub! Kevin and Melissa went into a McDonald's for drinks and ordered tea for me—it came out hot! They don't serve iced tea in England.

Some other quirky, fun, features of England:

- Jagged lines along the road near the curbs indicate "No Parking."
- Some other signs we saw: "To Let," "Give Way," "Caution: Lorries Turning"
- Kevin and Melissa have hiked miles of footpaths through private property—landowners have no right to keep people off their property.
- People are not allowed to have guns or protect themselves if someone breaks into their homes.
- Tea bags are called "tea pigs."

On the morning of the "Big Day" (Kevin's recognition ceremony), Melissa and I drove over to Lakenheath to get our nails done. She careened her little BMW at a speed of 60 mph along the "carriageway" (road). The salon gal, Lois, promptly instructed me to "pop" my fingers into the water! When we returned home, I scoured the grocery shop and found some local offerings: scones, digestives (graham crackers), crumpets, hot cross buns, and magazines revealing the "scoop" on the Royal Family.

We were over-the-top proud of Kevin's achievement. He previously had earned a chest full of medals and now would be installed as Chief Master Sergeant! This was a formal affair with all military personnel sporting their spotless dress uniforms. John wore his new navy blue suit, shiny new shoes, and classy red tie. I wore my new navy blue evening gown, new silver heels, and matching clutch—we wanted to present our best in honor of our son.

After the official photos were taken, John and I observed the room full of brass and bow ties while Kevin and Melissa mingled. The chiefs and their wives were introduced as they entered through a tunnel of sabers extended by uniformed airmen.

A massive white candle embossed with the blue Air Force Chief's insignia stood stately as the table centerpiece. Kevin's Chief Conley and his wife dined at our table, as did Major Colgate and his wife, Valerie. Valerie was a vivacious young woman who was, I think, eager to talk with an older, American mom. Her parents were welders in South Carolina who traveled around a lot. We compared our collegiate experiences, as she and her husband both had attended Colorado State University.

The food was first-class, and the speaker kept his oratory short and sweet. A solemn candle-lighting ceremony in which nine candles were lit represented the nine steps required for achieving the rank of Chief Master Sergeant. As Kevin's presentation ceremony began, he and Melissa were called forth, and his medal (hanging on a red, white, and blue ribbon) was placed over his head and around his neck, after which John and I were invited to join them in a photo shoot, followed by a receiving line.

Bobby, one of four senior airmen Kevin was mentoring, made it a point to sing Kevin's praises and tell how much he prized his command. Two more items of honor bestowed upon him included a bronze Indian chief's head mounted on an impressive wooden base with "CMS Kevin Hendershot" engraved on the plaque and a "Reserved" parking sign with his name on it!

We arrived home around 10:30 p.m. with full hearts and wonderful memories, but there was one more significant happening yet to take place—presenting Kevin with my deceased father's American flag. Kevin always had adored my dad, Robert S. Reese, who served in the Navy during WWII and died in 2003. At his memorial service, Kevin had taps played as he saluted a portrait of my dad and ceremonially knelt before me as he placed my dad's flag in my arms. It was the only time I lost my composure during the service—my heart trembled as I clutched that flag to my breast. I now, knelt before Kevin, and passed my Dad's flag on to him.

I looked forward to attending the Anglican church on Sunday morning—it was posted to begin at 11:00 a.m., but when I arrived at the church, like most all the Anglican churches I had seen in various villages, it was locked up and no one was in sight, so I decided to visit the Baptist church instead.

There were only about twenty-five worshipers (including children) sitting on narrow, straight-backed wooden benches with Bibles and hymnals that contained only words—making it an ordeal to harmonize with the organ. Though the congregation was seemingly straitlaced (with all the women wearing hats), the pastor prayed a long, heartfelt prayer and preached a good, solid sermon on the Holy Spirit. On my way out, a sweet elderly lady asked me to sign a petition protesting gay marriage, which I promptly responded to with my sprawling signature!

I came home and savored a scone and some tea before we left for Ely Cathedral. On the way, we passed a "boot sale," where people open the trunks (boots) of their cars and sell stuff! I spied another "local color" sign that read "Traffic Calming Area."

Ely Cathedral is enormous! Kevin and Melissa took an hour-long tour up to the top of the 217-foot tower. It was originally built in 672 as an abbey church; after the Reformation, it became an Anglican cathedral of outstanding architecture; Romanesque in style and Gothic in décor. This cross-shaped tourist attraction welcomes around 250,000 visitors a year. It is locally known as "the ship of the Fens" because of its prominent position above the surrounding flat landscape. This is not the place for a historical rundown—there literally are no words to adequately describe its grandeur, but it would be well worth the time to research it or visit.

John found a friendly guide who sat with him, and highlighted its history for about forty-five minutes (John always attracts interesting people who love to tell him their life stories). This new best friend lived in West Market and used to speak for Mercedes—he does archaeological digs in the summer!

I checked out the gift shop and bought a CD of the boys' choir and some postcards before ambling around the cathedral. The Lady Chapel's exquisitely brilliant lighting was awe-inspiring.[46] St. Catherine's Chapel is another delightful area I stumbled onto (although not spelled correctly in my opinion—but my namesake anyway). One other area of intrigue that I must acknowledge is a humongous wall of colorful fish netting. A prominent plaque explains:

When the Cathedral was built, Ely was an island in a sea of rivers and swamps; thus, fishing formed an important part of people's livelihood. Jesus' first followers were also fishermen. Yet Jesus called them to leave their nets and follow Him.

OFF TO LONDON

We were up and at 'em at 7 a.m. on Monday and out the door by 8:00 a.m. We drove an hour to Epping to ride the Tube[47] into London's Piccadilly Circus, a round, open space at the junction of five major streets, with a bronze fountain in the center that is topped by a winged archer. This bustling commercial area is a surcharged scene of buildings with neon displays that overwhelm the senses.

Sitting atop a red, double-decker tour bus, we wrestled with the too-cool wind on the way to Trafalgar Square on Haymarket (where hay used to be bought) and the Charing Cross area, which was crammed with galleries and historic buildings. The architecture of the 70-foot Charing Cross is itself huge, old, and amazing and is perceived as the geographical center of the metropolis. The eighteenth-century structure forms three stages: the first is a design of shields and panels bearing the arms of England; the second consists of eight statues of Queen Eleanor. The memorial is topped with a spire and cross.

We rode past St. Paul's Anglican Cathedral, which lays claim to being the highest point in London (365 steps to the top) and passed the modern replica of the Globe Theater, which was owned by Shakespearian actors and closed down by the Puritans in 1642. We exited at the London Eye, which is a giant Ferris wheel situated on the South Bank of the River Thames. Since its opening in 2000, approximately 3.75 million visitors a year have ridden this observation wheel, which is 443 feet tall and 394 feet wide. The thirty-two air-conditioned passenger capsules allow room for twenty-five people to walk around during its thirty-minute revolution.

It's impossible to even try to describe the vastness of this visual treat: the river traffic, the Westminster Bridge, Big Ben, the London Bridge, and the architecture of the skyscrapers, along with ancient and modern buildings beyond the North Bank cityscape. And then there were the scenes framing colorful people of all nationalities scurrying along the sidewalk parallel to the Thames—a man in a skintight gold suit, covered head to toe, wearing an FTD helmet and selling red roses; another man in silver; girls in black tights and shorts; and lots of brassy-looking red hair. Mickey Mouse and Donald Duck showed up as well.

Next, we cruised the Thames to view everything already commented on, except from a closer vantage point—of course with an additional view of the entire Eye. Then we wound our way over to the exquisite Westminster Abbey and at first were frustrated that it was closed, but then we found out why—the Queen was coming! She was about to meet with members of the Commonwealth in celebration of her Jubilee (fifty years as Queen).

We waited for a half-hour behind a gray, metal rail on the opposite side of the entrance, hoping for a glimpse of her. Heart-pounding bells were peeling, and bobbies were strolling casually around the spacious courtyard. It was quite exciting! Then a double-decker bus pulled up and blocked our view! We were thankful that Kevin was able to snap some splendid close-up shots of Camella and other dignitaries who were parading in, and at long last Queen Elizabeth appeared in a rose-colored suit and matching hat, with Prince Philip at her side!

Then we were off to the Tower of London, but it would be closing in an hour, and we would have needed hours to cover the entire complex. We opted simply to walk the outside perimeter, which did not seem that impressive to me compared to the ornate cathedrals, although it was surrounded by lush, green lawn. Maybe on our next trip we will try to explore the Tower of London.

We hopped back on the bus and rode past Buckingham Palace, Hyde Park, Speakers' Corner, Marble Arch, and Oxford Circle, completing our tour at Aberdeen Steakhouse in Trafalgar Square. I savored the best sweet potato fries, chicken fingers, coleslaw, and a pot of tea before our return trip on the Tube to Epping and then home. GREAT DAY!

On our last full day in England, Kevin took us to what he called "Bury St. Edmunds," which is actually called St. Edmundsbury Cathedral. Its construction began in 1503 and was completed about fifty years later. I am not a cathedral critic (maybe if I had seen this one before I experienced St. Ely, I would have found it striking), but alas, although it rendered several noteworthy features, I didn't expend much effort gazing upon its elegance. However, Melissa bought me a pair of "Holy Socks" (faith on your feet)! They represent the ancient idea of life as a pilgrimage and come with a story, meditation, or poem. Their playful leaflet sets the tone:

"Wherever you are on your life's journey, I hope Holy Socks make you smile—not least because one day, these might be the only clean pair of socks in the drawer!"

Our last stop of the day was New Market, where I spied the perfect souvenirs—a teapot with the English slogan from WWI, "Stay Calm and Carry On," for me and a red baseball cap with the word *England* stitched in gold across the top for John.

The perfect ending of our wonder-full week came at the end of our last evening together. A couple of nights previously, I had mistakenly thought Kevin said, "Good night, Sweetie" to me. We laughed because he actually had said, "Good night, Sleepy!" So this time, as I turned to head for bed, I distinctly heard him say, "Good night, Sweetie," and my heart melted.

Chapter Nineteen

INDIA (RAHAB'S ROPE) JANUARY 2013

THE CALLING

A fresh stirring for missions surfaced in my spirit as a result of reading *Kisses from Katie* by Katie Davis. Katie, a popular high school senior, reigned as homecoming queen and served as senior class president. She and her boyfriend looked forward to marriage after graduating from college—four years down the line. HOWEVER . . . Katie and her mother spent spring break that year serving at an orphanage in Uganda, where Katie's life took on a whole new trajectory.

Her love for the children and the village people filled her heart and soul—they were an undeniable magnet, pulling her to negotiate with her parents to put off college for a year. At the time, this seemed to be a sensible compromise, but that year evaporated like the morning dew and Katie was entrenched in her new lifestyle. But she dutifully returned home to fulfill her part of the bargain—only to experience an overwhelming reverse culture shock! Her soul no longer sought out a cute pair of shoes or the luxury of her upper-class world or the now obviously mundane college scene. Her worldview could no longer be confined to the current twenty-something values. Her heart's call was in Uganda, and back to Uganda she went! She bought a house, adopted fourteen little girls, helped village women market their goods, and raised support to keep hundreds of children in school.

This was not the first account of a nonconformist nature to catch my attention, but the way Katie expressed her love for the Lord captured my heart. As I read her conversations with Him, I sensed her mirroring my heart!

"God wanted more of me, and I wanted more of Him. He began to grow in me a desire to live intentionally and different from anyone I had ever known. So I quit my life. I quit college. I quit cute designer clothes and my little yellow convertible; I quit my boyfriend. I no longer have all the things that the world says are important. I do not have a retirement fund; I do not have electricity some days. But I have everything I know is important. I have a joy and a peace that are unimaginable and come only from a place better than this earth. I cannot fathom being happier. Jesus wrecked my life, shattered it to pieces and put it back together more beautifully. I am much more terrified of living a comfortable life in a self-serving society and failing to follow Jesus than I am of any illness or tragedy."

I emailed my good friend, Julie Broderson, the missions pastor at Centenary UMC. "Have you read this remarkable book?"

"No, but I am enthralled with a book I am reading called *Half the Church*."

This turned out to be another key of direction. I ordered the book immediately, and it eventually referred me to *Half the Sky,* another key. The first third of this book addressed trafficking in India.

One Sunday morning after a week or so of musing over Katie's book, I sat quietly in my home office meditating on her experience, when suddenly the Lord's familiar Presence entered the room—similar to what I had experienced in 2003 while I was in India doing research on Mabel Lossing Jones (in 1912 Mabel started an orphanage in Sitapur, India; it is still in operation today). Back then, God had impressed upon me that He was calling me to return to India at some point in the future.

God beckoned me, "Look into My eyes." I saw globes of the world and then tears running down His cheeks—then children in those tears. "I want your heart to break for what breaks mine." I accepted that He was calling me, and I blurted out, "But Lord, I'm not eighteen and single!" He said no more.

I left for church, where I heard the pastor say, "Your life could change in a split second," and he continued speaking about orphanages and the need of the church to step up and care for the children of this world. After church, John and I went out to eat, and as we sat there, I related what I believed the Lord was saying. John looked at me thoughtfully and then casually asked, "When are you leaving?" Startled, I let my response simmer on the back burner for a while.

John occasionally videotaped Gideon State Conventions in that season of our lives, and I would trail along to tape the Women's Auxiliary luncheons. The first weekend in May of 2012 we filmed a conference in Boca Raton, Florida. At the women's luncheon, I sat down next to a friendly-looking lady and proceeded to describe Katie Davis's captivating work in Uganda. When I wrapped up my awesome story, she asked, "Have you heard about my project?" Rather taken aback, I replied, "No, I haven't."

Carol Beresford continued to recount how the Lord had given her a vision of a home for unwed mothers on five wooded acres of prime land. She had no resources to accomplish this in the natural—her life experience centered on being a pastor's wife and mother of their now-grown children. Thus, everyone graciously smirked and smiled sweetly when she described her dream.

Determined to hold on to her dream, she bravely approached a successful land developer's office and explained her vision—SURPRISE! He donated the five acres of prime wooded land! Stirred by her success, she stopped by two funeral homes and shared her vision (I never did hear **why** funeral homes—perhaps they were friends). They each donated $1,000!

Carol's small prayer group caught her vision and began to pray over the project with her. They advised her to form a board. "What's a board?" she questioned. They patiently explained the function and the need to include successful people to help, such as a doctor, a businessman, an architect, a secretary/treasurer, etc. Aided by their wisdom and prayers, she wrote out her vision and sent it to several prominent people in the area. That very week a lawyer contacted her and asked, "When and where is your next board meeting?" She boldly replied, "How about next week in your office?" Voilà! Her vision was off and running.

This "project" manifested into one miracle after another until three years later, Hannah's House became a reality in Mentor, Ohio—a fully equipped and fully staffed home for unwed mothers. Such a God-thing! A dream come true! So, you can imagine her heartbreak when her husband accepted "a call" to pastor a church in Tequesta, Florida! Carol cried her eyes out—she was leaving her "baby" in someone else's arms!

However, once she arrived in Florida, the vision reappeared, and once again Carol followed the Lord's leading. Now there is a Hannah's House in Florida, and at the time of our encounter she was strategizing on building more in the Bahamas or Trinidad because she had discovered that those governments would donate land for this type of outreach. As Carol shared this incredible story, the Holy Spirit whispered in my ear, "And she's not eighteen and single!" Carol is my age and married to a pastor! She had no special training, no degrees, no dollars to fund her visions—she just followed the path the Lord led her on. Talk about challenging!

About a week later I received a phone call from a pastor friend, inviting me to preach in his church on Mother's Day (two weeks away). I *knew* this, too, was part of God confirming my calling. The preparation time alone solidified my understanding as I preached on "The Mother-Heart of God." He is calling us all to engage in some capacity to care for His motherless children. My youngest daughter and my eleven-year-old granddaughter were in tears at the end of the message, and several women who were called to minister to children at risk came forward for prayer. This was May 13.

On May 15, while reading articles in The Elijah List, I noticed one titled "Mother India." It is a real-life version of *Slumdog Millionaire.* I emailed the missions pastor at our church and asked if we could sponsor a showing of this film. He agreed to ask for permission but did not think we could. I immediately heard the Spirit whisper, "This is not a church thing I am calling you to—it's a Kingdom of God thing."

Dr. Ananthi Jebasingh, from India, stopped by my office one afternoon to share her amazing story about answering a knock on her door by a begging child in 1989. She took the child in, and another, and then another. The children kept coming. She soon began a school in the rooms of a slum toilet facility; her small beginning evolved into what is now a brand new, fully equipped, school with 1,100 students.

When sharing all of these "coincidences" with my secretary, she questioned, "Isn't Esther from India?" Duh! I had gone to seminary with Esther, and her office was only two doors down from mine at Asbury University! "Of course I need to talk with Esther."

I scurried straight down the hall and recounted my story to Esther. She immediately gave me the names of two women—Andrea, a realtor in Lexington who works with trafficked women and often travels to India, and Laura, an Asbury graduate who was heading to Mumbai for two years with two other young women to reach the children and women in two red-light districts. This was on May 24.

I continued to pray and seek the Lord daily, specifically trying to discern His voice more clearly. On May 25 I heard in my spirit, "Be a voice, not an echo." On May 27 John and I went to see *The Best Exotic Marigold Hotel* and I became homesick for India.

Andrea and I shared our passion to reach out to these women and girls who were being abused both here and in

India. Encouragement and seeds for future work were sown. When I connected with Laura Meyers in June, she directed me to Rahab's Rope, the missions organization she was serving under. Their website drew me like a magnet! My eyes immediately settled on an announcement of a ten-day outreach scheduled for Mumbai in January. One of these Christmas celebration outreaches was to take place in their Center (a room about 15 ft. x 30 ft. in the middle of a red-light district). I *knew* God was calling me to this, but what about the $3,000 I needed in order to go?

On Sunday morning, July 29, after praying on the prayer team at church I asked another team member to pray for me (she did not know what was going on in my life). In the midst of her prayer, she asked the Lord to help me to not be resistant to what He was saying! So I brought her up to speed on my current journey.

"But I don't have the money."

"I know. Money is tight right now; I'm so thankful for my Social Security check."

"How can you get Social Security when you are still working on staff?"

"Well, when you turn sixty-seven, you can collect your Social Security check without penalty, whether or not you are working."

"I did not know that! I turned sixty-seven last week."

"The local number is hard to find, but here, I have it on my cell phone."

I wrote down the number and called the next day for a phone interview, and by August 1st I had received my first Social Security check—not a biggie, but by December it would provide enough money for me to go on the outreach! I eagerly filled out the paperwork and submitted my application and was accepted.

A few weeks later, a friend invited me to meet Cindi Mendoza, who told of recently building a home for children who had been left on her doorstep in Kenya. The witness of

God doing something similar to what He was calling me to do filled my heart with hope and great encouragement.

It was only a few weeks later that the Morrisseys of Thailand Methodist Mission spoke to a small group at Asbury. They also had established a children's home for children at risk. Listening to their story wakened my understanding of how worldwide sex trafficking is and how many workers are being called into these fields and reinforced my desire to be part of the answer.

I determined to learn as much as possible in preparation for outreach in India. I watched the documentary *Born in a Brothel* and my heart broke when I realized that girls aged twelve and over have a high attrition rate when they are trying to come out of the slum/brothel lifestyle because that is all they have known. Through this, I felt the Lord calling me to concentrate on girls aged ten and under.

The Lord speaks to all of us in a variety of ways if we are attentive and choose to listen to His spirit via His written Word, circumstances, preaching, teaching, music, nature, billboards, books, movies, magazines, other people, etc. I usually begin my day in the Scriptures and prayer and then read from a couple of daily devotional books and any current prophetic words that come across my path. Most often, these develop into a pattern that serves as confirmation of what I believe the Lord is speaking to my heart that day, week, or month. When words jump off the page or ring a bell in my heart, I write them down.

One challenge came in the form of asking myself: "What do I see? What does God see?" Then my answer came when reading, "We may find ourselves in the wilderness praying for deliverance when God's desire is for us to plant gardens and call forth the springs in the desert."[48] "For, I will empower you to do what is necessary to fulfill that which is required of you."[49]

MUMBAI

And the adventure begins! My large bag was ten pounds overweight. I had to repack, putting some things in my carry-on. I departed from Lexington, Kentucky, on December 28 for Atlanta, where I met up with several other team members. The corps consisted of the three young women who had made the two-year commitment (Laura M., Rachel, and Laura H.—I will be referring to them as "the girls" for the sake of distinguishing them from the women we ministered to) plus Sean, a college student from Georgia; Sammy, a single mom from Arizona; Lisa, a single businesswoman from California; and me.

I loved our mixture of ages and gender and background! Yes, they were ALL young enough to be my children! None of them were married. Except for "the girls," none of us had met before.

We had a short stopover in Paris—classy terminal! For the next leg of the journey, I lucked out with an aisle seat, which would help me to move around a bit more easily and somewhat alleviate swollen hands and ankles. However, my seatmate left much to be desired. He was a young Indian man who drank a dozen whiskeys en route.

We arrived in Mumbai after midnight and hired a van to take us to the YMCA. I teasingly tempted the driver with a Twizzler, and he inhaled it! The girls told me that the Indians call it liquid gum. I don't know whether or not it was the Twizzler that distracted him from his driving, but he got lost. When we eventually ended up at the Y it was well after 2 a.m.

Lisa, Dani, and I were to share a room, and by the time we had settled in and shut up, another two-plus hours had passed. Laura Meyers picked us up at 10:30 a.m. for a late breakfast before joining the other girls at their apartment. During our devotional time, Dani shared that she has a nineteen-month-old son, and they live with her parents.

It took us a full day to shake off jet lag and be able to concentrate on Laura's training sessions and focus on our assignment! Each day would begin with a train ride, and then we would hustle to another train and disembark in groups of 3-3-2 so as not to attract a lot of attention. We would then cross the tracks of the departed train and begin an ascent up a narrow, dusty, dirt road with a variety of "stores" (more like lean-tos/shacks to an American eye). Various handmade wares and cheap trinkets were available, as well as tea and food being cooked over live fires.

I was intrigued and at first saddened over their living conditions—filthy and noisy, but as we walked our way to the Center (a rented room in the middle of the "activity"), I was stunned by the affectionate manner in which the girls greeted and were received by the women sitting outside their homes/places of business. I compare their warmth with the sight of a grandmother and grandchild embracing each other—such loving hugs of acceptance and the joy of seeing one another again!

On their way up the hill each day, the girls took time to stop and just be with them and chat. These women had never been to the Center. The girls had started their "labor of love" with about a dozen children—playing with them and teaching them about Jesus and hygiene. But the plan this week was to reach out to these women through a Christmas celebration.

In preparation for the big day, we shopped for hygiene products and then divided them into individual gift bags for the women. The shopping trip was expected to take one or two hours; instead it took about four hours—typical example of the inability to get things done at the "normal American" pace. "Hurry up and wait" became our M.O. (method of operation). The girls had already bought saris for each of the women, and local businesses had donated about 166 pairs of shoes, which we sorted by size. Rice meals were purchased, as well as a birthday day cake to celebrate our Guest of Honor —Jesus!

The day before the celebration, several of us canvased the village, passing out invitations. Of course, each stop was a love feast in itself! Such small acts of kindness were overwhelmingly received with great joy. We often do not realize what a treasure we carry around inside us—a treasure in earthen vessels that is powerful in touching the lost and lonely with hope. Never in my wildest dreams did I think I would be hugging women in brothels and children in the slums with the compassionate, accepting love of Jesus. Reaching out to them became a great privilege and joy.

So many women (more than a hundred) responded the next day, much to our delight. However, keeping them peaceful and happy while waiting their turn presented a challenge. The Center could accommodate only about twenty at a time. It quickly became apparent that the ladies did not know their shoe sizes. Chaos reigned! After serving the first round of ladies, we explained to the others that they would need to come back one by one sometime next week for their shoes!

I first told them of Christ's birth (with an interpreter). We fed them a rice meal, then cake, and sang "Happy Birthday" to Jesus. We passed out the hygiene bags, and I laid hands on them individually and prayed for them as they left. One woman sat at my feet with her arm and head on my lap most of the time. We did not talk—she just kept looking up at me and smiling.

The days we spent with the children who came to the Center were filled with energy—theirs! They were so bright-eyed and happy to see us! We celebrated Siba's ninth birthday American-style: we decorated with balloons, had tiaras for each of them to wear, played games, and ate cake and smeared chocolate frosting on each other's faces! I fell in love with another little girl named Ziba and longed to take her home with me—would have if I could have. Her mother had swallowed rat poisoning the day before in an attempted suicide.

When we ran to catch the train back to the girls' apartment, it was already in motion by the time we spotted the women's car (not always in the same section of a train). The girls grabbed the pole and jumped on, but my hand only reached over another's hand—she grabbed my wrist, but was not strong enough to pull me aboard. I slipped away and just missed falling beneath the train. However, this was the last car, so the "caboose" engineer spotted me and stopped the train from dragging me too far. My angels were on assignment! I ended up with only some bruises and swelling of my right knee and ankle.

Both Lisa and Laura jumped off the train before it started to roll again. They made sure I was only scraped up, and then we realized that Sean was on the train—with no one to direct him. He was in one of the men's cars at the front of the train and had no idea why the train had stopped and started again so quickly! Sean knew where to get off but was clueless on how to proceed from there. He would be searching for us.

Laura hired a tuk-tuk for us, hoping to catch up with Sean at the train's next stop, unfortunately the driver had to pull off the road two times to fix a faulty spark plug! Sean was nowhere to be seen when we got there. Laura walked one way down the platform. Lisa and I walked the other—no luck. We eventually gave up and boarded the train that would take us to our home terminal, where we continue our search. Lisa and I were praying as we walked, and just as I said "Amen," Sean jumped off the next train!

We went to In Orbit, an American-style mall, for dinner and shopping—for slacks to replace the ones I had ripped up while falling off the train! Driving back to the YMCA was a hoot—Dave (the director of Rahab's Rope) and Sean rode in one tuk-tuk, and Lisa, Dani, and I rode in another. For some reason, our drivers decided to race. Ours actually had two drivers, and they tried to switch seats while driving at top speed, while we were yelling "NO!" They continued to careen down the crowded road. Our guys were running out of steam, and then both tuk-tuks realized they were lost, and forced to stop and ask for directions! By the time we made it back to the YMCA, the rate had gone up to 250 rupees from the 125 set before we left the mall. We gave them 200 rupees each.

The next day, we met up with Pastor Manoj,[50] who directs the Hope Center in the same slum village where the Rahab's Rope Center is located. He and his wife also run an orphanage in Mumbai, taking care of fifty-two children. Thursday was a national blackout day due to demonstrations over a woman being gang-raped on a train in New Delhi the previous week. We did not go to the villages that day; instead, we met with a representative of the International Justice Mission who related ideas on how we could be helpful in rescuing these women and children.

On Friday we caught taxis at 8:30 a.m. and then quietly walked up to the Rahab's Rope Center, reminding the women along our path that we were hosting a medical clinic that day. Nine doctors from Mumbai came to our makeshift clinic (sheets were hung to cordon off the center into a couple of examination sections). We assisted the nine doctors as best we could by welcoming the women, performing administrative duties, saying prayers, and offering childcare. That day, 168 women were tended to. This was a big step for many of these women who had never had access to professional medical assistance before. I prayed with each patient on her way out.

The next day, Pastor Manoj picked us up at 10 a.m. and we stuffed his van full of gifts for the women at another brothel location, which was located about thirty minutes in the opposite direction from the last one. We stopped to pick up rice, but since the pot was too big for the van, the store owner ordered his truck driver to follow us to the brothels—some flat land they had taken over near a train station. Actually, there were four competing brothels lined up next to each other behind a series of bushes.

The madam of the first brothel encouraged us to set up shop in the front of her establishment and later invited us in—insisting on serving us rice and drinks! After I communicated the Christmas story, the girls henna-painted the women's hands with symbols corresponding to the biblical account. One of the women timidly asked to paint mine—I humbly agreed. We prayed for these precious souls and gave them gifts.

Several women from the other brothels hovered around me as I told the Christmas story a second time, while seated between two other brothels. Men walked in and out at will. One of the women would disappear for a while and then rejoin us. These women wore beautiful, colorful saris and treated us with sweet, gentle spirits. "Lord, may they and their customers come to know Your sacrificial love."

That night, we took a prayer ride (like a prayer walk) on a train from one end of the line to the other. We got off at the far terminal in Old Mumbai, ate in a trendy restaurant, and walked to the edge of the Arabian Sea, where we sat on a concrete wall taking in the exquisite view of the Queen's Necklace.[51]

On our last day, we attended the girls' church and heard a stirring sermon on Jonah, checked out of the YMCA, ate lunch with the girls in their apartment, and debriefed before leaving for the airport on our way to Bangalore, Paris, Atlanta, and then Lexington. John and Christi made up my welcoming committee, showering me with hugs and a bouquet of flowers. To my delight, I later discovered chocolate-covered pretzels in our refrigerator! GREAT TRIP! I was glad to be home, although I had to switch gears quickly, as John's first knee-replacement surgery was only two days away!

Prior to my time in Mumbai, I had thought the Lord's leading was to establish an adoption agency in the United States for little girls from India. But once I had walked the paths of the red-light districts, I realized that was not to be. I believe the Lord dropped into my heart the desire to build safe homes for them in India.

I kept thinking about Ziba. She represented all the little girls that are at risk of abuse in the slums. I sensed a meshing of what I had felt God was preparing me for through gender justice awareness, graphic documentaries He had brought across my path, and now this experience of meeting and loving some of these sweethearts up close and personal. "It will take faith to step into the fullness of what God has called and ordained for you. . . . You have an uncommon seed that will produce an uncommon harvest!"[52]

A week after I returned home, I Skyped with Laura and recounted what I believed the Lord was saying to me. She did the "happy dance" and then described the week at the Center after we had left. When the women came back one-by-one to get their shoes, they sobbed and begged the girls, "Take my children!" They yearned for better lives for their children. This cry was heartbreaking in itself, but even worse was the reality that there was no place to take them. Pastor Manoj and his wife were already caring for fifty children in their orphanage. Eventually they were able to squeeze in a couple more but could not stretch beyond that.

The need is SO great for homes for these children. The Indian government will not allow Americans to adopt Indian children anymore. The only answer would be to establish homes in India for them. I felt drawn to Bangalore because the air was healthier there. "When you decide on a course of action that is in line with My will, nothing in heaven or earth can stop it. Never give up. Do not expect an easy path."[53]

Chapter Twenty

INDIA (SHINING LIGHTS) JULY 2013

SETTING UP ITINERARY

On January 18th, I met with Mark MacDonald of Kentucky's branch of the National Christian Foundation in an effort to set up a 501c3. Since I had no structure in place at this point, he advised me to come under the Foundation until a more concrete plan evolved. I set up the "Shining Lights Fund" that very day and ordered calling cards! The Lord was assuring me, "I have lovingly planned every inch of the way."[54]

My part-time, year-round employment at Asbury University allowed for no extra vacation time other than that of the University schedule at large, but I knew something more was stirring in my spirit—God was up to something. I pressed into negotiations with the provost with my plan to hold longer office hours when the students were actually on campus, allowing me the month of July off. Now—**time** to network in India was available; I just needed to find the finances.

The plot thickens . . . I learned that a parent of one of our students ran an orphanage in Kolkata, and he offered to assist me, even to the extent of flying to Bangalore to help me search for property that would be appropriate for the first home. It seemed to me that flying to Kolkata and observing his work firsthand would be advantageous, even though my vision for Shining Lights was focused on the west coast.

In March, I received a letter in the mail from Prudential Life Insurance Company. I thought it was a solicitation to sign an application and almost threw it away—sealed! For some reason I did open it and found that my mother, who had died more than twenty years previously, had left two small policies. The letter informed me that if not claimed by April 26, the money would be transferred to the state treasury! Although far from a fortune, it provided enough money to fund my trip to India for the month of July! I knew my mother's heart; this was a faith-walk she would have been thrilled to finance. "Jehovah-Jirah"—God is my Provider!

In May, Alltech was hosting an international conference in Lexington at the Hyatt Regency Hotel. The Asbury administration and faculty were given complimentary access (worth hundreds of dollars) to dinners and seminars by elite entrepreneurs from around the world. At first I had no interest but could not seem to dismiss the invitation, thinking that with 1,500 people from various countries present, perhaps I could make some contacts and find opportunities for our students to fulfill their required cross-cultural experience.

The seminar on entrepreneurship was led by the president of Alltech and attended by several hundred people. He made reference to various success stories, one being that of a young man who had asked his father for $100 to start a business twenty-five years ago and whose business had become a multi-million-dollar success. The president then introduced the man from INDIA! My heart leapt. He was seated in the front row on the right. I was seated in the back row on the left. I whispered to the Lord: "If this is of You, I will walk over to him at the end of the seminar, and if he is busy, I will walk right on by and go home. If he is free, I'll introduce myself."

The aisle was completely clear. The path across the front of the room was also free of foot traffic—the Indian businessman was closing his briefcase and no one was talking with him. I introduced myself and explained that I would be spending the month of July in India, hoping to start a home for little girls rescued out of the red-light districts. G.B. handed me his business card with both hands and said,

"When you come, we will meet." I was taken aback. I had not expected such a response. He repeated, "When you come, we will meet." I thanked him and moved on out of the room. "Wow, God!" Surely this man was God's provision for starting Shining Lights!

Tammy Hutchins was another significant Asburian contact to whom several colleagues had drawn my attention. Upon graduating from the seminary twenty-four years earlier, Tammy had made her way to the streets of Bangalore, India, with six dollars left in her billfold and immediately had begun caring for homeless orphans. Her quiver expanded rather quickly as she joined forces with two Indian women, and the trio eventually gained legal guardianship of forty-six children.

My itinerary would begin in Bangalore with Tammy Ma for three days before I traipsed across town to spend time with the Rahab's Rope team, whose members work with intervention and aftercare for women (victims of India's slave trade). Then I would fly to Goa for three days to visit with that Rahab's Rope team, who work primarily with human trafficking prevention programs.

Next, I would fly to Mumbai for a week with the girls from Rahab's Rope with whom I had ministered in January, and from there fly to Kolkata to connect with the Indian pastor who kindly had offered to help me and to observe their orphanage. Then I would fly back to Bangalore with the pastor. My final in-country flight schedule was to Coimbatore to meet with the businessman before returning to Kentucky—via a night in the UAE!

I was finally on my way! The first stop was at O'Hare International Airport for a nine-hour stopover. I was lugging an extra suitcase full of requested supplies from the girls, and the check-in clerk charged me $75 for extra baggage! At least I wouldn't have to fiddle with it when I transferred at the Charles De Gaulle Airport.

As I boarded my flight in France, I was growing weary and eager to get to India. The legroom in the first seats of coach sure looked inviting, and it appeared that there was only one man sitting there. As I reflected on possible seating options, the man stood up and I recognized him! Darrell Whiteman had been my doctoral mentor! We spent over an hour catching up on the past seven years, as well as sharing our current schedules. We discovered that our journeys were going to overlap for a few days. He was teaching a seminar at SAIACS (South Asia Institute of Advanced Christian Studies) in Bangalore, and I had reservations to stay there in about a week. When we landed, he introduced me to Ashley, an associate who was to play an important part in my decision-making in the days to come.

TAMMY MA'S

Shontu, a young Indian friend of Tammy's, met me at the Kempegowda International Airport in Bangalore at 1 a.m. and drove me to KHome. Annie, one of the interns, had waited up for me, and she sleepily opened the gate and guided me to my room. Taylor and baby Lea met me in the morning, and we shared our stories as we walked to the Hillside Cafe, which was run by a couple of the older boys. I learned that Taylor is married to Harrison D'Jerrnet, whose parents were students at Asbury during the time John and I were there.

She attempted to acquaint me with some of the local color, such as the monetary system in India: 1,000 rupees = \$20; 1 lakh = 100,000 rupees. She and Taylor were seeking the Lord on His plans for their future, but she determined that if they stayed here she would definitely learn Kannada (the local dialect). Each district of India has its own dialect, making it extremely difficult to communicate. I thought that if I learned Hindi, I would be home safe—not so!

Tammy Ma is the perfect prototype in regard to caring for children who have lost their parents. Every child is embraced as being a vital part of the family. They are nurtured in love and taught how to love God and each other, as well as those who cross their paths. They eat together, worship together, study together, and go on outings and outreaches together as a beautiful family unit. The little girls share bedrooms, bathrooms, and a living room with an Indian woman who lives with them in their wing of the home. The same for the little boys, older girls, and older boys.

Each child has a special, intimate relationship with Tammy Ma, as she intentionally makes one-on-one time for them on a regular basis and plans special activities with them in smaller groups. Many are now Spirit-filled young adults, getting married and leaving home to minister with YWAM and plant churches, while others serve in a myriad of Christian endeavors. This was a model of the home I longed to establish through Shining Lights.

Tammy's root canal (which had occurred on the day before I arrived) was still causing her pain, but she invited me to chat with her a couple of hours. This woman offered me a wealth of knowledge that no book could ever teach me. She does no fundraising. She counseled me: "The way to start an orphanage is the same way you start a family—it develops organically. You start by building relationships with those who have a heart for this type of ministry and feel called to it. Be mentors to them, and be grandparents to the children. You must live among them at least a year, and plan on three years to set it up."

My shock came when Tammy Ma informed me that the Indian government would not let anyone outside of India establish a home for orphans. She and her Indian partners became legal custodians of the children in accordance with Cara[55] regulations. Her home also supports one hundred children living in single-parent homes. How could this be? God had been so confirming in my calling. I could not believe it. She made it clear that I was getting way ahead of myself. The first step would not be to buy property. Of course, I needed to contact the pastor from Kolkata and cancel his flight to Bangalore, but he had already purchased the tickets (at my expense). I had no choice but to continue my itinerary as planned, although I informed him of the change: we would not be looking for property. I sent him $575 for expenses.

Tammy cautioned me to set boundaries with my responses: "maybe later," "next time," and "I need to rest." Later in the afternoon, she took me upstairs to the new apartment they were building for her, and we hung out on the rooftop with a few of the older boys: Arumada, Mune, Shuiseter, and Moline. It was a joy to watch them easily interact with each other and with us.

Tammy encouraged me to visit various types of orphanages in Bangalore—private, government, and English. She suggested I take a box of apples, oranges, or treats as gestures of courtesy, and coached me on some questions to ask or observe:

What is the child/adult ratio?
What do they do on holidays/weekends?
Are the children fearful? Clingy? Self-confident?
Do they have individual space?

I began with Shalom Grace Children's Home, funded through Christ the King Human Development Trust. I had tea with the married couple who cares for these twenty-one children. The only two girls live with them, and the boys live upstairs with the headmaster. They appeared to enjoy their work and genuinely cared about the children.

The woman I spoke to at St. Charles Orphanage was suspicious of me and hard to talk with. She supervised sixty girls under the age of sixteen; when they turned sixteen, they were forced to leave. St. Mary's Orphanage is the same type of sterile-feeling institution. Since the priest was at lunch, I decided it was not worth the wait in this most unwelcoming atmosphere. On the contrary, I found ACCEPT to be a wonderful, clean facility with great outdoor areas for the children; it is run by a fine, discerning, Spirit-filled Christian man who supervises the care of eighteen HIV[56] children—nine boys and nine girls.

The time spent in these other orphanages served only to emphasize the necessity of establishing a loving, Spirit-filled family atmosphere for children. In the first fifteen years that Tammy spent in India, she watched fifteen different singles or couples try to start homes. They had both Western and Indian founders and directors. Ten failed miserably. She proclaimed: "It never works to have the person with the vision hire someone else to carry it out. The founder/director/visionary living in America and visiting several times a year is a recipe for disaster."

I enjoyed a great Fourth of July celebration with several missionary families who were Tammy's friends. Dustin and Mallory Covington were Asburians! Greg Haseloff, my chaplain friend, had officiated at their wedding—small world! Mickie and Mick Smith were another delightful American couple. He coaches boys' sports, and she is a designer. We dined on customary American-style hamburgers, beans, salad, chips, Coke, apple pie, and ice cream. We walked to a nearby park, where Mallory and I twirled fire batons to patriotic music (CD) as the guys set off firecrackers and the children squealed with delight. FUN!

Since Tammy's church had a vision similar to mine, her secretary, Shikina, arranged a meeting with their pastoral staff for me. I shared with them about my journey thus far, and they shared their vision for the same property I was previously drawn to, near SAIACS. We discussed their finances and how much they needed to raise to buy it and then rode out to look at the land. This was too coincidental to NOT be God! The pastor's name is Shine, and his wife's name is Glory—Shining Lights!

RAHAB'S ROPE: BANGALORE

I then moved in with the Rahab's Rope team, where Jill Johnson and Lydia Apple were hosting an amazing team of young women on a mission trip from America. We were all eager to bless the women who had been rescued from trafficking nightmares. The mission home we visited accommodated about twenty hurting women whom we tried to help express their feelings through painting their emotions: sad, mad, glad, afraid, worried, or happy. One sad little girl proudly presented me with a bracelet she had made out of black yarn.

Our next stop was ACCEPT, the orphanage I mentioned before for children with AIDS—several of whom had a mother dying of AIDS in a hospice hospital across the driveway. Jill shared a short teaching on character with the older girls while I listened in, and then we told stories to the younger ones. But I found it difficult to connect with them, perhaps because I was disillusioned over my own vision—WHY AM I HERE? The only connection I could see was the meeting in Coimbatore; perhaps I could serve as a conduit of finances needed.

We attended church at SAIACS the next day and listened to a sermon about Discipleship Essentials: "Come, follow Me . . . . I will make you fishers of men." I acknowledged that yes, it's an ongoing journey with the Master. After the service, Darrell introduced me to Bobbie. He didn't mention her last name because she goes into many Muslim countries to teach storytelling and must keep her identity hidden. She is about my age, and our kindred spirits refreshed my soul.

When the team returned to the guesthouse, we sat around the table while some members of the group cut up veggies for dinner. They were eager to learn about my journey and asked for more detail. The Holy Spirit encouraged their hearts as I spoke, which encouraged my own heart! They asked to pray for me and my vision—precious and powerful prayers.

RAHAB'S ROPE: GOA

I was off to the airport the next morning for a flight to Goa, after paying another $130 for excess baggage weight! I had not been informed that anyone was planning on meeting me at the Goa International Airport (in Dabolim), and since I saw no one holding a sign with my name on it, I hired a cab to carry me to a vague address. We drove around and around until finally I asked the Lord for a divine contact. Just then my driver saw Kevin (the guesthouse landlord) running down the road, waving both arms in a frenzy.

Melissa had gone to the airport ninety minutes early and thought she had enough time to grab a coffee. However, I arrived while she was in the restaurant! Not knowing she was there to greet me, I hailed a taxi. When she couldn't find me, she figured that I had taken a cab and called Kevin and urged him to leave the house and look for a cab! Great timing! When she arrived, we enjoyed a leisurely talk over tea in a little oceanfront restaurant (Joet's) located right next to the team's headquarters.

The Goa group focuses primarily on areas of prevention through a sewing center and a preschool. On my second day with them, we took a cab to the Bright School to help a preschool teacher—fun, but exhausting! That night I met the other seven members of the team. They do a "Stretch and Blessing" time each night in order to wind down and maintain support for one another, sharing how they were stretched that day and how they were blessed.

On my third day in Goa, Melissa and I went to the activities center and watched the girls and the team create crafts most of the day—macramé, knitting, and sewing. Their teacher was celebrating her birthday by cooking lunch for them, and they surprised her with gifts and a cake. Then

Julie taught a hair-styling class, using me as the model—got a good trim!

Susan and I ate at our favorite restaurant on the ocean for dinner, while the rest of the team went to meet Pastor Stilbo and his wife to discuss trafficking awareness strategies. In the middle of dinner, Susan received a phone call from Melissa inquiring if I had picked up my hearing aids. I had given them to Jessie when Julie was trimming my hair! By the time Susan and I returned to the Center, Sylvester had found one on the floor, and after a diligent search, he found the other one in the dustbin!

RAHAB'S ROPE: MUMBAI

Rain. Rain. And more rain! I was ready to move on to Mumbai. Melissa and I had teatime and prayer before she helped me repack my suitcase. The airline charged me only $40 for excess baggage this time! The girls were just wrapping up a meeting when I arrived. Laura and Rachel needed to leave almost immediately for the hospital to visit Lashmi, a woman from the red-light district who had been brutally stabbed. The team was her lifeline. Because of a murder in one village and death threats in the other, I was not able to visit the women on this trip.

Pastor Manoj picked me up at 10 a.m. to meet his family and tour his children's home (not his center in the slum). He and his wife care for fifty children there in Mumbai. The building they are renting is up for sale: $300,000. They can buy it for $60,000 as a token amount and pay $7,000/month for three years or $5,000/month for four years.

Over tea he shared his vision for a City of Hope: orphanage, church, school, old folks homes, fire department, hospital—the works! We went over the finances needed to purchase 30 acres about an hour outside of Mumbai (with plenty of room for Shining Lights homes). I was optimistic that my business connection in Coimbatore would open the door to this becoming a reality. A Mumbai businessman donated 10 acres free of charge and offered the other 20 acres to be bought over five years, interest-free.

Hope Center is his work in the red-light district. He has rented the building for four years, and the owner had decided to sell it—wanting $80,000 within six months. Little by little, his slum church has come up with the money. It houses a preschool, a study center, tutoring, and counseling and feeds 120 children lunch every day. Their vision is to provide sewing lessons and teach production skills. How I would love to help fund these outreaches.

Laura, Saronya, and I took off on a two-day excursion to Mukti Mission in Pune, where Pandita Ramabia established an orphanage for girls, destitute women, the blind, handicapped, and elderly. Pandita was a medical doctor, social reformer, champion for the emancipation of women, pioneer in education, an author who could speak seven languages, and she had translated the Bible into her native tongue!

Our nine-hour trek consisted of several transitions between cars and buses. Upon arrival, one of our first activities was to visit Margaret Williams, "Moshie," an eighty-eight-year-old Australian missionary who now resided at Mukti. We toured the 200 acres and met many of the elderly ladies in their modest homes and met beautiful, nicely dressed, young girls in their courtyards. Like bees to honey, these young ones immediately hovered over us. The facilities were clean and welcoming; however, twenty to twenty-eight girls per house felt way too crowded.

At the church service, we watched about three hundred girls file in and sit on the cloth-covered floor. The sermon centered on Colossians 1:9–18: "When Things Go Wrong" we are to walk worthy of Him. Do you think the preacher was reading my mail? He referred to Fanny Crosby, George Washington Carver, Nehemiah, and William Carey (uneducated, unfunded, inexperienced). He concluded: "There is no other way to be happy in Jesus than to trust and obey. Don't run away. Be wise." Printed on their cafeteria wall were these words:

Nothing to fear.
Nothing to lose.
Nothing to regret.

On my last full day in Mumbai, the girls took me to an American-style mall to celebrate my birthday in air-conditioning! I shopped, got my hair done, and lingered over lunch at TGIF. The guys sang to me: "I don't know, but I've been told, someone here is getting old! The good news is we sing for free. The bad news is we sing off key."

We proceeded to spend a good deal of money at the Clinique counter (things seem cheap when you are paying in rupees). I found a travel bag and a salwar/dupatta. We ended our excursion at Starbucks. When we got home, Laura gave me a massage while we watched several episodes of *So You Think You Can Dance*.

The girls attempted to enter the Center the next day, but they were not able to stay long—the police were on the scene where a woman had been strangled to death by her client. Tense darkness.

KOLKATA

On to Kolkata. The pastor's family met me at the airport. I found them to be gracious, loving, and focused on the future of their orphans. They live in a slum area but were able to provide me with my own room at the top of the stairs in their building—with an American toilet and great fan! The pastor took me on a wild motorcycle ride through Kolkata that night. It was quite a sight to see the field of homeless souls stretched out in a section of the airport parking lot.

The next day, a noisy bird woke me up at 5 a.m. We left for the orphanage at 7:30 a.m. to travel the three hours to their orphanage, which was home to about thirty neatly dressed, well-behaved boys and girls sitting in an orderly fashion on the front steps. To hear these winsome children worship in song was a heavenly treat. We ate lunch together, and then we all napped! Everyone quietly laid down on the carpet in the assembly room for about a half-hour. Later they performed skits and sang within the different age groups before the elaborate finale—children of all ages acting out the story of Joseph.

I noticed that the older boys were exceptionally attentive to the pastor and quickly obeyed his orders. The landscape of the large campus is lush with natural greenery—a picture of peace and rest. The main building is not finished, but what has been completed is impressive. I am not sure where they all were staying in the meantime.

This experience was tarnished for me by the way the pastor treated his wife: he was verbally altogether rude to her in front of me and the children. Embarrassment, hurt, and sadness pierced my heart for her, and his character was discredited in my eyes. I lost respect for, and trust in, him after that. It was a quiet ride back to Kolkata!

The next morning was more restful. I chatted with the pastor's wife for a while, expressing my concern about how she was treated, praying with her, and wondering if it would be appropriate for me to confront him. She obviously was hurting and encouraged me to do so. I sought him out in his office, but it was not conducive for such a showdown. Instead, his assistant took me on a rickshaw ride to get lassi (milk and yogurt). I probably would not have tried it if he had not been insistent—I loved it!

I spent the afternoon in my room, resting, praying, reading, trying to hear the Lord's direction. The pastor and I were distancing ourselves from one another, and looking back, I regret that I did not use the opportunity to visit Mother Teresa's Sisters of Charity. I did not sleep well that night and had to get up at 4 a.m. to leave for the airport. Descending the dark staircase with my luggage was rather scary; it seemed to offer an accurate picture of what was taking place in the spirit realm.

With overweight baggage again, even though I had unloaded a ton in Mumbai when I delivered the girls' supplies, the pastor's wife cajoled me into carrying a hefty care package back to her son in the States! And then the airport security confiscated my batteries and for some reason badgered me as to why I had them in my carry-on!

BACK TO BANGALORE

It was good to be back at SAIACS in Bangalore. Once we had settled into our rooms, the pastor and I took a leisurely stroll and talked turkey over chai. He convinced me that there were ways around the government regulations to set up a home for little girls. Thus, I agreed to accompany him to meet his sister and brother-in-law on the other side of Bangalore the next day. His brother-in-law would set up appointments for us to look at apartments.

We ran into Mallory and Dustin at SAIACS just before the afternoon church service. I was thrilled to espy the team from Rahab's Rope there too. The sermon was based on John 15:1–17 regarding Jesus as the Vine, and we are branches, but we must obey in order to abide (stay connected) to His Spirit flowing through us to produce good fruit. God has an expectation that our lives will be abundantly fruitful because of what Jesus has made available for us. The preacher made this comment: "A parasite sits on the tree and sucks the life out of it." In hindsight, I believe the Spirit was nudging me with a warning about the pastor from Kolkata.

At dinner that night, I introduced the pastor to Darrell, Bobbie, Ashley, and several other speakers who were holding the week-long seminar for missionaries. I understand the importance of networking, but something in me felt uncomfortable—like the pastor was hustling. Sometimes it is hard to discern how different cultures express themselves, so I hesitated to judge what I believed to be sinful actions.

The pastor's sister and her husband warmly welcomed us into their two-room apartment. They were both very hospitable and easy to talk with—not at all pushy like the pastor. Her husband is a professor at a local university and detailed in his preparations—he had forms for me to fill out that would be filed with the government and would establish me as a resident. The pastor's sister served us lunch before her husband, the pastor, and I left.

I thought we were going to look at an apartment, but instead we met up with three other men. They could not contact the owner of the apartment, so we were going to have to wait a couple of hours, although they did not tell me that. They were speaking in their own language as if I were invisible. Suddenly, the pastor motioned to me to get on the back of a motorcycle being driven by a stranger—to where, I did not know!

It turned out that we went to another pastor's house to wait with his family for a couple of hours. They also were very hospitable, although they did not speak English! They offered me a glass of water, but I could not accept it—it wasn't in a bottle. I guess my actions translated my problem correctly, because the son ran out and brought me back a bottle of Coke.

The married daughter proudly presented her wedding album, which I slowly pored over, trying to show appreciation. We smiled at each other a lot. The Kolkata pastor showed up about a half-hour later with a few sentences of explanation for me. I was trapped into listening to them talking in their language for several more hours. Eventually, they indicated it was time to go.

The three men scrutinized three apartments with me—they thoroughly considered how any one of them was conducive for starting a home for little girls. I did agree that one apartment was feasible. It was a new, nice, clean, two-bedroom apartment for $300/month. By the time we returned to SAIACS, it was 8 p.m. and I was exhausted. I had hoped to connect with Darrell, but almost everyone had already retired for the evening.

The next day was a red-letter day for me. I realized that I did not have an E-ticket for Coimbatore, and I did not know how much money was in my bank account since these ATMs do not give balances when you withdraw. I rushed down to the coffee shop to see if I could get online and find out. As I turned the corner, I saw Ashley and approached her to find out how she was managing. When she had checked in at the airport for her flight home, she had learned that her visa had expired!

As we continued in conversation, she said she'd been praying for me and felt she should give me a warning about the pastor. She discerned that he was not all that he was declaring himself to be. I immediately felt a witness in my spirit. The pastor was circling around the courtyard while we were talking. I called him over and told him I had a change of plans again and that I was releasing him to move on. He came on strong—trying to convince me that it would all work out. I stood my ground, with Ashley sitting beside me, and said good-bye. She was furious with him for trying to manipulate me. I was SO RELIEVED!

We were headed for lunch when Ashley received a message that an official from the police department was coming to talk with her. A couple of hours later, I checked back with her, but they still had not shown up. The Center was asking her to change rooms (since she had planned on being back in the States by now). I helped her transfer her belongings to another room before the authorities came to take her to the police station.

I finally caught up with Darrell, who had already discerned that something was amiss with the pastor. He was irate that they had pressured me into toting the care package that weighed at least 25 pounds. I learned a valuable lesson on this trip: Do not accept packages from others, no matter how hard-up they seem to be. I now had three confirmations that I was hearing the Lord correctly: Tammy, Ashley, and Darrell. Thank You, Jesus!

I woke up at 4 a.m. startled—realizing that the U.S. customs officials would not let me take in food from India. I hurried down to the desk and described to the clerk that this package was for the pastor. As I was talking, he showed up behind me. I quickly explained and eagerly transferred the package into his keeping and then left him standing there. Not only was I free of him, but now I would not have to lug around two suitcases.

I was also asked to switch rooms, as scheduled wedding guests were now arriving. I couldn't complain; SAIACS was charging me only $200 for five days—including the pastor's room. My "new room" was in the girls' dorm. I "adjusted" by spending the rest of the day shopping for gifts with Ashley.

COIMBATORE

My adventure in India was winding down—only two more days, but major challenges were still in store. My flight to Coimbatore was scheduled to leave at 9 a.m., and the clerk at the front desk had been instructed to wake me at 5 a.m. but forgot. I endured a fretful night and awoke on my own. I was almost ready to leave my room when the power went out. Of course my flashlight battery was dead, and I did not have a phone in my room. I inched my way down the darkened stairs only to find a metal gate strewn across the main hallway (it had not been there when I came in last night) and padlocked! I rattled the frame with all my might and called out as loudly as I could, but no one was around—maybe the Rapture had occurred and I was left behind! I began anxiously knocking on doors until one light sleeper awoke and found a key to open the lock.

I continued to make my way to the main building, only to find that it was locked as well. I jiggled the lock as hard as I could and yelled out, but to no avail. I decided to run around the building to the road and then back to the front of SAIACS, but by the time I had reached the parking lot, my taxi was waiting for me.

G.B.'s driver met me at the Coimbatore airport and escorted me to his office building at Jaya Enclave, a glassy high-rise building he owns. G.B. cordially welcomed me and invited me to have a seat in his conference room. His appearance was totally different from when I had met him in the United States. He had worn the appropriate business attire that I was used to, but here he wore slacks and a peach-colored *dhoti kurta* (long shirt) with a prominent red dot in the middle of his forehead, which indicated that he was a practicing Hindu, was very serious about his faith, and followed all their rules. Interestingly enough, none of his staff wore one.

He intently listened to my story from beginning to end, including details about the work of the Bangalore church and Pastor Manoj's work in Mumbai. He asked me point-blank what I wanted from him, and I faltered—I didn't know how much to ask for; I was only prepared to share the opportunity to help these women and girls being rescued out of sex trafficking. He frankly did not feel there was a need for another children's home. He said his government does a good job of taking care of its children; they provide food, shelter, medical attention, education, etc. He himself was active in a local Rotary Club that supported this kind of outreach.

G.B. offered to have Ravi (his HR man) and his driver take me to two designated orphanages in Coimbatore to ask questions, then come back and report to him what I had found. Since my flight back to Bangalore was not until 8 p.m., I had ample time to follow up on his suggestion. The two men took me to KFC—they use Suguna chicken, which is from the company G.B. owns. I was taken aback when the men sat and talked at a separate table. When I finished my eating, they arose and we continued on our assignment.

Families for Children was begun in 1978 by Mrs. Simpson, a Canadian woman. This special-education school houses 350 boys and girls and is self-financed, i.e., supported by local people, with NO government support. They are in need of 20,000 rupees per child, per year. The only food they receive from the government is rice, wheat, and sugar. The government provides a little support for medical emergencies but not for special needs or testing. The school pays for HIV testing. The government provides counseling, but it does not pay for it. The student/caregiver ratio is 60/1 and 4/1 for babies. They are proud of their sewing stations.

Our next stop was the Star Special School. It is St. Anne's rehabilitation school, which was started by the Mother Superior. The government does not support it—no medical aid, no testing, nothing. The student/caregiver ratio is 10/1. The caregiver is paid 6,000 rupees/month ($79.52/month).

Their teachers earn 10–15,000 rupees per month ($132.53–$198.79). The 250 boys and girls are between the ages of four and twenty. The school needs 2,500 rupees ($33.13) per child, per month, to provide for all the needs of the children. One hundred of these children live in the hostel; the others come in for the day. There is NO government rice, wheat, or sugar. The school takes care of all the students' food, clothing, and medical needs.

G.B. became blatantly defensive in response to my findings, although Ravi had accompanied me in every conversation and also had witnessed the living conditions of the children. I told G.B. that India was the #1 country involved in sex trafficking according to world statistics. He ignored me. I expressed my desire to focus on eight girls and give them a quality living environment in every aspect of life. He thought my ideas were unsustainable and that I should help one of the existing homes. When he thanked me for coming, I took the hint—our visit was over. His driver took me back to the airport at 3 p.m. I read for five hours!

G.B. is a kind man, and I believe if he were confronted with the facts about the sex trafficking in his area of India, he would generously respond. I offered to do more specific research and get back with him on the statistics. **I believe this was a divine appointment.** Please continue to pray for this Hindu man to seek truth for the children and for himself.

LAST DAY IN BANGALORE

Rather stunned and disappointed about my time with G.B., I awoke the next morning to further frustration—I was locked in my room! The lock on my dorm door had broken. Remember, I had no phone. I called out the window for help, but no one was around. I kept rattling the door until finally someone heard me and tried to open it from the outside—no dice. Someone roused the groundskeeper, who fiddled with it for the greater part of an hour before freeing me.

Ashley arranged for us to meet with Tammy at the Hillside Cafe for lunch, after which we left for Tammy's and a loooong debriefing. I loved hearing their hearts and wisdom about missions and missionaries. When I shared my frustration and feelings of failure, they encouraged me and laid hands on me and prayed. Tammy asked one of her boys to take me back to SAIACS on his motorcycle, but my taxi was already waiting for me, and SAIACS paid the fare as a gesture of regret for all the "inconvenience" of my dorm room.

My bags were too heavy yet again! I think I am the wiser for my next trip—I'll take my toothbrush and a pair of clean underwear! A sweet Indian girl sat next to me on the flight to UAE; she is going to be a freshman in college in Houston, Texas. My hotel room in Dubai was luxurious; it soothed my body, soul, and spirit. I slept in until 10:30 a.m. My flight to Atlanta would not take off until 10:30 p.m. I went back to bed at noon and slept another three hours. Then I caught up on my devotions, had a prayer time, filed my nails, wrote in my journal, and took another hour-long nap.

Stepping outside even in late evening takes your breath away in Dubai—it is so hot! I leisurely enjoyed a cup of coffee in a small cafe at the airport. I was pleased to meet my seatmate for the flight, a sweet young girl from Afghanistan who was going to be a freshman at Wake Forest University. This was her first time out of Afghanistan—WOW! Was she in for some culture shock! I watched *Roman Holiday* and reruns of *Downton Abbey*.

During my stopover in Atlanta, I read all about Kate and William's newborn son, Prince George. It was soooo good to be back in the good ol' USA! Christi and Alan picked me up at Lexington's Blue Grass Airport, and we spent a couple of hours sharing stories. They had just returned from visiting Kevin and Melissa in England, with a side trip to Scotland. John would not be back from a Gideon conference for a few days, which gave me some time to unpack and sort things out on multiple levels.

More than a hundred friends and family members had been praying for me. Their prayers had carried me through: **thirteen flights in thirty days**—no missed flights, no lost bags! But more importantly, they had kept me safe and sound, discerning, and greatly blessed to experience a glimmer of what God is doing in India. The trip was **a complete joy** even though it did not look at all like what I was expecting. I have no doubt that the Lord orchestrated every step of my journey, and He has only just begun!

A huge thanksgiving to the Rahab's Rope teams who hosted me in three different cities. They have an incredible ministry to women and children caught in the sex-trafficking industry, those coming out of these dark places, and those who are at risk of being captured. God is working powerfully through these teams. I encourage you to look at their website: www.rahabsrope.com.

Chapter Twenty-One

INDIA (ASBURY/RAHAB'S ROPE) 2014

Hoping my love for India would overflow to some students, I advertised the Rahab's Rope trip to Goa in January 2014 and was delighted when two females responded: Christa Stone and Katie Oostman. David Moore, a founder of Rahab's Rope, led the team. The rest of the team consisted of a young married couple, Dani and Sammie; and five single women: Farah, Morgan, Hannah, Leah, and Joanna.

Christa and I flew from Lexington to Atlanta and joined several others on the flight to Amsterdam. We all arrived in Mumbai around 5:30 p.m. but my bags were missing! After a seven-hour stopover, we flew on to Goa, arriving at 7 a.m. I rejoiced when I found out that I was getting my old room back! Leah, my new roommate, would not join us until the next day.

We ate at an oceanfront cafe prior to our two-hour orientation prep-talk and then took a bus[57] to Vasco for the girls to buy some Indian-style garb. When we returned, David had a spaghetti dinner spread out for us.

The next day, we toured a fascinating spice farm and watched a man shinny up a tall palm tree and leap over to another tree, then slide down with ease. Our big thrill was to climb up a hill and mount elephants for short rides down to the water (the elephants sidled up to the hill, and we straddled over the elephants from the top of the hill). To round out our day, we traveled to St. Xavier's tomb—his mortal remains have been restored as a mummy that has been placed in a decorated casket inside a huge church.

The team split up on Thursday—half going with an NGO that Rahab's Rope had partnered with to provide a medical clinic. Hannah, Leah, and I went with David to the sewing center to sort beads with the women and organize the product. After lunch we led a life-skills group on self-confidence. Sarah picked us up at 5:30 p.m. to join the rest of our team in a slum where Rahab's Rope rents an educational center. We broke into small groups and visited the families of children who attend.

Friday was one of my favorite days; we spent several hours doing house visitation in the slums and offering to pray with people. The people were so hungry for someone to care enough to stop and pray for them! Their countenances changed on contact. We worked with thirty-six kids in the afternoon doing crafts, reading stories, and playing balloon games. At the Dollar Store in the United States, I had bought bead kits that contained 9-inch-wide paper flowers and fish that the kids could decorate. They were so proud of their creations that we hung them on strings from the ceiling. At 5 p.m. we met with ten young girls in a life-skills class to talk about goal setting for the next year. Two more bus rides back to the guesthouse for dinner at 7:30 p.m.—great day!

On Saturday we assisted a clinic for school-aged children; my assignment was basically to observe and pray. That night we returned to the slums for a children's New Year's celebration. It was delayed because of microphone problems—out in the middle of a field. A youth band led in an extensive time of praise and worship, and then the kids performed songs and dances they had learned at the educational center. One little girl who was about six years old parked on my lap for the duration!

On Sunday we split up and taught Sunday school lessons—I was so thankful for Christa's energy! She did an outstanding job of relating to the kids. She, Joanna, and I went to church with Sarah. Again, great praise and worship and a solid salvation message, but I kept falling asleep! After an hour-long bus ride back to the guesthouse and a nap, we left at 3:45 p.m. for the other school's New Year's celebration. This one took place inside a community hall. Several of us performed a dance and song to a CD—hilarious! The crowd was pleased—little did they know that when I did the jumping part, I literally had tears running down my pant legs! Oops! It was a soggy ride home.

Monday's breakfast was at 7:30 a.m., followed by three bus rides to Hahen's preschool. Leah, Morgan, Farah, and I went with David. The Lord choreographed our creative genius in a unique way. Our theme was "Thanking God." We sang "There's a River of Life Flowing Out of Me." We taught them John 3:16. We did a recitation on salvation and explained it with colors:

Black = Sin
Red = Blood of Jesus
White = Clean
Yellow = Heaven
Green = Grow/Life

The children made "Thank You" cards to take home for their mom or dad, and we ended by singing "Thank You, Jesus."

From there we went outside to a small lean-to and taught a class for the slum children who do not go to school. We taught them several songs, and I acted out an impromptu rendition of Noah's Ark—GREAT FUN!

Half of our team was sick—coming up and out, as well as down and out at the same time. AND we needed to pack up and head out to the airport by 3 p.m. Christa seemed to be struggling the most, and she was my traveling companion. The toughest part was at the Mumbai airport—baggage checks, immigration, etc. Long, slow-moving lines. She could hardly stand on her own; she leaned on me and laid on the floor. It took our whole team to help her. Once on board, she slept most of the way to Amsterdam and felt slightly better after that. By God's grace, we made it through Atlanta and home!

John was eager to have me home, as he was facing his second knee-replacement surgery the next day, and I was glad to be home—this was not my favorite trip. I believe a major missing piece was the fact that we did not meet each morning for prayer as a team nor did we debrief at night. Thus, the team did not bond to the degree I had experienced on other trips, leaving a hole in my heart, even though the Lord was faithful to provide opportunities to bless those we met along the way.

Chapter Twenty-Two

THE ENDING & THE BEGINNING

I found myself hungering for more of the Lord. I felt like I kept missing what He was trying to tell me—more like hearing His voice but misinterpreting what He was saying. When I caught up with an old friend at a Christmas party, she was bubbling with excitement over a new video class taught by Bill Johnson that she was taking at Destiny Community Church. She captured my attention, and thus began years of worshiping with the congregation at Destiny.

At Destiny, I found the freedom in praise and worship I had been longing for, plus I began learning the significance of the prophetic ministry that God is raising up across the Body of Christ in our day. After a few months, I was occasionally invited to preach on Sunday mornings, which is what I believe I was made for—it's a place where I feel God's pleasure.

This was a year of adjusting to the initial (hopefully not final) death of a vision. What about Shining Lights? The struggle was truly spiritual warfare, and I was worn out but not giving up on praying and believing for an eventual breakthrough—although it may manifest through someone else. But the Lord blessed me with new expectations and special plans in several areas to look forward to in the near future.

On September 27, 2014, our eldest granddaughter (Anna) got married—she and Mark offered me the honor of officiating at their wedding ceremony. I flew down to Clarendon, Arkansas, to spend a weekend of premarital counseling with them a couple of weeks before the wedding, and then on their big day I married them on the steps of the stately Waveland Museum in Lexington. What a privilege!

A few months later, on February 17, John turned seventy, and I planned a surprise birthday celebration for him at the high-class Greenbrier Inn in West Virginia. He knew we were headed for a surprise when we left home, but he did not know the destination until we arrived. When we walked into our Greenbrier suite, all of our children and grandchildren[58] were already there to yell "Surprise!" What a wonderful weekend we had—we took a tour of the once-secret government underground bunkers, sat in on a special *Antiques Roadshow* presentation, shopped, swam, and ate at several of their superb restaurants.

Kevin wore his Air Force dress uniform to John's birthday celebration dinner. Afterward the owner spotted him and offered to treat us all to dinner, but since we had already dined, he paid for us to have a family portrait taken! A memory to cherish forever.

Then on September 4 we celebrated our fiftieth wedding anniversary. Our children told us to be prepared for another surprise. Our youngest daughter, Christi, was the assigned chauffeur who picked us up and drove us to our destination—the famous boutique CASTLE! They paid for us to spend the night at this lavish Kentucky landmark. They furnished our already upscale room with a basket of goodies and a decorated box of anniversary cards and well-wishes from family and friends—and a formal written invitation to dinner, but they did not reveal where the dinner was to take place. We would be picked up at 5:00 p.m.!

At 5:00 p.m., Christi came back with the paparazzi (our eldest daughter, Kimberly). Our youngest granddaughter (Tatum) knocked on our door to announce that it was time to depart and escorted us down the elegant staircase to the waiting transportation (our van, duly decorated with "50 Years" signs). Then we were instructed to follow them as they led us to The Distillery, where they had made reservations for us to dine. After lingering over our truly delicious dinner, we returned to the Castle and found a bottle of champagne on ice, rose petals on our pillows, and a CD with our favorite love songs!

The next event of note that year came at the end of April, when I retired from Asbury University. My heart really wasn't in my work after the July trip to India in 2013. I had spoken of my plans to establish Shining Lights Inc. with the provost before I left, thinking I was just being above-board about moving on—not wanting him to be caught unawares when the time came. With that in mind, he had hired an assistant for me while I was in India, in order that she could learn the ropes, so to speak, of the Cross-Cultural Experience.

Upon my return home, I found her already settled in the office across the hall from mine—a rather awkward couple of years ensued. She was a lovely, well-qualified young woman, and when it came to technology, her abilities were way above my capabilities. The provost assured me that I could stay on as long as I liked, but from that point on I felt out of place, yet not released by the Spirit.

By the end of April in 2015, the Lord had confirmed that it was now time for me to move on. On one particular day I had been fervently praying over His timing all the way to work, and later as I sat in chapel, the Lord spoke clearly through the speaker—it was time to JUMP! And I did.

RUPP ARENA

After some R&R, I began to sense God's heart for bringing the wider Body of Christ together in Kentucky. I have forever been a true patriot and proud of my country. Of course that also means I am grieved as I watch us lose our Christian moorings as a nation. For years, every time I saw a picture of Rupp Arena, I saw it FULL of people praying together—no special speaker, no fancy praise band, just a

Spirit-led gathering of the people crying out to God in prayer for our country.

For months I prayed over this vision and ended up investing another six months in an attempt to rally the troops—sensing the Lord's leading each day. "United We Stand in Prayer" was to take place on 10-16-2016 at 3 p.m.—leading up to our national elections and in accordance with 2 Chronicles 7:14:

"If My people who are called by My name will humble themselves, and pray and seek My face, and turn from their wicked ways, then will I hear from heaven, and will forgive their sin, and heal their land."

Admission and parking were to be free. John created an inspiring 3x5 card with an American flag in the background and an eagle's head in the foreground. We printed about a thousand, with the pertinent information provided on the back:

This MULTI-GENERATIONAL gathering is to pray for our nation. As a physical manifestation of UNITY in PRAYER, we will invite the Presence of God to forgive, heal, and restore our land.

What you can expect:

- 12 pastors from different Christian denominations leading in prayer, along with prayer leaders of Christian organizations
- No names—no pastors or churches promoted
- A prayer meeting, not a church service
- We will humble ourselves before God in prayer.

I began calling on thirty-six pastors in May and soon discovered that many of them had already made commitments for that date, but I remained convinced that

God was daily leading me to press on. Following is just a smidgen of the words God was speaking to me in September leading up to October 16:

Endure and change history.
Stand.
Do not freak out!
Do not panic.
Do not become discouraged. He is leading the way.

Sound the alarm.
Shout at your wall.
Erupt with praise.
I will pour out My power for all to see.
Childlike worship.

Say yes to the journey and see what impossibility you may have the privilege of making happen.

Come together as one.
The magnitude will be global.
Supernatural chemistry—step up, believe, cross over.

Keep going with it. Don't give up.
Ezekiel 36: I will not change My mind.
Stand firm—He is fighting for you.

Mobilize.
My holiness will be displayed.
They will know that I am the Lord.

Lean on God—it will be the most glorious recommendation to trust in God.

Mark 10:29–30: It must have sounded like the most outrageous assignment!

That is Jesus every time telling you to do what is beyond your natural abilities.
He is there to make it possible.
He will equip you.

A God-sized goal.
All I can do is get out of the way.
God has big plans.

One yes from God is all you need.
Trust the process.

Rise to your full stature and call on that gritty something bigger within you—that all the earth may know there is a God in Kentucky & the U.S.A.

When He is quiet it is intermission—the scene is about to change!
Ezekiel 44: Don't sweat it!

Moving into unfamiliar territory—trust Him even when you feel like you are moving blindly.

Relinquish any control.
Delayed answers are so you can go through the process.

Take a stand.
Fight for unity in the Body of Christ.

Ezekiel 45: The Prince will provide the offering.
God has no plan B!

Keep praying that many will see your good works and glorify your Father in heaven.
Keep the faith—look at the big picture.
You've got to jump.

Expect Blessings.
Commit to finish.
Unconventional methods/resources.
Look past what doesn't fit in your box.

Don't talk yourself out of your vision—God put it there.
Don't give up in spite of impossible odds.
Uncommon faith opens gateway cities.
You must work in prayer.

No matter what it looks like, trust Him.
One voice until the city shakes with the sound!

God wants to use you to do the impossible.
Shake off what you need to shake off.

Do not look at the circumstances—trust in the outcome that
is coming to you.
He does what He plans.
We have long awaited for this day and it is finally here!

There will be a completion of the vision—it is being
purified with fire.
Endure the process.
Move forward.

New territory is awaiting—a call is pulling you on.
The fullness of My plan is ahead of you.
I am calling you to leave behind the reasoning of this
world, the opinions and traditions of men.

Stand your ground.
Hold onto Jesus' hand.
You are about to land on your feet.

It's time to live out on the water—in the significant,
unexpected changes, even when you do not understand why
He is asking you to do what He is asking.
Today starts a new chapter—things are shifting.
The fog has lifted—new direction.
Dare to hope.

GREAT IS HIS FAITHFULNESS!

Wait quietly.
Sit alone in silence.

I invited forty women leaders to join me at the Prayer Room in downtown Lexington to pray over the gathering at Rupp—ten women showed up, and of those ten, five stuck with me in prayer over the next few months.

The CEO of the arena management and I exchanged phone calls for several weeks before I met with him the first time. No one could have been more gracious, encouraging, or helpful than this man. He took the time to thoroughly explain to me what was needed to bring this about in the natural scheme of things.

Rupp Arena seats 25,000 people and use of the arena would require forty policemen, 125 security personnel, 150 ushers, a first aid crew, a cleaning crew, and a fee for video equipment usage, lighting, and air-conditioning.

The base fee, depending on how many we expected to show up, would be $25,000–$75,000 plus confirmation of insurance coverage. The minimum cost for the assisting staff would be another $5,000, and for video personnel, another $5,000. Plus, they would need to build a special platform to suit our requirement—in the round. Fundraising is not my forte—I believed the Lord was going to tap a wealthy someone on the shoulder to foot the bill. We put a tentative hold on Rupp Arena for October 16.

Our license agreement stated: "This agreement and full deposit of $25,000 must be executed and returned by

October 7, 2016. . .. All remaining expenses will be due within seven days after the completion of the event."

In my vision, I saw the ministers/leaders sitting in a circle with their backs to each other; they would then pass the microphone to the right as they covered pre-assigned areas of prayer:

- Church
- State Government, Governor
- National Government—Legislative
- National Government—Judicial
- National Government—Executive
- Elections
- Police, Fire Dept., EMTs
- Military/Veterans
- Business
- Education
- Family
- Youth
- Senior Citizens
- News Media
- Entertainment/Sports
- Drugs
- Homeless/Poor
- Medical Personnel

After an official welcome, the Honor Guard was scheduled to present the flag, followed by the Pledge of Allegiance, the reading of 2 Chronicles 7:14, and the giving of thanks and praise accompanied by a concert pianist, before the ministers/leaders prayed over their assigned areas. We would close with the Lord's Prayer and Nancy Cox singing "God Bless America."

I contacted the radio stations and TV stations, but their schedules, like the pastors', were set months in advance, even a year ahead of time. Kent Ostrander announced it in the Family Foundation's Newsletter that went out to more than four thousand people in Kentucky. I produced a five-minute promo and prayer-walked around the building every Sunday for three months.

I waited until five minutes before 5:00 p.m. on October 7 to call Carl Hall and **cancel** the event. I truly believed, up until the last minute, that God was going to work a miracle. I drafted and sent out the following letter to those who had come alongside me in prayer:

It is with deepest regret that I must cancel the October 16th "United We Stand" prayer event. Today was the deadline for submitting a $25,000 deposit for Rupp Arena, and the finances did not come in.

*My **heartfelt appreciation** for all of you who have stood with me over these past nine months of preparation in prayer, encouragement, and getting the word out—I know that NO SEED IS WASTED. I trust the Lord to water it, grow it, and manifest the fullness of fruit in His timing. I will be contacting as many people as I can through Facebook and ask that you do the same. May Sunday the 16th **still** be a day when we individually or in small groups "humble ourselves, pray, seek His face and turn from our wicked ways."*

Although I do not understand the "why," I know WHO does, and I trust Him!

Peace & Joy,
Kathryn

The miracle in all this is that I did not become depressed or angry with myself or anyone else! Of course I was disappointed, but I was not overwhelmed, *"perplexed, but not in despair"* (2 Corinthians 4:8). I knew that God used a donkey to talk to Balaam and a colt to carry Jesus into Jerusalem—therefore, He could certainly use me if He so desired. I always believed that the Lord "uses the foolish things to confound the wise," and the wise were certainly confounded as they watched me walk through this—just not quite the way I had imagined!

It might appear to be a bridge to nowhere, but God knows my heart and sees my perseverance. Things are not always what they seem—perhaps I was the seed-planter and someone else will come along and bring it to pass. I have learned that we must walk in faith and obedience even when we see no results, and we must "press on until we no longer are afraid to lose."[59] Anthony Nelson (our Associate Pastor) quips, "No guts—No glory—No missionary story!"

Did you know that Strong's Concordance lists ninety-seven occasions in the Bible where the word *nevertheless* appears? The writer is always describing an impossible situation, then inserts *nevertheless*—like it didn't matter what was going on; the opposite was now going to take place.

I have noticed there are numerous instances of "BUT GOD" intervening and turning the tables around. No matter what your challenging circumstance is today, I would say to you, "NEVERTHELESS, God has a way out, around, over, under, or through for you!"

If you love God, He will work ALL things together for your good (Romans 8:28). Just don't get discouraged in the process.

"At the right time, I, the LORD, will make it happen."
Isaiah 60:22b (NLT)

END OF MY SECOND DECADE OF JUBILEE

The end of my second decade of Jubilee had officially ended in July, but this challenge was already in the works and provided a segue into the beginning of my third Decade of Jubilee, which I anticipate being the best of the best, because I am continuing to grow up in the Lord and am learning more of His ways that are not my ways—and I am secure in that. I can never do anything to make Him love me more, and I can never do anything to make Him love me less. "When we become little enough, naked enough, and honest enough, we find that we are more than enough just the way we are."[60] Nothing to prove. Nothing to protect. No grades!

I learned that the Celts during the time of the Welsh Revival called the Holy Spirit "The Wild Goose!" Aha! I have been on a Wild Goose Chase! And I do not intend to stop following Him as best I can. I read that Ruth Bell Graham's tombstone reads, "END of CONSTRUCTION: Thank you for your patience." Well, I'm not quite there yet! So, PLEASE CONTINUE to be patient with me!

I leave you with this Scripture from the Song of Solomon 2:11–13 (TPT):

*"**The season has changed**, the bondage of your barren winter has ended, and the season of hiding is over and gone. The rains have soaked the earth and left it bright with blossoming flowers.*
*The season for singing and pruning the vines has arrived. **I hear the cooing of doves in our land, filling the air with songs** to awaken you and guide you forth.*
Can you not discern this new day of destiny breaking forth around you? The early signs of my purposes and plans are bursting forth. The budding vines of new life are now blooming everywhere. The fragrance of their flowers whispers,
***'There is change in the air**.'"*

A New Decade has descended! And I am eager to embrace the Joy of my third Decade of Jubilee with Jesus!
I will to savor "the wink" of His favor for the rest of my days on this earth.

Love and blessings,
Kathryn

[illegible]

Love and blessings,

Kathryn

ABOUT THE AUTHOR

Dr. Kathryn Hendershot has served for over fifty years in various ministerial roles, including the pastorate, teaching, and counseling. She has authored several books, and has been blessed with divine appointments in eleven uniquely diverse countries on six continents. Kathryn and John married fifty-five years ago, and take great delight in their three married children and five grandchildren.

Connect with Kathryn at: Kdmiss@gmail.com

ENDNOTES

1. *Life Lessons of a Desperate Housewife* is a later version of *Obedience: The Road to Reality* (a more fitting title)! John and I were not Christians when we met and married in 1965. I had just turned nineteen, and John was twenty. We survived our first year of marriage as sophomores in college—a year of suffering a series of disappointments as unrealistic expectations of "happily ever after" stung our souls. The Viet Nam War called for a more concentrated workload on the family's heat-treat company, and required our relocation to Wickliffe, Ohio for John to supervise the night shift. These two years were followed by several two-year transfers as new family plants were constructed across the Southeast.

In Simpsonville, S.C. we visited a small country church to meet some "nice people." Little did I know that Jesus was going to meet me at that altar and my life would be forever changed. My eighty-year-old Sunday School teacher, Mrs. Pollard, mentored me, and encouraged me to teach the Word of God. The Lord answered my cry to draw even closer to Him when we transferred to Reidsville, N.C., where I received the Baptism of the Holy Spirit.

Our final transfer with the family company was to Charlotte, N.C., where John received Jesus as his personal Savior. During this earth-shaking season John also received the Baptism of the Holy Spirit; we were both baptized by immersion (the believer's baptism); and John received a call from the Lord to come out of the business world and follow Him in ministry. We moved to Wilmore, Ky. to attend Asbury College, while living in student housing with our three children, ages four, six, and eight. Thus began a walk of faith for the following sixteen years (in our hearts and minds it was simply a walk of obedience).

This was a season of much inner healing from my childhood wounds, revelation of marital sin, and the rebuilding of our marriage. We both finished our degrees; John in psychology, and me in elementary education. Upon graduation he began volunteering with Gospel Graphics (a faith-based media ministry) for a couple years before founding Christian Ministries.

2. Based on a Graham Cooke teaching.

3. Doctorate of Missiology: "This is a doctorate in missions that will prepare one for working in the field and the academy."

4. Women could not teach men and must remain silent.

5. My husband has never been chauvinistic.

6. Known as "slain in the Spirit," when a person is touched by the power of the Holy Spirit and falls to the ground, often not able to move for some time, as the Lord heals or speaks words of direction, comfort, wisdom, etc. Biblical examples: soldiers who came to arrest Jesus (John 18:6), Paul on road to Damascus (Acts 9), John (Revelation 1:17).

7. The Bible names four Herods: the Gospels mention two, and the Book of Acts speaks of two:

#1 Herod the Great built Caesarea and killed baby boys, hoping one of them turned out to be Jesus.

#2 His son, Herod Antipas, ruled Galilee during the time of Jesus' trial.

#3 The third-generation Herod is first mentioned in the Book of Acts and ends up being eaten by worms.

#4 The great-grandson of Herod the Great had Paul brought before him and was almost persuaded to accept Christianity.

8. Hookah: a stemmed water pipe used for smoking.

9. Some traditions describe it as a cave.

10. The Bridge: A method of explaining salvation:

- Draw a straight line—man and God having fellowship
- Draw two cliffs—establish separation of God and man by sin
- Show what is available on God's side—John 5:24
  1. Eternal Life
  2. No Judgment
  3. Passed from death to life
- List God's description of everyone's condition—
  Romans 3:23: Separated by sin
  Romans 6:23a: Wages or consequences of sin
- Good people and self-made men and their "security"
  1. Giving themselves to others and community
  2. Excellent moral character
  3. Religious church attendance
- These things are GOOD works but not enough to be THE answer to man's problems. Ephesians 2:8-9
- God's answer to man's hopeless situation:
- Draw the cross, representing Jesus Christ as the Bridge between God and man. Use Romans 5:8.
- How does man cross this Bridge to receive all that God offers? The answer is in John 5:24: hear and believe.
- What does it mean to believe? Revelation 3:20
  a. Commitment to the Living Savior
  b. Open the door

- THE QUESTION: (Knowing man's condition and God's prescription, where are you in this illustration?)
- (If on man's side, is there any reason why you would not want to be on God's side or why you would not cross the Bridge now?)

11. A board game.

12. Ditty bag: a bag to hold small articles, usually toiletries.

13. Russian streets were hardly what we would refer to as streets: no lines, potholes, bumpy, no street signs or traffic lights.

14. Christi and Alan graciously offered me housing on the second floor of their home. John or I would make the trip one way or the other on weekends until he was able to relocate.

15. Her biography, *The General Was a Lady* by Margaret Troutt, is available on Amazon.com.

16. Pastor Samuel Lamb was seventy-two at that time. He served more than twenty years in prison for being a Christian in China. In 1990 the government closed his house church on his property, but he still averaged four hundred worshipers per service in other locations and led four services a week. He explained why he was not in prison then: "Every time they arrest me and send me off to prison, the church grows." He served as leader of the Chinese house church movement. He was known for his resistance against the state-sanctioned Three-Self Patriotic Movement.

17. A three-wheeled little golf-cart-like type of transportation similar to an open taxi.

18. A cloth-dying technique: hand-printing textiles by coating with wax the parts that are not to be dyed.

19. https://place.asburyseminary.edu/cgi/viewcontent.cgi?article=1015&content=ecommonsatdissertations

20. Read *Life Lessons of a Desperate Housewife* for details.

21. "Healthcare for a Lifetime" Oasis Hospital, Abu Dhabi, UAE.

22. Christians for Biblical Equality is a nonprofit organization comprised of individuals from more than eighty denominations who believe that the Bible, properly interpreted, teaches the fundamental equality of men and women of all ethnicities and all economic classes, based on the teachings of scripture as reflected in Galatians 3:28: *"There is neither Jew nor Greek, there is neither slave nor free, there is neither male nor female; for you are all one in Christ Jesus."*

23. Dissertation address: same as #19.

24. Kevin Giles, Th.D. was Vicar of St. Michael's Church (Anglican) in North Carlton, Australia. He has published numerous scholarly articles and books, including *Trinity and Subordination.*

25. Dowry is a gift of money, goods, or property a woman brings to her husband in marriage.

26. Richard Howell, Ph.D., Professor Emeritus of Philosophy and Apologetics at Southern Evangelical Seminary in Charlotte, North Carolina. Dr. Howe has a

B.A. in Bible from Mississippi College, an M.A. in Philosophy from the University of Mississippi, and a Ph.D. in Philosophy from the University of Arkansas.

27. Robyn Claydon, an evangelist and Bible teacher. She was the Lausanne Movement's Senior Associate for Women in World Evangelization.

28. Kuruvilla Chandy, a graduate in philosophy, went on to study theology at Union Biblical Seminary. He is a contributor to CBE's Priscilla Papers and is the author of several books.

29. Chae Ok Chun, D.Miss., an ordained minister who has served in various positions, including Dean of the Graduate School of Theology at Ewha Womans University in Seoul, Korea.

30. Wes@iliteam.org; Joy@iliteam.org; 770-832-1244.

31. Eight Core Values:

1). Intimacy with God

"For you did not receive a spirit that makes you a slave again to fear but you received the Spirit of sonship. And by Him we cry, Abba, Father." Romans 8:15

2). Passion for the Harvest

"And Jesus was going about all the cities and the villages, teaching in their synagogues, and proclaiming the Gospel of the kingdom, and healing every kind of disease and every kind of sickness. And seeing the multitudes, He felt compassion for them, because they were distressed and downcast like sheep without a shepherd. Then He said, 'The harvest is plentiful, but the workers are few. Pray therefore to the Lord of the Harvest that He may send laborers into His harvest.'" Matthew 9:35–38

3). Visionary Leadership
"Where there is no vision, the people perish." (Proverbs 29:18)

4). Culturally Relevant Evangelism
"I have become all things to all people that I may by all possible means save some." (1 Corinthians 9:19–27)

5). Multiplication of Leaders
"What you have heard from Me in the presence of many witnesses, these entrust to faithful men and women who will be able to train others also." (2 Timothy 2:2)

6). Family Priority
"Let each individual among you also love his own wife even as himself, and let the wife see to it that she respects her husband." (Ephesians 5:22–6:9)

7). Stewardship
"His master said to him, 'Well done, good and faithful servant; you were faithful with a few things, I will put you in charge of many things, enter into the joy of your master.'" (Matthew 25:14–30)

8). Integrity
"I have fought the good fight, I have finished the course, I have kept the faith." (2 Timothy 4:7)

32. Julie is the missions pastor at Centenary United Methodist Church in Lexington, KY.

33. ECWA, Evangelical Church Winning All.

34. Isaac Lim is the founder and head of the Energy Psychology Centre of Malaysia. He is also the leader of the Malaysian EFT Chapter under AHPM/FCNMAM, a Ministry of Health-approved T&CM association.

35. Recorded in *Life Lessons of a Desperate Housewife,* Chapters 9, 10, 16.

36. ILI National Conference Notebook, p. 41 (Everett Rogers).

37. Pages 163 & 164 are excerpts from *From Graveyard to Vineyard* by S. Devasahayan Ponraj and Chandan Kumar Sah; Mission Educational Books, Chennai, India 2008.

38. 1947, after WWII.

39. Temperatures ranged from 108° to around 120° most days.

40. Basically the same teaching as in Nigeria.

41. Lyrics by Cliff Richard.

42. Thomas Chisholm & William Runyan, 1923.

43. A four-page paper required within 30 days following the Cross-Cultural Experience.

44. A trident is a three-pronged spear serving in classical mythology as the attribute of a sea god (as Neptune).

45. Source unknown.

46. The work on the ornate, Gothic chapel began in 1321. It is located on the north side of Ely Cathedral. A life-size statue of the Virgin Mary was installed in 2000.

47. London's public rapid transit system.

48. Nic Billman, December 12, 2012.

49. “Small Straws in a Soft Wind,” Marsha Burns, November 30, 2012.

50. More information on his mission at www.raysofhopeindia.org.

51. The Queen’s Necklace is a three-mile, six-lane, concrete road that curves around the coast, which forms a natural *C.* At night, the streetlights in the median shining forth is what gives it its name.

52. Angela Greenig, January 8, 2013.

53. *Jesus Calling*, Sarah Young, January 9, 2013.

54. *Jesus Calling*, Sarah Young, January 18, 2013.

55. Central Adoption Resource Authority is India’s governmental monitor and regulator of in-country adoptions.

56. “Human Immunodeficiency virus over time causes acquired immunodeficiency (AIDS), a condition failure of the immune system that allows life-threatening opportunistic infections and cancers to thrive.” (Wikipedia)

57. Bus rides were dangerous for several reasons. Passengers are literally packed like sardines—you cannot avoid rubbing up against another human, which makes bus rides ripe for unholy touches. They even have signs that read: “Eve teasing is a recognizable offence: For help call #0191.” Of course, this would be impossible to enforce.

58. Our eldest granddaughter, Anna, lived in Arkansas and couldn’t make the trip.

59. Movie: *Art of Racing in the Rain.*

60. Richard Rohr, August 8, 2019, Daily Devotions, Center for Action & Meditation.

www.ingramcontent.com/pod-product-compliance
Lightning Source LLC
Chambersburg PA
CBHW071317090426
42738CB00012B/2716

9781732529335